LIST OF ILLUSTRATIONS
VOL. I

LIST OF ILLUSTRATIONS

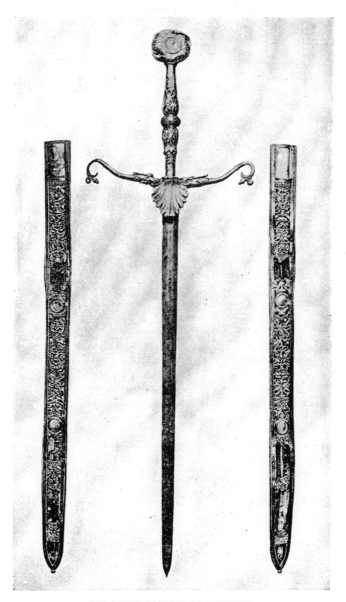

THE SWORD OF STATE OF SCOTLAND.
A present from Pope Julius II. to James V.

MARY QUEEN OF SCOTS

CHAPTER I

CHILDHOOD IN SCOTLAND

MARY QUEEN OF SCOTS—third and only surviving child, and the only daughter, of James V. of Scotland and Mary of Lorraine—was born in the Palace of Linlithgow, either on October 7th or 8th, 1542.[1] The birth took place at a very dark crisis of Scottish history. Abashed by the humiliating disaster of Solway Moss, and perturbed by bodeful expectancy of what might follow it, the spirit of the Scottish nation had sunk to an exceptional depth of dejection. Yet the birth was, whether the nation realised it or not, a mitigation of the disaster.

To Henry VIII., then apparently purposing the annexation of Scotland, either by violence or guile, the birth could hardly have been welcome, and it must have been less gratifying after he learned of the death of James V. Had no immediate heir to the throne, in the senior line,

---

[1] The 8th was kept as the official birthday ; but Chalmers, in his *Life of Mary*, gives as authority for the 7th the Register of the official of Lothian ; and the 7th is the date given by Bishop Leslie, who had special access to official documents, and by Holinshed. Knox gives the 8th, probably because he knew that it was Mary's custom to celebrate the 8th ; but if the birth happened late on the 7th, there was a strong temptation to make the 8th the birth-date, since it was the festival of the Conception of the Virgin Mary.

been born, the peril of Scotland's annexation by Henry would have been even greater than it was : the groundless rumours that were current as to the birth and the child's illness, are a sufficient evidence of the English hope that the Scottish throne might be left, in a manner, vacant.

Some days before the birth happened, it was reported to have occurred prematurely. The first rumour was that the child was a son ; then it was said to be a daughter, but not like to live ; later it was declared to have died ; but although on the 19th Sir George Douglas was able to report that it was both alive and likely to live,[1] Chapnys, the imperial ambassador in London, was on the 23rd writing to the Queen of Hungary that both mother and child were very ill and despaired of by the physician.[2]

The importance of the birth was incalculably enhanced by the death, within seven days afterwards, of James V. at Falkland Palace, where, a few days before the birth, he had taken to his bed. The variety of dates assigned to his death is partly to be accounted for by the fact that the occurrence was for a time concealed from the nation ; but Sir George Douglas, who had the information from a servant, was probably correct in stating that he died on Thursday at 12 o'clock at night, although he wrongly supposed that Thursday was the 15th instead of the 14th of the month.[3]

From an early period of his illness the King's mind had been affected. His nerves were highly strung, and when the disaster occurred he was apparently so ill as

---

[1] See *Hamilton Papers*, i. 323, 328, 337, 340, 342.
[2] *Spanish State Papers*, vi. (ii.) No. 87.
[3] *Hamilton Papers*, i. 339. Chalmers (MSS. in the University of Edinburgh) gives as authorities for the 14th the Register of Lothian, the Household Book, and the tombstone.

to be unable to accompany the army. There is no proof that he was a mere craven-hearted sentimentalist ; but, on account of his illness, the disaster completely upset his mental balance, and Douglas, on the authority of his servant, who was present with the King, reported that from the time he took to his bed, " he did rage and crye out, and spake but fewe wysse wordes." [1] Having taken to his bed on the 6th of the month, he was in the full grasp of the fever, or of the mental alienation, before a messenger arrived from Linlithgow with tidings of the Queen's delivery of a daughter. Had the child been a son the news might have given him some comfort, but that it was a daughter seemed but the climax of his misfortunes. " The King," writes Lindsay of Pitscottie, " inquyred whidder it was a man or woman. The messinger said it was ane fair dochter. The King answered and said, ' Fairweill, it cam with ane las and it will pas with ane las ' : and so he commendit himselff to the Almightie God, and spak litle from thenforth, but turned his back to his lordes, and his face to the wall." [2]

The forebodings of the dying King were not to be fulfilled ; for though in their efforts against Mary's sove-reignty the Protestants finally succeeded, the sceptre of Scotland did not then pass from the Stewarts. On the contrary, Mary's son, James VI., by ascending the throne of England, was to be the fated agent in accomplishing the great political purpose which was then baffling the wit and might of Henry VIII. Nevertheless, the King's forebodings that exceptional misfortunes would await his daughter were fully justified. Almost from the earliest moments of her existence, she became an object of dire

[1] *Hamilton Papers*, i. 340.   [2] *Chronicle*, ii. 406.

conflict and contention, and even what her immediate fate might be seemed to hang in very uncertain balances.

Among the more potent personages to whom her future was a subject of intimate concern, a first place must be assigned to the portentous Henry VIII., the most strenuous and self-willed personality of Europe, and at this juncture conscientiously bent on the appropriation of her kingdom. Nor could Henry's great adversary, Pope Paul III., nor his chief political rival, the accomplished and dissipated Francis I. of France, be oblivious to the issues dependent on the infant's fate, although their interference in the great intrigue was meanwhile of a more obscure and indirect character than that of Henry. For the results they might be able to achieve, Henry, Paul, and Francis were also largely dependent on the purposes of Scottish notabilities who had their own particular ends to serve.

Arran, recognised as next heir to the Crown, though his claims were, on account of asserted bastardy, disputed by Lennox, became, as Regent, a person of high official consequence. He desired, if he could, to turn the providential opportunity to account for the advancement of his house, and nothing could have gratified him more than the betrothal of the infant sovereign to his own son and heir; but he was constitutionally unfit, however nominally high his position, for any hazardous adventure. His wits were so limited, and so mild and facile was his temper, that he had no distinct individual influence, and was bound to become the mere tool of subtler and more resolute plotters.

It was as the tool of others that Arran was a formidable opponent of Henry's scheme; but, unlike Arran, the Queen-Dowager was exceptionally fitted for playing her own game, though her peculiar gifts were as yet unascertained.

After a picture in the collection of the Duke of Devonshire.]

JAMES V. AND MARY OF LORRAINE.
The Father and Mother of Mary Queen of Scots.

[Photo by Frans Hanfstaengl, Munich.

CONTENTS OF VOL. I

ERRATA

VOL. I.

Page 306, line 9, *for* " Wemmys " *read* " Wemyss."
Page 308, line 18, *for* " Wemmys " *read* " Wemyss."

of human nature, and these details are the mere trappings of the subject. It is the heart of the nation that we desire to understand ; and on account of the tension and stress of the great contest that centred round Mary Stuart, the hearts of all the main actors in it are laid bare with exceptional completeness.

The aim of the present biography is, therefore, to deal with the more personal aspects of the Marian period, and to deal with them apart from ecclesiastical prepossessions, and on the understanding that the praise and blame of the twentieth century are not quite applicable to the sixteenth. Indeed, the more the present writer has concerned himself with the career of Mary Stuart, the more has he been impressed with the inapplicability to it, in the strict sense, of praise or blame. Whatever may be the rights or wrongs of Protestantism or Catholicism, Mary appears to have been very largely the mere victim of a bitter religious quarrel.

While it has been deemed inadvisable to overload the text with references to authorities, they have been added on all the more important and disputed points.

The importance of portraiture and other illustrations as an aid to the realisation of the past is becoming more and more recognised ; and it is hoped that the special attention devoted to this in the present volumes will meet with the reader's approval.

September 25th, 1905.

T. F. HENDERSON.

labours in calendaring the Spanish State Papers all students of this period of English and Scottish history are under a debt of obligation ; but the volume deals mainly with a special aspect of the Queen's character and career. Of recents works, less strictly biographic in form, a first place must be assigned to Father Pollen's *Papal Negotiations*, which, besides supplying much new and varied information in regard to minor details, has made known the suggestive fact that Mary dared to marry Darnley without a Papal dispensation. But for Father Pollen, also, we probably should not have had Mr. Lang's bright and ingenious *Mystery of Mary Stuart*, with its remarkable Casket Letter theory, which I have dealt with in an appendix ; and, again, Mr. Lang's volume has been the apparent begetter of Mr. Hewlett's clever and realistic *Queen's Quair*, which is, however, of course, romance rather than history, and, vividly suggestive though it be, rather provokes biography than supplies it.

For the student of human nature, the career of Mary Stuart must ever have a special fascination, as a striking example of a strong personality the issues of whose life seem to have been persistently determined by an adverse fate ; while the whole range of human history affords no better opportunity for the study of the moral and social influences that determine a nation's destiny. It is all very well to insist on attention, in the study of history, to external customs, habits, social conditions, progress in art and science and industry ; but after all, history is the history

PREFACE

MY explanation for seeking to add to the numerous works on Mary Stuart may be stated in a sentence. The recent concise biographies—whatever their special merits—and the more important works, lately published, on special aspects of the subject, so far from forestalling, rather suggest the desirability, of a biography dealing in a somewhat detailed and critical fashion with the main episodes of her career. True, among recent contributions to Marian literature is the first volume of Dr. Hay Fleming's notable example of biographic spadework. That book is, however, more a dictionary of the errors of other biographers of the Queen than a biography in the strict sense of the term. It has, it is to be hoped, done valuable service towards dissipating many persistent and venerable delusions about Queen Mary; but its method is entirely exceptional, and only to be justified by the exceptional peculiarities of the Marian controversy; while its effect is necessarily, on the whole, negative rather than positive, and perhaps more unfavourable to Mary than is actually intended. Another recent biographical work of importance is the lively and graphic volume on the *Love Affairs of Mary Queen of Scots*, by Major Martin Hume, to whose

First Published 1905

HASKELL HOUSE PUBLISHERS LTD.
Publishers of Scarce Scholarly Books
280 LAFAYETTE STREET
NEW YORK, N. Y. 10012

Library of Congress Catalog Card Number: 68-25241

Standard Book Number 8383-0163-0

Printed in the United States of America

MARY QUEEN OF SCOTS

HER ENVIRONMENT AND TRAGEDY

A BIOGRAPHY

BY

T. F. HENDERSON

With 102 Illustrations, including 2 Photogravure Plates

VOL. I

HASKELL HOUSE PUBLISHERS Ltd.
Publishers of Scarce Scholarly Books
NEW YORK, N. Y. 10012
1969

From a miniature by François Clouet at Windsor Castle.   Allen & Co. Lo.

MARY QUEEN OF SCOTS

VOL. I

arrogance as Henry, was hardly regarded with horror. They were already, many of them, weary of the yoke of Beaton and other ambitious ecclesiastics, even if most of them were yet untainted by the new doctrines ; while the prospect of a union of the kingdoms was already a by no means unwelcome idea to the more enlightened Scots. There was nothing in itself abhorrent in the proposal of Henry to the principal nobles taken prisoners at Solway, that they should do their utmost to effect the betrothal of the young Queen to his son Prince Edward. To them and to Scotland there was even in the proposition a certain specious air of magnanimity. Yet it scarcely veiled the real character of his intentions—the virtual seizure of the Scottish government.

That Henry's purpose could then, even in opposition to the efforts of the Cardinal and the churchmen, have been accomplished by methods which would not have done violence to Scottish susceptibilities, was perhaps impossible ; but his best chance of success was by endeavouring to offend these susceptibilities as little as he could.

But besides that Henry had never learned to curb or temper his strong desires, he was probably convinced that he had no choice of methods—that the only adequate guarantee of the marriage and the union was the immediate possession of the Queen and Scotland. His providential capture of so many Scottish nobles afforded him, he thought, an exceptional chance of effecting his purpose, and he was resolved to make the most of it. This was all very good from his point of view, but what he demanded of the nobles was of course shameful treachery to their country. It is but a sorry excuse for them, that when they consented to the bargain they were wholly at his mercy ; of more relevancy was the consideration that he was really proposing to them the impossible, and that on their arrival in Scotland the force of circumstances would compel him to modify his demands.

The treachery now mentioned the nobles were asked to perform openly. Henry calculated that, if willing, they, with the co-operation of Angus, had sufficient power to compel the accomplishment of his wishes. They were therefore, on their arrival in Scotland, publicly to demand the delivery of the child to Henry's guardianship, and the transference of the principal fortresses to his keeping ; and should those comprehensive requests be refused, they were to effect Henry's purpose by force. In addition to this, ten of the principal prisoners signed a secret article by which, in the case of the child's decease, they promised to aid Henry to the best of their power in taking "the whole rule, dominion and government of Scotland upon him " ; and the Earl of Angus, by a separate article, undertook to aid Henry in this, whether Henry obtained the guardianship of the child or not, or whatever fate might befall her.[1]

It so happened, however, that the astute Sir George Douglas had not been asked to sign any of the articles. His brother Angus had signed them without consulting with him, and Lisle perceived that Sir George was "verye angrye in his mynde " on learning that his brother had done so, without representing to the King the imprudence of imposing an agreement on him which could hardly be kept secret, and if known would do much mischief in Scotland.[2] This could only mean that Sir George deemed

---

[1] *Hamilton Papers*, i. 374-6.   [2] *Ibid.*, i. 390.

Probably alone amongst the intriguers unselfishly devoted to the infant's welfare, she could not be expected to favour the ambitious hopes of a mere noble like Arran ; and, apart from its worldly advantages, she was not likely to be biased towards the marriage to a son of the heretic Henry VIII. The eldest child of Claude, Count and afterwards Duke of Guise, and also, before her Scottish marriage, the widow of Louis of Orleans, second Duke of Longueville, her sympathies were necessarily with the French and Catholic party. That Henry's proposals offered no temptation to her is, however, by no means certain ; but in any case she had meantime to dissimulate her preferences, and to remain outwardly almost as impassive to the designs of others as was her helpless infant.

Next to Arran and the Queen-Dowager in official power, but much more to be reckoned with than either, was Cardinal Beaton, the virtual prime minister and more of the late King, and the main director of the policy which had resulted in the Solway disaster. This powerful prelate was, even for his own time, a quite notable specimen of the secular ecclesiastic. No such astonishing development of worldly ecclesiasticism is perhaps now possible, and amongst the ambitious ecclesiastics of that exceptional age Beaton occupied a high pre-eminence. Like many great prelates of his time, he lived in open violation of his priestly vows of chastity ; but he violated them with as much decorous restraint as if he had been the husband of one wife, and, it may be, was quite faithful to the lady who had won his affections. Nor could there have been any prelate more resolutely devoted to the interests of the Catholic Church as he understood them ; but, whilst he was more or less the slave of ecclesiastical fetichism, his inordinate conceptions of priestly power had a strong secular colouring, so that practically in his eyes the Church was hardly more than a Divine institution for gratifying the pride and ministering to the avarice of the higher ecclesiastics. His face indicates polish and refinement rather than coarseness; but though also full of intelligence, the expression is disdainful, and there are indications of temper, if not of cruelty.

Haughty and ambitious, and contemptuous of his intellectual and social inferiors, he viewed the spread of heresy among the friars and common people with aristocratic contempt, and punished it with much the same lofty rigour as that exercised by the secular justice against the crime of deer-stealing. But, possessed of a tireless and dauntless energy, and an expert in unscrupulous craft, he was, by the aid of his ecclesiastical position, by far the most formidable opponent that Henry had in Scotland, and much more than a match for the half-hearted band of Scottish nobles which Henry, by mingled bribes and threats, had lured into his service. The triumph of his diplomacy over that of Henry was inevitable, for, in addition to his great talents and his ecclesiastical prestige, he had, owing to the overweening assumption of Henry, the peculiar advantage of posing as a devoted and high-minded patriot.

Of the sincerity, and even fanaticism, of his patriotism there can hardly be more doubt than of that of the majority of his fellow-Scots; but, in his efforts to thwart Henry, his patriotism was largely the slave of his ecclesiasticism. That Henry was seeking to tamper with the ancient independence of Scotland was perhaps cause enough, in itself, to rouse the resistance of Beaton to his policy; but any terms that might have been proposed for a union of the two kingdoms would have been strenuously opposed by Beaton so long as they implied alliance with a king at feud with Rome ; while, had Henry appeared in the guise of a Catholic deliverer to a Scotland infected with heresy, Beaton, on almost any terms, would, we must suppose, have welcomed him with open arms. Yet, matters being as they were, Beaton was the means of rendering priceless service to his country in a political crisis of exceptional gravity ; for the aims of Henry, though in some respects well meant, were vitiated by his too passionate impatience, and his too lofty contempt for Scottish national sentiment.

The main direct opponent of the Cardinal in Scotland was Henry's agent, Sir George Douglas, brother of the Earl of Angus. Both in boldness and subtlety, Douglas was more than the equal of the Cardinal. The part he had to play, being that of, in a manner, bamboozling at once Henry, Arran, and the Cardinal, was an almost impossible one ; but in playing it he showed a fertility of resource suggestive of wizardry. Like Angus, he really wished to do his best to oblige the English King, who for many years had sheltered the two from the wrath of James V. He was driven to deceive and bamboozle Henry, simply by the unreasonable character of Henry's demands. Notwithstanding the rivalry of the Douglases with the royal house of Stewart, and their consequent alliances with England, even they were not without a tincture of patriotic prejudice, and by no means relished the brutal attitude of Henry towards their country. The task which Henry sought to impose on them was really an impossible one ; and on this account alone they had hardly other option than to plot for a modification of its stringency, even if they had not had chiefly at heart their own rehabilitation in Scotland.

Finally, a good deal was to depend on the Earl of Lennox, though more in the remote future than in the immediate present.   Recalled by the Cardinal from France, where he had been in the service of the French king, he was, on account of his claims against Arran for the next heirship to the Scottish Crown, to play a part of high importance as the tool of the Cardinal ; and, after the Cardinal had cast him off, he was to become the tool of Henry VIII.   But, admirable soldier though he was, and a great proficient in manly exercises, he was not fitted by nature to shine much more brilliantly than his rival Arran as a politicial diplomatist ; and he was mainly to be reckoned with after his marriage to the ardent and irrepressible Lady Margaret Douglas, daughter of Angus and the Queen-Dowager, Margaret Tudor.   The great results of that marriage were as yet unforeseen, but it was to have a more vital effect on the relationships between the two countries than either the unprincipled intrigues of Henry or the savage exhibitions of his unbridled wrath.

As regards the immediate political outlook in Scotland, the death of James V. was fortunate rather than otherwise, for it induced Henry to suspend active operations against it when it was very much at his mercy, and to seek, in the first instance, to compass by guile what he had purposed to win by force of arms.   Instead of proceeding to the immediate conquest or chastisement of Scotland, he now proposed to effect the transference of its government to himself, through a proposal for the betrothal of the infant Queen to his only son Prince Edward.   There was of course the difficulty of Henry's quarrel with the Pope ; but by many of the Scottish nobles a close alliance with such a flaunting heretic, and such a bridler of ecclesiastical

After the picture by Holbein.

HENRY VIII.

Henry's policy impossible. If Angus was resolved to fulfil his oaths to the letter, Sir George had hardly other option than to support him ; but then Angus was entirely under the influence of the much cleverer and more resolute Sir George, and Sir George, being bound by no oaths, felt himself free to do his utmost to modify, and in a sense to thwart, the policy of Henry, in the interests at once of Henry, the Douglases, and Scotland.

His strength in thwarting Henry lay in his plea of *non possumus.* The Solway nobles could do nothing without the support of their followers ; and in his first interview with Henry's ambassador, Sir Ralph Sadler, Sir George affirmed that if "we shoulde go about to take the Governour from his state, and to bring the obedience of this realme to Englonde . . . there is not so lytle a boy but he woll hurle stones ayenst it, the wyves woll com out with their distaffes, and the comons unyversally woll rather dye in it." [1] Further, the Solway nobles could plead that before their arrival in Scotland, a Governor of Scotland had already been chosen, and that Henry's best chance of securing his purpose was by peaceful negotiation through the Governor.

There has been some obscurity as to the time and manner of Arran's succession to the regency. As the nearest heir to the throne after the infant, he had a legal claim to the governorship of the kingdom, while the guardianship of the child fell to her mother, as her nearest female relative ; but, on December 18th, Lisle learned from Sir George Douglas that "the gret men of Scotland," who were then convened in Edinburgh, intended to choose four governors of the realm—Arran, Moray, Huntly, and

[1] *Hamilton Papers,* i. 477.

Argyll—" and the Cardinall to be governer of the Prencys and cheyff rewler of the cownsell." [1]

On December 21st he further wrote that the above arrangement had been willed by the King on his deathbed ; and on December 24th he announced that on the previous Tuesday (the 19th) proclamation had been made at Edinburgh that all " men sholde be obydient unto " the persons named " as the only governors of the realme," etc. Yet on January 5th he was able to report that Arran had, on the 3rd, been proclaimed Protector and Governor of Scotland.[2] According to Knox, this latter proclamation was authorised by a convention of the nobility specially called by Arran, and the decision was arrived at in despite of the Cardinal.[3]

It was also, after the Cardinal's imprisonment, confirmed by the Parliament which met on March 17th, certain noblemen being at the same time nominated " as keepers of the Quene's grace." [4]   Disagreeing in regard to minor details, contemporary writers, such as Knox, Buchanan, Lindsay of Pitscottie, and Bishop Leslie, fully corroborate the testimony of Lisle that the Cardinal made a bold but futile attempt to oust Arran from his legal right to the regency, by adducing, for another arrangement, the authority of the late King on his deathbed.   Lisle further reported that Arran, in protesting against the attempt, had not scrupled to term the Cardinal a " false churle." [5]

The only question, therefore, remaining for consideration is whether the Cardinal intrepidly rested his case on his own report of the King's statement to himself, or

[1] *Hamilton Papers.*, i. 340.   [2] *Ibid.*, i. 345, 346, 360.
[3] *Works*, ed. Laing, i. 93-4.   [4] *Acta Parl. Scot.*, ii. 414,
                    [5] *Hamilton Papers*, i. 349,

on a written document to which the King's signature was attached. There is abundant testimony to the effect that Beaton produced a supposed will ; and the statement of Buchanan that he forged a will by the aid of a priest, Henry Balfour, has been so far confirmed by the discovery at Hamilton of an instrument signed by Henry Balfour, and narrating that James V. had appointed Beaton, Moray, Huntly, and Argyll to act as tutors testamentary to the Princess and also as Governors of the kingdom.[1] The instrument of Balfour was of course of no legal efficacy unless supported by an actual will ; it was only a warrant for the existence of a will, and in all probability was sent to Arran as the warrant for the Cardinal's proclamation.[2] The omission of Arran's name from the document is in agreement with a statement of Knox, and is apparently referred to in a letter of Henry VIII. to Sadler. " Can youe think," he advises Sadler to say to Arran, " that youe shal contynue a Governour when thadverse partie that wold have made themselfes by a forged will regentes with youe, *or rather excluded youe,* shall have auctoritie." [3]

The only excuse for Beaton's unwarrantable use of the King's name is that he was probably convinced that the King would have coincided with him as to Arran's unfitness, at such a perilous crisis, to have charge of the

---

[1] *Hist. MSS. Report,* Appendix, part vi. pp. 219-20.

[2] It is impossible here to discuss fully the curious theory of Mr. Lang (*History of Scotland,* i. 467 *sq.*) that this document may have been a forgery of Arran. Suffice it to state that Arran was no more likely to be guilty of a forgery than Beaton ; that Beaton could have no warrant for his proposal unless he could adduce evidence of the King's wishes ; and that Arran's case was that the evidence, on account of the condition of the King's mind, must be false.

[3] *Hamilton Papers,* i. 527.

government. A strong man—in the interests both of Catholicism and the country's independence—was required for a position of such overwhelming difficulty ; and we need not, therefore, impute it altogether to personal ambition, that Beaton deemed it advisable to neutralise the weakness and pliancy of Arran by causing him to share the great responsibility with other four persons, including Beaton. But Beaton, by the means employed by him to secure his purpose, only revived the old jealousy of the nobles at his interference in the government, and their suspicion that he was seeking by fraud to retain his old ascendancy.

In addition to this, not only had the Solway disaster placed his political reputation under a cloud, but by confirming him in the high position to which he aspired, the nobles would have provoked the special indignation of Henry. The open quarrel between Beaton and Arran was perhaps the only thing that could have reconciled Henry, even for a time, to tolerate Arran as Governor. Henry's real aim was to obtain his own recognition as Governor and Protector of Scotland, and he was by no means pleased that, without his sanction, a Governor had been chosen ; but a Scottish Governor at loggerheads with Beaton, might be a convenient medium for the attainment of his purpose.

The Solway nobles found in the fact that a Regent had been chosen, a convenient excuse for the modification of their methods of implementing their promises to Henry. The fortresses could not be delivered into Henry's hands, nor the young Queen transferred to his keeping without a revolution ; while, owing to the feud between the Regent and Beaton, Henry might be able to obtain

After the picture by Holbein, formerly in the possession of the Earl of Egremont.

KING EDWARD VI.

the substance of his desires through negotiation. Having also been compelled to break with the Cardinal, Arran was largely dependent on the Solway lords and Angus for support, and was induced, notwithstanding his own private ambitions, to represent himself as friendly to the English marriage.

Negotiations, therefore, now assumed the form of an endeavour at a compromise, all parties in Scotland being, through the diplomacy of Sir George Douglas, induced to combine either to baffle or delude Henry, or to obtain an arrangement which would guard the country's independence. Necessarily those inclined to the new heresy were prepared to go very far in meeting Henry's wishes. Others, opposed to the worldly predominance of Beaton and the ecclesiastics, were inclined to favour Henry's matrimonial scheme, provided the independence of the country were secured; whilst even the most devoted adherents of Beaton had little stomach for a continuance of the war. There was thus now manifested towards Henry, on the part of the Scots, a very deceptive kind of friendliness; but for the lack of sincerity in much of their pretence, and the steadfast efforts of many to beguile him, Henry had chiefly to thank the extremely arrogant character of his original demands.

Sir George Douglas, on whom Henry mainly depended for the accomplishment of his sinister purposes, thus became the chief agent in their frustration. It was at his instance that Henry had arranged terms with the English prisoners; but he far from approved of the terms that had been arranged, and when asked to repair to Scotland to aid Henry's scheme, he wrote to Parr: "Good my lord, this is no small bording that is laid upon my balk,

and I ame very waike to accomplishe the same."[1]
Nothing could, in fact, be accomplished except by greatly
lightening it.

Therefore, although Henry, on learning of the proclamation of Arran as Regent, sent, on January 8th,
instructions that the Solway nobles should at once co-
operate with Bothwell and Huntly in getting possession of
the child and seizing the fortresses, the first endeavour
of Douglas was to induce Henry to forego the realisation
of both of these aims. He consequently got Arran to
dispatch him, on January 18th, with a letter to Henry's
agent, Lisle, in which Arran was made to express a zealous
desire by "the grace and help of God," to "put sum
reformatioun in the stait of kirk of this realme to the
honour of God, furtht setting of his trew worde," etc., and,
for this most godly end, asked Henry for a safe-conduct
for certain ambassadors he proposed to send to him.

Whatever may have been Arran's antecedent bias
towards the new doctrines, the sequel was to show that
he was more concerned in retaining the Regency than in
the setting forth of God's "Holy Word." As for
Douglas, he made no profession of religious zeal. Asked
by Beaton "whether he was a good Cristean man or not,
or whather he was gyven to the new lerning after the fassion
of England or not?" he replied "that he was cristened, and
if he were not a good Cristean man, he praid God to
make hym one ; but, as he thought, the best of them two
might be amended, and wished that the realme of Skotland
were no worse Cristeans than the realme of Englande."[2]

At this impartial attitude the Cardinal, we are told,
gave "a great sighe," a sigh which doubtless represented

---

[1] *Hamilton Papers*, i. 353.   [2] *Ibid.*, i. 389.

rather a political anxiety than any great solicitude for the welfare of Douglas's soul. Nor was his sigh without justification, for Douglas, having obtained from the Council a decision in favour of the retention of his and his brother's lands, now, with a view of allaying Henry's suspicions and impatience, decided on the clever ruse of arranging with Arran for Beaton's apprehension, which was accomplished on January 28th, while the Cardinal was sitting in the Council. As Douglas further intimated that the arrest was but a prelude to the reform of "the hole Churche of Scotland into the same sorte that the Kinges Majeste has reformed Inglond,"[1] it was difficult to charge him with lack of enterprise in Henry's service.

As early as February 13th, Suffolk also reported that Arran had caused a sermon to be made by a "blacke friar," in favour of the reform of the abuses of the Church and the dissemination of the Bible and Testament in English; and, a little later, a black friar was appointed to preach the gospel alternately in the Abbey of Holyrood and the "great parish church."[2] The names of the two black friars were, we learn from Knox, Thomas William and John Rough, whose preaching caused the Grey Friars to "rowp" as "thei had bein ravinis : yea, rather thei yelled and rored as devellis in Hell 'Heresy ! heresy, Guylliame and Rought will cary the Governour to the Deville.'"[3]

Arran was, however, to be plucked as a brand from the burning, as soon as he discovered that the support of the Reformers was hostile to his political interests. Meantime, he immediately discovered that mere Reforming zeal

---

[1] *Hamilton Papers*, i. 401.　　　　[2] *Ibid.*, i. 418, 426.
[3] *Knox's Works*, i. 96-7.

was not enough for Henry, who instructed Sadler to warn
Arran and the Scottish lords against sending ambassadors
to him merely "with things of entretaynment," and to
remind them of what might ensue if it appeared that he
and the lords went about to trifle with him.

Nevertheless, the policy of Douglas was producing an
impression on Henry, who gradually became persuaded
that the immediate accomplishment of his aims would
be well-nigh impossible ; and, in deference to susceptibilities
with which he did not profess to have any sympathy, he
was induced ostensibly to adopt a policy less fitted to
wound them.

On his arrival in Scotland, Sadler found that the
Parliament had just ratified the governorship of Arran,
and had appointed ambassadors to state to Henry the
terms on which they were prepared to negotiate for a
marriage. To Henry, who had not even expected that
the Parliament was to be assembled, the whole of this
news was a very unpleasant surprise, and he even instructed
Sadler to remonstrate privately with Angus, Douglas and
the Solway lords for permitting the parliamentary ratification
of Arran's governorship.

This being his frame of mind, the actual terms of the
marriage arrangements, when he came to know them, must
have struck him with sheer amazement. Not to mention
various important, though minor, provisions, the ambassadors were enjoined to represent the necessity of the
young Queen remaining in Scotland until the completion
of the marriage ; to refuse the delivery of " any strengths
of the realme in pledge and securitie " ; and to stipulate
that Scotland should meanwhile, and until the young Queen's
marriage, continue to be governed independently under

a Regent, and that even after the marriage, it should retain all its ancient rights and privileges. To condescend even to the formality of considering terms so entirely in the teeth of his bargain with Arran and the Solway lords implied the intention of secretly persisting in his original purpose, whatever might be the results of the negotiations ; and, on the other hand, the sincerity of the majority of the Scots in promoting the negotiations, was necessarily qualified by a lack of faith in Henry's intentions. In fact, there was among the Scots a kind of tacit conspiracy to delude Henry, by pretended acquiescence in negotiations which were not meant quite seriously.

Even the Queen-Dowager, whom Sadler was instructed to visit in order to " desire her frankly in all things to open her heart to him," Sadler found " most willing and conformable," in appearance, to the King's purpose : not only was she, seemingly, greatly flattered by the honour Henry proposed to do her daughter, but she even advised that Henry should stand fast " upon the point to have her delivered into his hands," if he really wished the marriage to take place, the real purpose of Arran being, she said—truly enough—to marry her daughter to his own son.

To impress Sadler the more with the sincerity of her desire for the English marriage, she indicated anxiety that he should send to his master a favourable account of the young Queen's appearance, and she therefore let him see for himself that the infant was not the weakling rumour had reported her to be, but a strong, well-developed child, and likely to prove a bride worthy of the great destiny Henry was proposing for her. Taking him, therefore, into the chamber where the child was, she " caused the nurse to unwound her out of her clowtes," that he might see her naked. "I assure your Majesty," wrote Sadler, "it is as goodly a child as I have seen of her age, and as like to live with the grace of God." [1]

That the Queen-Dowager was entirely hostile to the English marriage has generally been taken for granted ; and it is certain that to Sir George she expressed her anxiety lest the child should be immediately delivered into England, " because she was too young to be carried so far " ; but this natural maternal solicitude did not imply any necessary hostility to the match ; and those who can see in her conduct nothing but guile appear to forget that Francis II., to whom her daughter was to be married, was not then born, and that, at that time, there was no likelihood of any child being born to Catherine de Medici.

True, the Queen-Dowager wished the liberation of Beaton ; as how, being Catholic, could she do aught else ? But there is at least the possibility that she thought the Cardinal might succeed in arranging suitable terms for the English marriage, to the desirability of which, from a worldly point of view, she could hardly have been blind ; and his liberation would, she doubtless hoped—though on this point she proved in the end to be wrong—hold in check Arran's ambitious hopes in regard to the marriage.

In whatever way the seemingly daring *coup* of the Cardinal's arrest is to be explained—whether it was really meant seriously by Douglas as well as by Arran, or was only a ruse to delude and pacify Henry, or a contrivance of Douglas to commend himself at once to Henry and Arran— those who had him in keeping had no intention of handing him over to Henry : as Arran playfully put it to Sadler, " the Cardinal had lever go into hell." [2]

[1] Sadler's *State Papers*, i. 88.   [2] *Ibid.*, i. 110.

MARY OF LORRAINE, QUEEN OF JAMES V. AND MOTHER OF
MARY QUEEN OF SCOTS.

This picture was for some time believed to be a portrait of Mary Queen of Scots,
but it is now (though without certainty) supposed to be that of her mother.

It may be that the aim of his captors was to come to some kind of terms with him : to induce him either to assent to the parliamentary decision as to entertaining the marriage proposal, or to prevent him being in a position immediately to object to it ; and they may have hoped to induce him to combine with them in their endeavour to procure, meanwnile, a continuance of the truce with Henry. Little faith can be placed in the statement of " Sandy Pringill," an English spy, that the Cardinal obtained his release by bribing Douglas; but we may well believe that Douglas had charge of the stage-management of the release —a stage-management so artful as fairly to bewilder Sadler.

We have first his removal from Dalkeith—not to Tantallon, as the impatient Henry suggested, but—to Lord Seton's place, followed by nothing less than his transference, under Lord Seton's nominal care, to his own castle at St. Andrews in order, so Arran was made, perhaps quite ingenuously, to explain, that the government might obtain possession of the castle as well as the Cardinal ; then his confinement at St. Andrews on the bonds of four lords that he should not pass beyond its boundaries ; and finally the discovery that, bonds or no bonds, and whether he could leave his castle or not, neither his ecclesiastical nor political influence was diminished, but rather increased. True, Beaton's fiat that the sacrifice of the Mass should remain suspended throughout the kingdom, so long as he was not in a position to exercise his ecclesiastical office, may have so appealed to the superstitions of the people as seriously to endanger Arran's rule ; but of course, had Arran been as sincere a Protestant as he was then pretending to be, the cessation of " idolatry " ought to have ministered rather to his satisfaction than to his disquiet.

Deeply involved as we must suppose Douglas to have been in the liberation, as in the arrest, of the Cardinal, he, in conversation with Sadler, avoided responsibility for it by throwing this on Arran, who, he asserted, truly enough, was " the most wavering and unstable person " ; and he further affirmed that Arran had been led astray by Huntly, whom he described " as the falsest and wiliest young man of the world " [1]—a definition which, apart from the qualification " young," would have applied with special aptness to himself. If Arran was concerned in the Cardinal's liberation, it must have been because he could not help it ; for he was still doubtful as to the Cardinal's attitude towards himself, and for some months they remained unreconciled.

The next stage in the intrigue, so far as it concerned Scotland, was—minor under-plots being left out of account—marked, on the one hand, by the efforts of Arran, while seeking to avert the suspicions of Henry, to adapt his policy in Scotland to the new situation created by the Cardinal's release, and, on the other hand, by the finessing of Beaton to consolidate his position in Scotland either by means of Arran's ruin, or by compelling him to terms. The influence which the Cardinal exercised was at first indirect. It was exercised through Arran's bastard brother, the Abbot of Paisley, who had lately arrived in Scotland from Paris. The expectation at first was that the Abbot and his companion, David Panter, had been brought to Scotland by Arran that " the one and the other " might " occupy the pulpete, and trewly preach Jesus Christ " ; [2] but either the Abbot was the special emissary of his Catholic superiors, or Arran had sent for him to help him in arranging terms with Beaton. As early as April 12th he

---

[1] Sadler's *State Papers*, i. 105.   [2] Knox's *Works*, i. 105.

had dispatched him as an envoy to Beaton, who, Arran told Sadler, was now desirous of "leaving utterly the cast of France," and being wholly, as Arran professed to be, "given to the cast of England." Yet Arran professed to have little faith in the sincerity of his professions, and hardly believed that he would, as he had invited him, come to Edinburgh, "fearing lest I should eftsoons lay hands on him."[1] Arran proved to be right in his conjecture ; but shortly afterwards Arran—doubtless on the Abbot's advice—adopted the remarkable resolve of resiling from his Protestantism, though in the March Parliament he had got an Act passed for the free circulation of the Scriptures, and was supposed now to be "the most fervent Protestant in Europe."

Some time before Arran's recantation, Henry, in order still further to bind Arran to his interests, had offered the hand of the Princess Elizabeth for Arran's son. Towards this great bribe Arran's attitude was, however, irreproachable. Acknowledging his deep sense of the honour Henry proposed to do him, he said he would consult with his friends before he gave a definite reply. After consulting with them, he reported that they were as much gratified as he was, at the proposal ; and he added that he could not doubt that the marriage between the young Queen and Edward would be easily agreed upon, "unless the King's Majesty go about to take away the liberty and freedom of this realm, and to bring the same to his obedience and subjection."[2] Whatever weakness may, however, have characterised Arran's policy, he was necessarily as desirous as the Cardinal to outwit Henry. Indeed he was, through the influence of his brother the Abbot, coming

[1] Sadler's *State Papers*, i. 137.   [2] *Ibid.*, i. 130, 139.

more and more into line with the Cardinal's policy ; and,
on April 22nd, Douglas announced that he had put away
his friar preachers, and would undoubtedly join the French
party.[1] Not only so, but, as has now been revealed, this
fervent ecclesiastical recruit of Henry, as early as May 14th
assured Pope Paul III. that "he would strive with all
his strength for the safety of the Church " ; and on the
14th he wrote, to commit his country to the protection
of his Holiness, and to beg him to undertake " the defence
of its rights and privileges." [2] The truth was, that for
Arran to continue to champion the cause of Protestantism,
unless he could depend on Henry's help, would be suicidal ;
and convinced, as he could hardly help being, of the
sinister purposes of Henry, both towards his country and
himself, he had hardly other option than, while continuing
meanwhile his friendly pretences towards Henry, to return
secretly to the Catholics, and seek succour for his country
and support for himself by a renewal of the alliance with
France.

In his desire to come to terms with Beaton, Arran
had doubtless also been quickened by the arrival from
France of Lennox, who against him claimed the next
heirship to the Crown, and whom Beaton and the French
party were bringing forward as a possible Regent, should
Arran continue to persist in his Protestant folly. His
main difficulty was doubtless distrust of Beaton, whose
illstarred attempt to deprive him of the governorship could
not be easily forgotten. Their alienation was also, meanwhile, apparently aggravated by the very methods adapted
by Beaton to bring Arran to terms ; but it being now

[1] Sadler's *State Papers*, i. 144, 158.
[2] *State Papers, reign of Henry VIII.*, ed. Gairdner, xviii. (11) No. 542

impossible for Beaton to establish the original contrivance of a Regency Commission, with himself as head, Arran, apart from the consideration of kinship, which then counted for much, was the most pliant tool for his own purposes which Beaton could select. The real aim of Beaton in patronising Lennox—who, it was even suggested, might marry the Queen-Dowager—was merely so to alarm Arran about his position, as to make him realise the advisability of definitely throwing in his lot with Beaton and the Catholics.

Meanwhile, although the English marriage was anathema to the clergy, Beaton made no open objection to the negotiations, and from the time of his liberation he was, through Sadler, seeking to commend himself to Henry's favour. Towards the end of April he invited Sadler, through the Bishop of Orkney, to visit him at St. Andrews, adding that if he did so, he trusted he would have good cause to think his "journey well bestowed." But at this time Arran, on account of Beaton's support of Lennox, was specially distrustful of Beaton, and Sadler was afraid that the visit to Beaton would be taken by Arran in bad part.[1]

Henry could hardly have been deceived by Beaton's professions ; but Beaton's attitude explains the general assent to the marriage negotiations. These negotiations were, in fact, proceeding much too smoothly to be consistent with sincerity on either side—the enormous character of the original differences being considered. As the first Scottish ambassadors affirmed that they lacked commission to make certain alteration in the terms, without which alteration Henry expressed his inability to proceed further, Glencairn and Sir George Douglas were sent with certain

---

[1] Sadler's *State Papers*, i. 104, 133, 189.

compromises, which Sadler, influenced by what he deemed his knowledge of the peculiarities of the situation, strongly urged Henry to accept; "more than hath been done, being," he said, "impossible"; although, once a definite arrangement had been formally reached, Henry, though the actual terms of the treaty did not guarantee all that he desired, might, by "gentle means," soon have "all the nobility" induced "to his will and devotion."[1]

Such a view of the situation was of course absurdly sanguine, but Henry, from whatever motive, ostensibly acted in accordance with Sadler's advice; and thus a treaty of marriage was completed between him and the Scottish Commission on July 1st.

Strangely enough, also, the Scots had obtained the substance of their demands: the young Queen was to remain in Scotland until she had completed her tenth year; Scotland was to retain its name and continue to be governed by its ancient laws; and although it was agreed that neither country should afford assistance to the foreign aggressor, on the other hand, Henry failed to induce the Scots to dissolve their ancient league with France.[2] So far as appearances went, Henry had waived his claims to overlordship, had foregone his ambitious purpose of virtually seizing the Scottish sovereignty, and had done his utmost to avoid offence to Scottish national prejudices. If Henry's part in the arrangement had been entirely *bona fide*, the Scots had been without excuse for the rupture which soon after followed.

Much, indeed all, turned on the attitude and procedure of Beaton: unless he were again overthrown, or unless Henry could buy him and convert him to his own

[1] Sadler's *State Papers*, i. 187.   [2] Rymer's *Foedera*, xiv. 786, 796.

ecclesiastical opinions, Henry knew that the treaty was mere words, and that, treaty or no treaty, he was as far as ever from gaining his purpose ; but since even Arran and his friends had, whatever their professions, resolved not to further the sinister ends of Henry, the prospects of the Cardinal renouncing his old faith in order to become the bosom friend of the heretic king could not be termed bright. Thus the main hope, meanwhile, of Henry was that Beaton and Arran should again quarrel, and appearances seemed at first to favour its realisation.

On June 7th Sadler reported that Arran was staying proceedings against Beaton until the conclusion of the treaty, and that Beaton was making great suit for Arran's favour, or for leave to go to France.[1] Sadler continued to press him, by all the " means and persuasions " he could, to the apprehension of Beaton, Lennox, and their adherents ; but he now found that Arran was making the enterprise " more difficile than he was woont to doo." [2]

The truth was that neither Sadler nor Henry had gauged aright either Beaton's abilities, resolution, or influence, or the possibilities of Arran's pliability, insincerity and self-regard. In addition to this, the close connection of Arran, the Douglases, and the Solway lords with the intrigues of Henry had so alarmed the nation as to enable the Cardinal to regain much of the old influence he had lost through the Solway disaster.

Nor was Beaton strong only in Scottish support. On July 2nd, Sadler reported that the French navy was lying off the east coast—with the view, Sadler suspected, of carrying off the young Queen—and that Angus and Arran were in force near Linlithgow, till they saw what

---

[1] Sadler's *State Papers*, i. 214. [2] *Hamilton Papers*, i. 548.

the naval visit might portend.[1] Henry thereupon proposed
that the child should be sent to a place within reach of
English help, but it was explained that she was then troubled
" with the breeding of teeth." Sadler thought Arran was
as much concerned for her health and wellbeing as if she
had been his own child ; and no doubt this was so, though
his reasons for this were of course selfish rather than
benevolent. But he was on the horns of a great dilemma.
On the one side there was the devil, as represented by
Henry, and on the other there was the deep sea of Beaton's
as yet unfathomable intentions. Unseconded by Beaton,
Arran's appeal for Papal or French help was vain ; and
without French help he could not hold his own, either
against Henry or against Beaton.

Instead, however, of Arran succumbing to Beaton, Beaton
was now making a show of revolting against Arran.
Assembling, on July 26th, six or seven thousand of his
adherents at Stirling, Beaton next day marched with
them to Linlithgow, arriving there at ten o'clock at night ;
but Arran having taken the precaution to fortify the Palace
with men and artillery, the insurgents contented themselves
meanwhile with lying in the town. Arran's party, reinforced
by Angus and the Solway lords, were, according to Sadler, of
"joylie courage " ; but since they were also desirous to
settle differences by " wisedom and pollicie withoute the
effusion of bloode,"[2] an arrangement was soon come to which
must have been as "gall and wormwood " to Henry.

The demands of the Cardinal were too reasonable and
too accordant with general Scottish sentiment, to be objected
to. His avowed purpose was not to head a revolt, nor
remove the Governor from power, nor oppose the ratification

---

[1] Sadler's *State Papers*, i. 228.   [2] *Hamilton Papers*, i. 584-5.

LINLITHGOW PALACE.

of the treaty, but merely to secure the safety of the child, by placing her in Stirling Castle under the care of guardians in whose fidelity the nation could put full trust. The secret bond, which he got his adherents to subscribe on July 24th, at Linlithgow,[1] was, notwithstanding its references to Arran's weakness, a most moderate as well as cogent document. While adroitly indicating the lack of policy and justice under Arran's administration, it justified their muster by the need to guard against the subjection of the country to England, as well as against the transference of the young Queen into Henry's hands, to the "hie dishonour, perpetuall skaith, dammage and rewyne of the libertie and nobilness of this realm." Not only, indeed, were these proposals unobjectionable : they were so advisable that even the Protestant Glencairn was disarmed by them ; and, discerning the possibility of a temporary reconciliation among all parties and a peaceful and unanimous acceptance of the treaty, he made himself the medium of arranging the agreement.

Nor, however disconcerted Henry may have been by Beaton's apparent triumph, was it possible for him to object to the terms of reconciliation, for the primary aim of Arran and his party in agreeing to it was stated to be, the desire of obtaining the willing and unanimous assent of the nation to the treaty. The professed object of the Cardinal and his friends was merely to secure that the provisions of the treaty should be properly carried out.

They objected, and with reason, to the Queen-Dowager and the young Queen being wholly in the hands of Arran's creatures, and it was finally agreed that she should be placed with four guardians—Lords Graham, Erskine,

---

[1] *Hamilton Papers*, i, 630-1.

Lyndsay, and Livingstone, two being nominated by Beaton's party and two by Arran's—under whose care she was to reside in Stirling. Stirling being the jointure-house of the Queen-Dowager, assigned her by the Parliament, she was quite entitled to remove the child there, should she think fit ; and it was diplomatically explained to Sadler that " the house of Lythcoe is so little " that the new guardians, with their attendants, could not all " be well placed and lodged in the same."

On the same day—July 26th—that the young Queen left for Stirling, the treaty of peace and marriage was proclaimed at Edinburgh, apparently to the entire satisfaction of the citizens ; and immediately thereafter it was also proclaimed throughout the country. But the sanguine hopes of Glencairn as to its ratification in a full and unanimous Parliament were not to be realised. Had the professions of Beaton to Angus and others, as to his " moche " dedication " to the peax and mariage," led to a formal reconciliation between him and Henry, it might have been otherwise ; but Henry would not even pretend to tolerate the Cardinal and his followers, unless they followed Henry's example in revolting from the Pope. Despite Beaton's profuse professions of goodwill to Henry, Henry continued to advise Arran against him ; and it is therefore small wonder that Beaton and his followers ceased to pretend any zeal for the treaty, and declined to stultify themselves by taking part in the ceremony of ratification. Difficulties were raised as to the place of meeting, Beaton standing out for Stirling, and Arran insisting on Edinburgh. All the while Henry was continuing to bombard the bamboozled Arran with advice against Beaton—that he should not permit him on the new Council unless he renounced his "red hood" and allowed God's word to be preached ; or that he should send a man secretly to capture him ; or at least deny him or his followers admission to the Queen. Not only so, but, in dread of the Cardinal's possible reconciliation with Arran, he now offered to make Arran king north of the Forth, on condition that he delivered up to him the southern strongholds ; and in addition to this he, in July, induced Angus and Maxwell to sign a "secret device," by which they bound themselves to secure the delivery of the child "as soon as may be" ; to acknowledge Henry as lord of the kingdom in case of her death ; to support Arran only if he kept the treaty, but to acknowledge no other Regent ; and to secure, if possible, to Henry the strongholds south of the Forth.[1]

Thus, hardly was the ink of the treaty dry when Henry was endeavouring to go behind its provisions and to secure the fulfilment of the conditions—and even of much more—to which the Scottish Commissioners objected. But so far as Arran was concerned, the inevitable result of Henry's proposals was gradually to drive him towards the Cardinal's net : Henry was making his submission to the Cardinal immensely easier than it would otherwise have been. That Beaton would oblige Henry by renouncing the "red hood," Arran could not believe ; on the contrary, he was of opinion that he "wolde rather embrace and recyve the three crownes."[2]

Nevertheless Beaton continued to finesse with Henry, protesting that, so far from seeking to offend him, there was nothing he so much desired as his favour. His protestations were backed up by the Queen-Dowager, who,

[1] Sadler, i. 237.
[2] *State Papers*, Henry VIII., v. 319.

however, never pretended any friendship for Arran, her aim
being to convince Henry that since the Cardinal, unlike
Arran, had no private ambition to serve with the young
Queen, he was much more worthy of Henry's trust. She
now sent for Sadler to visit her at Stirling, not only to
let him know her constant devotion to the match, but
that Beaton's party were all "well-minded and dedicate"
to it.[1] She further, tactfully, expressed her delight with her
new residence, as, alone on account of the surpassing nature
of its prospect, she well might ; and, as before, she wound
up the interview by gratifying Sadler with a sight of the
child, " who," she said, " did grow apace, and soon she
would be a woman if she took of her mother,"—" who
indeed," adds Sadler, "is of the largest stature of women."
All this seems to show that Beaton, so far from wishing,
meanwhile, to provoke an open rupture with Henry, was,
if anything, desirous to soothe him into quiescent assent
to the *statu quo*. But for the fact that Henry meant to
use the treaty as a mere blind to conceal his secret intrigue,
immediate action on Beaton's part against him was not
called for, for much might happen within ten years.
Henry's main difficulty, on the other hand, was that he
could not trust the Scots, so long as Beaton retained his
"red hood," and thus the treaty had complicated rather
than improved the situation.

Peace thus rested on the forlorn hope of converting
Beaton to Protestantism ; and on August 24th, Henry
suggested to Sadler that he should, "as of himself," seek
to allure Beaton by fair promises of Henry's unbounded
favour if he "wold be faithful unto us and serve us."
True, it would be incumbent on him to leave "his red

[1] Sadler, i. 250.

cappe," but he should still be "an archebishop and prymat over the rest." [1]

But who was Henry that he should thus take upon him to set up his own archbishop in Scotland ? And what peculiar honour lay in becoming the subservient tool of the English king, that it should tempt Beaton not merely to abnegate his great ecclesiastical office and his still higher ecclesiastical ambitions, but both to renounce his faith and betray the liberties of his country ? It may be that Beaton was never told by Sadler of devices at once so shameful and so crude, and in any case they were conceived too late to affect the attitude of him or his followers towards the ratification of the treaties, which took place, on August 25th, in their absence ; but without any direct dissent from them.

All the while that Henry was suggesting such high honours for Beaton, he was urging Arran to " go roundly to work " against him, and on August 25th, the English Privy Council recommended that unless Beaton and his party were present at the ratification, they should be attacked before the arrival of the Papal Legate, Cardinal Grimani,[1] who was bound to exercise an influence adverse to Henry's purposes. Immediately after the ratification, Arran went to St. Andrews for an interview with Beaton, who, however, refused to leave his castle to speak with him in the town, alleging that " he durst nor for fear of his life." Arran therefore, on August 29th, proclaimed him a traitor, and instructed his supporters to levy their forces against him.

How much in the attitude of Beaton and Arran towards each other was now mere pretence is hard to say ; but

---

[1] *Hamilton Papers*, i. 652-3. [2] *Ibid.*, i. 656-7.

scarcely had Arran's proclamation been issued when the
enigmatical Sir George Douglas was expressing to Sadler
his apprehension that Arran would " slypp from them and
beestelie put himselfe into thandes of his ennemyes." [1]

Whatever chance there might have been of postponing
an alliance of Arran with the Cardinal was in any case
lost by Henry's arrest of certain Scottish ships, sailing
with provisions to France, Henry's preposterous plea being
that this was a violation of the treaty, and that some of
the crews belonged to the Cardinal's party and had spoken
disrespectfully of the Governor.[2]   In fact Henry was virtually already assuming the direction of Scottish affairs, with
the result that the nation was immediately swept with a
violent storm of wrath at his interference. So indignant
were the citizens of Edinburgh, that Sadler could not
venture to appear in the streets, and had fears lest his
house should be burned over his head. Arran had thus
reached the limits of his temporising policy, and if anything further had been needed to compel him to a decision,
it was supplied by the revived pressure of Henry for the
delivery of the Scottish strongholds.

Nor was the Cardinal the man to be blind to his
remarkable opportunity. His refusal to meet Arran meant
that he had burnt his boats. Immediately after Arran's
proclamation he and his friends assembled their forces
at Stirling, their intention being, it was said, " to crowne
the yong Quene, to make four Regentes of the realme,
and to depryve the governour of his auctoritie." [3]

Faced by a revival of Beaton's original conspiracy,
Arran could not hope to repeat his triumph over him
except by the English help, for which he would have to

---

[1] *Hamilton Papers*, ii. 4.   [2] *Ibid.*, ii. 4.   [3] *Ibid.*, ii. 4.

pay Henry's own price. On September 3rd, therefore, he rode suddenly out of Edinburgh, with only a few attendants, who included, however, significantly enough, the two ecclesiastics, his half-brother the Abbot of Paisley, and Dr. Panter ; and, after a long interview with Beaton at Callendar, he accompanied him to Stirling.

The gentleman who informed Sadler of the startling change in the situation, stated that the Governor told him that " his goyng to Sterlyng shulde be for the best, for he shulde make all well " ;[1] and the Abbot of Paisley also assured him that he now " trusted the Cardinall and thother noble men of that partie woolde concurre with the Governour and his partakers in and for thacomplishment of the treaties, in all poyntes and condicions."[2]

As yet, be it remembered, the treaty, though ratified by the Scottish Parliament, had not been confirmed by Henry. Henry had declined to confirm it until the dispatch of hostages, which, he wrote to Sadler, he regarded as " the knot of the holl treatie."[3] Arran, pleading the disturbed state of the country, had not as yet been able to send hostages ; but, whether the hostages were sent or not, it was plain that Henry wished to cajole or concuss Arran into compliance with his original demands ; and therefore, instead of Arran winning over Beaton to support Henry, Beaton had won over Arran to his own French and Catholic policy.

That this was the true character of the situation was almost immediately made manifest by two striking occurrences : (1) on Saturday, September 8th, Arran, in the church of the Franciscans at Stirling—after doing penance for his apostasy and obtaining solemn absolution from

---

[1] *Hamilton Papers*, ii. 19. [2] *Ibid.*, ii. 22. [3] *Ibid.*, ii. 7.

the Cardinal—received the sacrament in token of his restoration to membership in the Catholic Church ; and (2) on the Sunday the young Queen was crowned in the chapel of Stirling Castle. It can hardly be doubted that, before his renunciation of his heresies, Arran, through his brother the Abbot, had made a bargain of an entirely secular import with the Cardinal, and that his price was an assurance of the marriage of his son to the young Queen. Indeed the English Parr, before August 2nd, learned from a spy that "bitwene the Cardinall and the lordes of his parte was secret commynicacion with the governour, that if he wolde in all causes applie and followe theire myendes, his sonne and heire shulde marrie theire quene."[1]

The complete understanding now arrived at between Arran and the Cardinal caused the revolt from the Cardinal of his protégé, the Earl of Lennox, who, seeing already how matters were drifting, had become a suitor for the hand of Lady Margaret Douglas, daughter of Angus and niece of Henry, in order that he might have Henry's aid " for the recoverie of his rights and title to this realme, which the governor now usurpeth." Strenuous efforts were made by Beaton to prevent such a formidable coalition, by effecting an understanding between Lennox and Arran ; but Lennox would be content with nothing less than the overthrow of his rival. Lennox did obtain the hand of Lady Margaret ; but it was mainly in after years that the political results of the marriage were to be fully manifested—in the marriage of his son, Lord Darnley, to the same queen, Mary Stuart, who was now the subject of such squabbling negotiations between Henry and the Scots.

[1] *Hamilton Papers*, i. 615.

THE CROWN OF SCOTLAND.

Immediately on learning that Arran had " put himself into the handes" of the Cardinal, Henry directed Angus and the " English lords" to attack them at once while their power was weak. Fearing also that Angus would not " so extremely execute" the enterprise as he wished him to do, he suggested to Suffolk a sudden raid on Edinburgh, in order to seize Arran and Beaton, or, if they were not there, to burn the city and waste the country of their supporters. Those hostile projects were not, however, carried out during the autumn, mainly owing to the great ingenuity of Sir George Douglas in raising objections to any immediate action by England, and to the resourcefulness of Angus and the " English lords"—while professing themselves entirely at Henry's service—in finding excuses for at least deferring the adoption of extreme measures against Arran.

Meanwhile the attitude of Arran and Beaton towards Henry continued to be outwardly conciliatory. On their arrival in Edinburgh, Beaton informed Sadler courteously, but ambiguously, that they would " doo what shulde becom them to doo " towards Henry, " not offending the honour and lybertie of the realme,"[1] while Arran sought weakly to turn away Henry's wrath by assuring Sadler that, while the Cardinal's supporters were " very styffe against the treaties," he " for his part remayned the same man he was," and would do all that he could for the performance of the treaties.[2] On the 23rd, however, the Cardinal, in the presence of the Council and on their behalf, complained to Sadler of their violation by the detention of the Scottish ships and other acts of hostility, and also expressed surprise that Henry had not yet ratified them. As regards the

[1] *Hamilton Papers*, ii. 59.   [2] *Ibid.*, ii. 59.

ratification, Sadler reminded him that the hostages had not
been sent, whereupon Beaton countered with the queries
whether, on hostages being sent, Henry would accept them
and ratify the treaties, and whether, also, he would not
only restore the ships and goods, but cause redress to be
made for the attempt on the Borders.[1]   Beaton further
informed Sadler that no man was more desirous to adjust
matters to Henry's satisfaction, " not offending his duyte
of allegiance "; but this qualified profession was mere fuel
to the fire of Henry's wrath.   So far from being able to
direct all things in Scotland as he himself would " appoynt
and determine," he saw, so he wrote to Sadler, " oon man
and he our ennemye to drect and determyn all together
at his oune arbitre."[2]

Henry therefore now definitely declared himself to be
at liberty " to take or leave the treaties," to which declaration the Scottish Parliament, in December, responded by
declaring that by the seizure of the Scottish ships the
treaties had been violated, and also that, by the refusal of
Henry to ratify them, they had ceased to be binding on
Scotland.   By the same Parliament the alliance with France
was renewed, and Beaton was confirmed in the office of
Lord High Chancellor.

The definite rupture of negotiations with Henry may
be regarded as the first decisive turning-point in Mary's
life ; it decided that French and not English, Catholic and
not Protestant, influences were to be the formative agencies
of her character.   The savage outrages by which Henry
now sought to glut his fury at the failure of his intrigues to
get the infant into his hands, only confirmed the worst
opinions that had been formed of his intentions : they but

[1] *Hamilton Papers*, ii. 70.   [2] *Ibid.*, ii. 83.

served to rouse among the Scots an almost unprecedented hate of their "auld enemies," and for the time being to bring into disrepute the Protestant opinions of which the great English ogre was the conspicuous champion. As for Beaton, he must at least be allowed the main merit of defeating Henry's sinister purposes. His triumph over the intrigues of Henry was complete ; or, if anything was needed to complete it, it was supplied by the savage excesses by which Henry sought to reap revenge. As Suffolk assured Henry, by a mere process of furious chastisement he could only cause all Scotland to say, "Whate fals traytours ar those or unhappye men ar theye, that will take the Kynge of Englandes parte, or thynke that the Kynge of Inglande entendethe any goodnes to the yonge Quene his nyece or the realme of Scotlande, but oonlye to the distruccion of the same. By reason whereof, after Edynburghe so brownte, your highness shall have nothinge in Scotland but by the sword and conqueste." [1]

At the same time, the policy of the Cardinal was as extreme as that of the English king, and it was enforced by cruelties which in great part neutralised the advantages accruing to his cause from the wanton excesses of the English. Beaton must of course be judged by the religious axioms of his time : burning, drowning, and torture were then the recognised methods of promoting outward conformity to a supposed Christianity, whose original message is said to have been that of " Peace on Earth and Goodwill towards Men."

" Adopting the most approved devices for stamping out heresy, Beaton discharged his task with a cool thoroughness which, had his task been other than it was,

---

[1] *Hamilton Papers*, ii. 285.

and the means necessary to its accomplishment of a different
character, might have entitled him to high renown instead
of, as the fates in Scotland were to determine, to a quite
peculiar infamy. But it cannot be said that, judged even
by the standards of that age, the infamy was insufficiently
earned. Had the zeal of Beaton been strictly religious, or
even, as in the case of Calvin, theological, some kind of
excuse might have been pled for his severity as a persecutor.
For the cruelties perpetrated at the instigation of extreme
religious fanaticism, or narrow theological persuasion, there
is the plea—akin to that which absolves the madman—of
overmastering impulse or indubitable conviction. Such a
plea is hardly available for Beaton. Extremely loyal
though he was to the traditional conventionalities of
Catholicism, it is difficult to believe that, neglecting, as he
did, some of the weightier matters of the law, and engrossed,
as he seemed to be, mainly by the " vain pomp and glory of
the world," his devout soul was really so utterly harrowed
by the violations of ecclesiastical use and wont as the
ruthless punishments with which he visited them would
seem to imply. At any rate, among the mass of the people
his persecuting fervour aroused a detestation of him, that
was largely inspired by a sense of the incongruity between
his zeal and his manner of life. The antipathy it awakened
against him was really more pungent than that felt towards
Henry VIII., for the reason that Henry's motives were those
of the average man, whereas the ecclesiastical campaigns
of Beaton could not be accounted for by that excess of
ecclesiastical piety which alone could have excused them.

A detailed consideration of the inhuman achievements of
Henry or the Cardinal does not, however, fall within the
scope of a book mainly concerned with the fortunes of Mary

CARDINAL BEATON.

Stuart. What we have mainly here to do is to note their effect in creating the circumstances that were to shape her career, and their results on the Scotland which it was to be her future lot to try to govern. When Arran and Beaton finally broke with Henry, the nobles of the English party—including Angus, Cassilis, and even Glencairn, though apparently not Lennox—thought fit, in order to escape the possibility of forfeiture, to sign a bond both to support Arran against England, and to defend " the liberty of Holy Church." Sir George Douglas, who was surety for Angus, explained to Suffolk the nature of the paction, un-scrupulously adding : " Nochtheles I assure your grace ye have the hartis of all thir greate men more surely nor evir ye had." But the aim of Douglas was, of course, to ward off Henry's wrath from himself and his brother, and, as he put it to Suffolk, to induce the English commander " to be gude to my frendis and powre servandis in the Mers." [1]

Henry was, however, as little able to regard with seriousness the excuses of the Douglases as he was the renewed overtures of Arran and Beaton. On May 9th he sent instructions to Wharton and Bowes to enter into an arrangement at Carlisle only with Lennox and Glencairn, the former instructions in regard to Angus and Cassilis being cancelled on account of their having joined the party of Arran and the Cardinal.

The overwhelming descent, early in May, 1544, of Hertford on Edinburgh, and his " wise, manly, and discreet handling " of the charge committed to him of devastating the country [2] had, however, no better result than to promote the general exasperation of the nation, to cause the temporary removal of the young Queen for greater safety to Dunkeld,

[1] *Hamilton Papers*, ii. 251.   [2] Haynes's *State Papers*, p. 32.

and to confirm Angus and other lords in their resolve to
hold aloof from Henry.

Lennox and Glencairn had been induced to take up
arms against Arran ; but on May 26th, after " a conflict
cruellie fochtin," [1] were completely defeated by him near
Glasgow, Glencairn taking refuge in Dumbarton Castle,
while Lennox, moved, perhaps, as much by love as by fear,
set sail for England.

On May 10th, Angus wrote to Hertford to advertise
him " of the gud mynd that I beir to do service to the
King's Majeste " ; and Sir George Douglas, after diplomatically congratulating Hertford on his arrival in Scotland
—even adding that but for the expedition both he and
his brother would have lost their heads—began to persuade
him to " leave thextremitie of the sworde and fyre now
extended here." But the time was past for either Hertford
or his master being influenced by the mere professions or
counsel of Angus or Sir George, and Sir George avoided
a definite proposal for the deliverance of Tantallon by
finding it impossible, on account of his situation, to give
a reply until Hertford had left Scotland.

Now, however, took place in Scotland a political muta-
tion, in some respects as singular as ever happened in that
country. A convention of the nobility, summoned to
meet at Linlithgow, on May 23rd, to consider the critical
condition of affairs, adjourned to meet next day at Stirling,
where, if we are to credit Sir George Douglas, the nobles
on June 3rd resolved, at his instance, to deprive Arran
of his office, because, by the counsel of the Cardinal, he
had broken " the peice and contract of mariage," and was
thus mainly responsible for the country's miserable plight.[2]

[1] *Diurnal*, p. 32.   [2] *Hamilton Papers*, ii. 409-13.

Sir George's account of the transaction was, however, coloured so as, if possible, to win for it Henry's approval. The original resolution was that the Queen-Dowager should be made joint Regent with Arran; but Arran, having declined to agree to this, was meanwhile suspended from his office.[1] The most notable features of the arrangement were (1) the apparent overthrow of the Cardinal, (2) the apparent breach between the Queen-Dowager and him, and (3) the apparently close alliance between the Queen-Dowager and Angus, who was made lieutenant-general south of the Forth.

That the Cardinal had again lost repute by the disastrous results of his anti-English policy is pretty certain. While Hertford and his staff were standing on "the hill without the town" (the Calton Hill, most likely), they heard "the women and pore myserable creatures of the towne make exclamation and cryenges out upon the Cardynall in thies words : 'Wa worthe the Cardynall!'"[2] and doubtless these words expressed the sentiments of very many Scots ; but it is also probable that the arrangement was in part another effort to beguile Henry; and there were other considerations involved.

The Queen-Dowager had both persistently warned Sadler against Arran's purposes and expressed her own strong desire for a marriage-treaty with England ; she may therefore not have been so hostile to the English marriage —with its magnificent prospects for her daughter—as is usually supposed. If, at any rate, the only choice was between it and her daughter's marriage to Arran's son, she could not but prefer it ; indeed, the rupture in her

---

[1] *State Papers*, Henry VIII., v. 301-4.
[2] *Hamilton Papers*, ii. 369.

friendship with the Cardinal can hardly be explained except
by the Cardinal's support of the Arran marriage, for, be
it remembered, the Cardinal was as strongly opposed to
any French marriage as he was to the English one.
Still, if Sir George Douglas, as he asserted to Hertford,
was the main instigator of this peculiar revolution, it
may have been, as regards many of the nobles, chiefly
a stage arrangement to delude and pacify Henry. That,
at any rate on the part of Sir George, it was largely
this is beyond question. To have succeeded in driving
both Arran and the Cardinal from power was also a
notable service to Henry, if the facts were as Sir George
represented them to be ; but yet it was not quite what
Henry desired. Henry's real aim was to have the
government himself ; and the selection of the Queen-
Dowager as Regent was in appearance one of the most
effective steps against this purpose that could have been
taken.

The Queen-Dowager's overtures, in the name of her
daughter, on behalf of peace met, therefore, with a worse
than indifferent reception. On the ground that the authority
of the "late governor was suspended," and that there rested
no such power either with him or her as could give sufficient
commission to ambassadors to treat of peace, Henry
declined to grant an abstinence except on what he must
have known to have been, in the circumstances, impossible
conditions : (1) that the Solway prisoners made their entry
within twenty days, and (2) that hostages of the next-
of-kin of Arran, Argyll, Huntly, and others were sent
as pledges for the maintenance of the abstinence.[1] At the
same time he assumed that it was quite beneath his dignity,

[1] Henry to the Queen-Dowager in *Hamilton Papers*, ii. 418-20.

in dealing with the Scots, to make any mention of pledges for his own good faith.

Thus the ruse of the Scots—if ruse it was—came to nothing, so far as Henry was concerned ; but his unbending attitude necessarily turned the thoughts of the Queen-Dowager, if they needed turning, more decidedly towards a French marriage, and also impelled the Scots towards an entirely French policy. Until she received Henry's uncompromising reply, no application had been made by her for French help. That, on July 20th, her envoy was caught with letters of her own to the French king, does not necessarily imply any insincerity in her peace overtures to Henry, for the circumstances had been altered by Henry's almost impossible terms. The same messenger carried letters " from the Governour, the Cardinall, and other noble men of the realm, addressed to the French King " [1] ; but their exact import has not been disclosed, so that it is impossible to tell whether they were acting in concert with the Queen-Dowager or not. Yet Henry's attitude was bound to effect a reconciliation between the rival parties, which took place after a meeting of separate conventions. As to its exact nature, there is no definite information ; but to represent it, as historians have lately done, as the triumph of Arran and the Cardinal is hardly justifiable. On the contrary, it seems to have been based on the practical acceptance by Arran of the Stirling resolution of June 3rd, whereby the Queen-Dowager was admitted to joint authority with him as Governor ; for while, before her election as Regent, she seems to have taken no part in public business, not only does her name, from the earliest meeting of the council in the first volume

---

[1] *Hamilton Papers*, ii. 434.

of the Register appear thus, "*Presentibus, Regina, et Gubernator,*" but, as a matter of fact, she henceforth took a very prominent part in the management of affairs.

The triumph of the Cardinal and Arran was mainly a triumph over the Douglases. On giving their formal submission to the new arrangement, the Douglases, on December 12th, received full pardon for their past treasons; but this necessarily annihilated any faint faith of Henry in their professions of loyalty to him, although Shrewsbury, on February 17th, reported, on the word of "Patie Grime," a Scottish spy, that Angus affirmed "he loved the Kynges majestie best of all men," and that since Lennox was married to "the woman whom he most loved in all the worlde," he would do his utmost to make Lennox "chief ruler in Scotland."[1] Presumably Angus, when he uttered these edifying sentiments, was unaware that the English warden had already been offered by Henry 2,000 crowns to trap him, and 1,000 crowns to trap Sir George; but when he learned that Sir Ralph Eure had received from Henry a grant of any lands he could conquer in the Merse and Teviotdale, he affirmed that if he came to take seisin, he would write him an instrument of possession "on his skin, with sharp pens and bloody ink." Something like this feat he was also able to accomplish, for when Eure penetrated into Melrose and disgraced the tombs of the Douglases, Angus had his revenge on him on February 27th at Ancrum Muir, where this "fell cruel man and over cruel," as Arran, on witnessing his body, described him,[2] was numbered amongst the eight hundred of his followers who were slain.

---

[1] *Hamilton Papers*, ii. 552.   [2] *Ibid.*, ii. 563.

The Ancrum triumph was, however, Scotland's solitary
stroke of good luck, and it did little to alleviate its
condition, although Henry, now in dread of a French
alliance, gave intimation that he would refrain from taking
revenge for Ancrum provided the nobility, at their convention to be held on April 15th, would agree to the
treaties of peace and marriage. As was, however, almost
inevitable, this proposal at more than the eleventh hour
was rejected.[1]   Its rejection led to the formation of a
plot against Beaton's life, to which Henry gave his consent ;
and though the dastardly political device was not immediately fruitful, it at least encouraged the successful conspiracy
against Beaton's life in the following year.

Meanwhile, any advantage Scotland might have gained
by the French contingent of three thousand foot and five
hundred horse was neutralised by the treachery of Angus
and the Douglases, who, having revenged their own private
wrongs on Sir Ralph Eure, found it advisable still to pose
to Henry as his friends. They therefore took care that a
strong invading force, of which the rearguard was commanded by Angus, should retire before much inferior
numbers, after the capture of a few unimportant strongholds ;
and they even followed this up by advising the occupation
in harvest time of the south of Scotland by a strong
English force, in order to terrorise the Scots into a renewal
of the marriage negotiations. Charity almost compels the
supposition that the Douglases believed that the presence of
Hertford in force, would be sufficient to induce the Scots
to treat, or at least that they had but a faint idea of what
their suggestion might result in—a wholesale devastation
of southern Scotland ; five abbeys and market towns, forty-

---

[1] Thorpe, *Scottish State Papers*, i. 49-50.

three villages, and sixteen fortified places being left in ruins by the English hordes.

Such wanton outrages only, meanwhile, strengthened the hands of the anti-English party. Even the assassination of the Cardinal, on May 29th of the following year (1546), in no degree assisted Henry towards the attainment of his fond ambition. What might have been the results of Beaton's survival on the future of the two kingdoms, or the fortunes of Catholicism, is of course rather a matter of conjecture than of positive conviction; but the sequel seems to show that he had already done most of the good or evil which it was possible for him to do either to Scotland or Catholicism. To him probably belongs the main credit of saving Scotland from Henry's clutches; but this had been practically achieved before Beaton's death, for, although the furious efforts of the English to concuss Scotland into obedience were to be continued even after the death of Henry, the foundations of resistance that had been laid by Beaton remained secure. Then, as for Catholicism, the persecutive methods of Beaton could not, in the long run, have been of advantage to it, or have stayed the operation of the manifold causes that were hastening its fall. Even, also, had not the Cardinal, when his life was snatched from him, been well advanced in years, a national ecclesiastical confederation dependent largely on the existence of one man must, should that man do nothing to breathe new life into it, be regarded as already doomed. As it was, his removal tended, for the time being, to strengthen rather than to weaken the French party. It gave an additional turn to the "adamantine spindle" on which the fate of the infant Mary was being wound, and rendered it more certain than ever that her husband was to be a French prince.

The regency of Arran now became more insecure, and he had well-nigh to abandon hope of obtaining the hand of the young Queen for his son. This was significantly indicated by a remarkable incident at a meeting of the Privy Council on June 11th : " The quhilk day, my Lord Governour in presens of the Quenis Grace and Lordis of counsel, for gude concurrence to be had for the commoun wele of the realme and stanching of divisioun, hes dischargit the contract and band maid to him be quhatsomeuir noble men of the realme, anentis Our Soverane Ladyis meriage, and sall distroy the samyn, and dischargis all noble men that hes consentit thairto of the said band, and siclik the Quenis Grace hes dischargit all bandis maid to hir be all maner of noble men in contrair the said contract," etc.[1] At the same meeting the Earls of Angus and Cassilis, Lord Maxwell, and Sir George Douglas declared their adherence to the Act of Parliament of 1543, dissolving " the pece and the contract of mariage maid between the realm of Englande and this realme."[2] There was thus outwardly manifested among the majority of the nobles a general desire to sink their differences in a combination against the common enemy.

The Scots were then probably in ignorance of England's conclusion of a treaty with France[3] on June 7th—ratified by Henry VIII. on July 28th—in which they had the option of being comprehended, provided they accepted the treaties of England of 1543 ; but the Privy Council, in July or August, resolved to accept the comprehension, without prejudice to the liberties of the realm.[4] From

---

[1] *Register of the Privy Council*, i. 27. [2] *Ibid.,* i. 29.
[3] Rymer's *Foedera*, xv. 93-7. [4] *Register of the Privy Council*, i. 35.

this time, therefore, a kind of armed truce prevailed until after the death of Henry.

In September, ambassadors were sent to enter into negotiations with him, but the political situation was complicated by the fact that the assassins of the Cardinal, who were holding the Castle of St. Andrews, had applied to him for help and had accepted his conditions—that they should undertake to advance the marriage between his son and the young Queen. Henry therefore demanded that "the Governor and Lords of Scotland," as a proof of their sincerity, should abandon the siege of the castle.

Since Henry had himself been concerned in a previous conspiracy against the Cardinal, he could hardly, of course, admit that the holders of the castle had done anything deserving of punishment ; but then his whole conduct towards the Cardinal's assassination was a flagrant interference with the internal affairs of Scotland ; and this, followed by the barefaced attempt to forbid the punishment of the malefactors, meant that he had abated no jot of his pretensions to make his will the supreme law in Scotland, though he did not live to resume the old violent methods of seeking to obtain his purpose.

The death of the great English king on January 28th, 1547—within less than seven months of the removal of his great enemy the Cardinal—did not materially affect the Scottish situation. Like the Cardinal, Henry had as regards Scotland really finished the work given him to do. Had England on his death immediately resumed its allegiance to the Pope, and had this been coupled by a more sincerely friendly attitude towards Scotland, the marriage alliance might very well have been accomplished.

But, meanwhile, there was the impassable barrier of

religious differences, which, if not created, had been made more unsurmountable by the two great opponents who had just left the scene ; and some fifteen years were to elapse before this particular barrier—and by this time others had arisen—against a permanent alliance between the two countries was to be removed. With a personality so distinctive and overmastering, Henry was bound to leave a strong individual impress on the general policy of the nation he had governed for nearly forty years. By himself also nominating the Council of Regency, he had a pretty certain guarantee of continuity in his policy.

To some extent, it is true, his intentions were frustrated by Hertford. After inducing the Council to nominate him Protector of the Realm, Hertford virtually assumed the functions of a sovereign ; but, as it happened, this made no material difference in the relations between England and Scotland. Hertford's bent was rather towards a more definite Protestantism than that of Henry, and he had thus even stronger reasons than those of Henry for adopting towards Scotland what was a coercive policy, by whatever specious pretensions it might be coloured.

On his deathbed Henry had urged that the efforts to concuss the Scots into the English marriage should be persevered with ; and the elevation of Hertford—henceforth known as the Duke of Somerset—to the protectorship insured that nothing would be wanting to the accomplishment of Henry's last wishes that could be effected by mere resolute brutality. But Somerset did not, as Froude supposes,[1] advance claims to an authority over Scotland not advanced by Henry. That Henry refused to call in question the feudal independence of Scotland can hardly

[1] *History of England*, cab. ed., iv. 274,

be admitted ; if he pretended to resign rights to overlordship which he had never been able to exercise, it was merely
that, by means of the marriage, he might obtain definite
possession of them.

On the other hand, Somerset did not, as Froude affirms,
" resolve to distinguish his protectorate by reviving the
pretensions and renewing the policy of Edward I., by
putting forward the formal claim of England to the
dominion of the entire island." This claim, in its naked,
unabashed form, Somerset sought to revive at a later period ;
but, meantime, he merely proposed to continue the forcible
but disingenuous policy of Henry : according to the instructions of " Norroy " herald, sent to the Queen-Dowager
and Governor after Pinkie, Somerset's invasion of Scotland
was " only to bring to good effect the godly purpose of
the marriage between King Edward VI. and Queen Mary."
But for Somerset, as for Henry, to take upon him
practically to decide the whole question of the Scottish
marriage and to prescribe to Scotland what course of political
action she ought to regard as most to her advantage, virtually
implied the old assumption of overlordship.

Of more important consequence, both to the Scottish
nation and to the fortunes of the young Queen, than the
death either of Henry or the Cardinal, was the death, on
March 31st, 1547, of Francis I. of France ; for not only
was his successor, Henry II., a more strenuous opponent
of England than his father, but the Guises, brothers of the
Queen-Dowager of Scotland, already exercised great ascendancy over him, and were bent on utilising it to the utmost
for the advancement of their family. The marriage of
their niece to the Dauphin was a matter of prime concern to
them ; and since they could bring special influence to bear

After the picture by Holbein.

EDWARD SEYMOUR, DUKE OF SOMERSET.

both on Henry II. and their sister, the chances of a French marriage became likelier than ever. The first result of Henry's accession was the arrival in Scotland of the French ambassador, the Sieur d'Oysell, in order to confirm the ancient league between the two countries. He remained at the Scottish court, and it was he who arranged that the French king should do the Scots the friendly act of sending galleys for the capture of St. Andrews Castle, which capitulated on the last day of July.

Though the capture of the castle could hardly be termed an act of hostility to England, it probably hastened the purpose of Somerset for an invasion of Scotland. Somerset's resolve only tended to strengthen the Scottish connection with France ; England's only chance of success now lay in the subjugation of the country ; [1] and though Scotland was no doubt weakened by internal discord, it was not so weakened as to enable Somerset to crown his enterprise with triumph.

In addition to Lennox and Glencairn, whom Somerset could entirely depend on, Bothwell, Cassilis, Marischal and Lord Gray were favourers of England ; but the discovery of their names in a register book of Henry Balnaves, found in St. Andrews Castle,[2] had revealed their intended treachery ; Bothwell, the most dangerous of them, had been sent to prison ; and the discovery only tended to redouble the efforts of the Governor and the Council in the adoption of measures for resistance.

For the first time since the death of James V. a great

[1] Professor Pollard (*Somerset*, p. 147) describes Somerset's invasion as "an imperative measure of defence" against the Scottish compact with France ; but it was the "aggression" of England that drove Scotland into the arms of France.

[2] *Scottish Papers*, i. 14.

combined effort was made by the Scots to dare the might of England in open conflict and to hurl back the encroachers on the country's liberties.   At an Edinburgh Convention on July 1st, all present pledged themselves that, should the country be invaded in harvest time, as was expected, they would be "reddy to defend their auld liberties" to the utmost of their power.[1]

All between the ages of sixteen and sixty were therefore ordered to be ready by August 1st to obey the summons to assemble in arms after eight days' warning ; and to render the summons as effectual as possible, the sacred symbol of the Fiery Cross was sent throughout every district of the country.   As the result of the exceptional efforts that were put forth, and of the deep resentment at previous outrages, the country was agitated throughout by a strong wave of enthusiasm ; and no fewer than thirty-six thousand Scots hastened from all parts towards Edinburgh to be mustered under the several leaders.   The muster included representatives of every rank, calling and persuasion, both zealous "professors of the Evangel" from Fife, Forfar, the Mearns, and the "Westland," all under the previous English dependent, Angus, and an immense number of priests and canons "with their shaven crowns and black jackis,"[2] who fought under a sacred white banner.

The Scottish army, on September 8th, 1547, drew up on a strong position behind Musselburgh : and, in order to encourage every one to do his utmost against the foe, it was decreed at a Convention, held at Monkton Hall, that if any kirkman, abbot, prior, or "any religious man" should perish in battle, his next-of-kin should have his benefice ;

[1] *Register of the Privy Council*, i. 175.
[2] Knox's *Works*, i. 210.

and that in the case of laymen, whether nobles or commons, special facilities should be given for inheritance by their relatives.[1]

The position of the Scots was a very strong one, the Esk extending in front, while their left was protected by the sea, and their right by a deep morass stretching towards Dalkeith. In numbers they were two to one of the English, and had they waited the attack, the victory might have been theirs; but the very enthusiasm to which they had been wrought up was their undoing ; for, consisting so largely of men almost unused to arms, they were no match in fair fight for the disciplined and experienced English ; and their attempt, on September 10th, to overwhelm their foes by mere weight of numbers resulted in utter disaster.

Had the day, however, gone otherwise than it did, the chances of the English marriage had possibly not been rendered so hopeless as they were by Somerset's victory and the butchery that followed it. An overwhelming defeat of the English, involving the death or capture of Somerset, might possibly have led to a more considerate treatment of the Scots by their " auld enemies " ; but the one main consequence of the disaster of Pinkie Cleugh was to make the English marriage impossible.

The vengeance wreaked on over ten thousand of the fugitive Scots, the conflagration of Leith, the occupation of Inchcolm and Inchkeith, the capture of Broughty Castle, were the only tangible results of Somerset's great expedition. Although a force under Wharton and Lennox overran Annandale, it effected no permanent occupation of it ; and when Somerset, from lack of provisions, retired with his victorious army across the Tweed, he left behind him mainly

[1] *Laws and Acts of Parliament* (Edinburgh, 1682), part i., pp. 265-6.

exasperation, detestation, and a firmer determination than ever to make no terms with the English.

The advance of the English to Leith, after Pinkie, caused the Queen-Dowager and her daughter to remove from Stirling to the monastery of Inchmahone, a secluded island in the lake of Menteith. There was, in those days, a decided advantage in having for a place of refuge the defence of a large circular sheet of water ; but whither the child had been spirited was evidently kept a profound secret. The English spies knew nothing of it ; it is not mentioned even in the *Diurnal of Occurrents* ; and all that was known to de Selve, the French ambassador in London, was that the child had been taken " dans le pays des sauvages." [1] An oval space in the grounds of the ruined monastery surrounded by boxwood—traditionally known as " Queen Mary's Bower "—suggested to Dr. John Brown, author of *Rab and his Friends*, the charming, but groundless, fancy that it preserved the outlines of " Queen Mary's child garden."

Mary remained but a week or two at Inchmahone. Bishop Leslie states that she and her mother returned to Stirling as soon as she had news of the retirement of Somerset ; and as Stirling is within a few hours' ride of the Lake of Menteith, Leslie's statement is supported by probability. In any case she had probably returned early in October, for in the middle of that month the Queen-Dowager was in Edinburgh. [2] But the invasions of Grey of Wilton and of Lennox, the one by the East and the other by the West route, as well as the suspicion that Grey's expedition included the siege of Stirling, caused the child's transference to Dumbarton, which, with ulterior

[1] *Correspondance Politique*, p. 204.   [2] *Scottish Papers*, i. 20.

aims, the Queen-Dowager induced Arran to deliver up to her. Writing from Cockburnspath Feb. 22nd, 1547-8, Grey reported that she had already been removed thither;[1] but the news was premature. De la Chapelle states that she was removed when the approach of the enemy was imminent;[2] Robert Moffet announced to Wharton that she had entered Dumbarton on the last Friday of February;[3] and, according to the Treasurer's Accounts, her guardians, Lords Erskine and Livingstone, departed with her to Dumbarton on the last day of the month.[4]

Though an arrangement for the marriage of Mary to the Dauphin had now become inevitable, there is some dubiety as to when the Council agreed to recommend it. According to Labanoff,[5] a definite decision was arrived at on February 8th, and Dr. Hay Fleming[6] even infers from certain condensed references in Thorpe's *Calendar* that " the removal of Mary to France was discussed, as well as the propriety of placing the principal strongholds in the hands of their allies," at a Council meeting at Stirling on November 2nd ; but the references on which he founds his opinion merely embody rumours and surmises, and, even so, they do not support his inference.

On November 5th the laird of Longniddry wrote to Somerset that there was great peril of the Queen and Governor resolving to adopt such momentous decisions. On November 2nd Luttrell wrote that a spy had just brought news that the Scots were to send ambassadors to France and Denmark for help, and that it was proposed

---

[1] *Scottish Papers*, i. 81.
[2] Teulet's *Relations*, i. 167.
[3] *Scottish Papers*, i. 93.
[4] Note in Knox's *Works*, i. 219.
[5] *Lettres de Marie Stuart*, i. 3.
[6] *Mary Queen of Scots*, i. 194.

to "ally the young Queen with Denmark rather than England."[1] The report of Ninian Cockburn to Grey of Wilton was merely that on the second day of the Council meeting the Queen-Dowager said that she had, with the Governor's advice, written urgently to France for speedy help, and that if she did not get it the Scots would seek to obtain the best terms they could from England;[2] and although Grey conjectured that the conditions offered to Henry II. were "the strengths of Scotland and the princess to be at his pleasure,"[3] it is clear from the sequel that no such conditions were agreed to by the Council either in November or the following February.

According to various reports, certain French officers landed at Dumbarton towards the end of December, but most probably they were volunteers. The version of Sir Ralph Bulmer, that they were fifty captains, who had brought with them sufficient money to pay for a year ten thousand Scots whom they were to command, had evidently as little foundation in fact as the statement that six thousand Frenchmen were then only waiting for a fair wind to embark for Scotland.[4] The difficulty of the Queen-Dowager was to induce the Scots to agree to terms that would suit the King of France, and the utmost caution was necessary in dealing with the subject.

An attempt had been made to win Arran by bestowing on him, in February, the Duchy of Châtelheráult; but Arran, from very weakness, was notoriously fickle, and the Queen-Dowager perfectly well knew that even yet he would seek to defeat her purpose if in any way he could. Further, it was only necessity that could induce

---

[1] *Scottish Papers*, i. 37.　　　[2] *Scottish State Papers*, i. 41.
[3] *Ibid.*, i. 42.　　　[4] *Ibid.*, i. 55.

him, or the majority of the Scots, to place themselves, in
any degree, in the power of the King of France, and this
necessity did not become urgent until the occupation of
Haddington by Lord Grey of Wilton in April. Previous
attempts to gain a permanent footing in the country had
caused some concern, but a permanent occupation of
Haddington threatened its subjugation.

The transference of Mary to Dumbarton at the end of
February was caused by Grey of Wilton's early expedition,
which also led the Scots to send more urgent appeals to
Henry II. of France for help ; but it was the resolve,
manifested in the April expedition, to make Haddington
a military depôt, that convinced the Scots of the desperate
nature of their case unless they obtained artillery and
ammunition, as well as skilled aid, from France. Yet as
late as June 25th—after the actual arrival of French aid—
the Queen-Dowager could only promise to do her best to
meet the French king's wishes,[1] and was praying him not
to withdraw his army if all his desires could not formally
be granted.

A good deal of course depended on the attitude of
Arran, but Arran's attitude depended largely on that of
others. If, also, his only choice were between the French
and the English match, he now much preferred the former.
After all that had come and gone, to have placed himself
in the hands of Somerset would have been little short of
madness. But he naturally hesitated to bid farewell to
his long-cherished ambition as to the royal marriage.

Huntly—who, having been captured at Pinkie and
having obtained his liberty on condition of secretly aiding
the English cause, was now acting a double part—told

_____
[1] Teulet's *Relations*, i. 173.

Grey of Wilton that the Queen-Dowager had been asking
his brother's help to convey the young Queen to France,
which he stated he would not do, because the Governor
held Dumbarton ; [1] but we learn from another source
that the Governor was enraged at now finding it in the
hands of the French ; [2] and on June 7th, Grey reported
that " the Governor was so grieved at the spoil and
devasting of Dalkeith, passyoned by his unadvised rendering of Dumbarton to the Queen, tormented at his son's
delivery to France, his estimation abated, his vain expectation
at an end, the French aid so slow, some say gone back,
that he has thrown himself into a sharp sickness, and lies at
the point of death." [3]   He was at last face to face with the
inevitable, and his daydream was rapidly dissolving.   Yet,
greatly as he had been influenced by a quite pardonable
family ambition, he probably, notwithstanding his own keen
personal disappointment, felt, like the majority of the Scots,
a sincere satisfaction in having so far been able to thwart
the overweening purposes of Henry VIII. and Somerset.

Before any binding agreement had been made with
France, the French transports, with a splendid force of six
thousand men, under the Sieur d'Essé, and with all necessary
siege material, appeared on June 12th off the Scottish
coast, though, on account of adverse winds, a landing was
not effected until five or six days later. [4]

On the 18th d'Oysell was able to assure the Duke
d'Aumale of the excellent impression produced by the arrival
of such powerful succour—that the Queen-Dowager and
Arran were better disposed than ever to the deliverance
of the strongholds, and would do so as soon as possible ;

[1] *Scottish Papers*, i. 107.   [2] *Ibid.*, i. 97.
[3] *Ibid.*, i. 117.   [4] Teulet, i. 164.

and that after the meeting of the Estates, " which would be brief," the young Queen would be sent to France.[1]

But even the Queen-Dowager was very much concerned lest, on account of her inability to persuade the Scots to meet all the French demands, the French troops should be withdrawn.[2] Still, by June 24th she had secured the written consent of Angus, Sir George Douglas, Cassilis, Seton, the Sheriff of Ayr, several other lords and barons, and seven or eight bishops, not merely to the Queen's marriage to the Dauphin, but to her being sent to France—all this on the promise of certain French rewards;[3] and we also learn from Knox,[4] that Huntly and Argyll—who had previously been following devious courses, were, as well as Angus, made French Knights of the Cockle.

The presence of the French auxiliaries—who, in concert with six thousand Scots, now began to encompass Haddington and on June 30th commenced entrenchments[5]—necessarily induced a greater readiness among the more strictly patriotic to comply with the French demands; and thus, at the meeting of the Estates in the Abbey of Haddington on July 1st, it was carried with seeming acclamation that the ancient alliance and friendship between the two countries should be perfected by the marriage of the young Queen to the Dauphin, and that, in preparation for this consummation, she should now be sent to France.[6]

As, in all likelihood, involving the permanent union of the two crowns, the decision was for Scotland of momentous consequence; for although the Estates stipulated that

---

[1] *Teulet*, i. 165.
[2] Letter, *Ibid.*, i. 173-4.
[3] *Ibid.*, i. 171.
[4] *Works*, i. 217.
[5] *Hamilton Papers*, ii. 597.
[6] *Scottish State Papers*, i. 136

Scotland's ancient laws and liberties should be preserved, the precise meaning of this proviso was another matter ; it did not greatly qualify the anticipations of the Queen-Dowager that "everything would be put into the hands of the King " [of France].[1] The main matter, as it seemed to her, was that the child should be in French hands ; and thus, as soon after the meeting of the Estates as she decently could, she proceeded to Dumbarton to arrange for the departure of the child, who, she hoped, would herself carry to the French king the news that Parliament had agreed to send, in the words of d'Oysell, "la chose qu'il désire le plus de recouvrer." [2]

But man proposes and God disposes. All that Mary of Guise and Henry of France expected from the decision of the Estates was not to be realised. She counted that it would result in Scotland becoming the mere appanage of France, and it was quite on the cards that it might even finally lead to the union of France, and not merely Scotland, but Britain, under one crown. Had the Dauphin not been the weakling that he was, and had Mary's eldest son been a French king, how different might have been the future complexion not merely of British, but of European history !

As it was, Scotland had hardly made her bargain with France than she began to repent of it. For the next twelve years she was virtually to be engaged in a struggle against annexation by France, as she had previously been in a struggle against annexation by England. Combined with this struggle there was the great religious revolution championed by Knox, and supported from various motives by those termed " the Lords of the Congregation." Jealousy

[1] Teulet, i. 179.   [2] *Ibid.*, i. 165.

of French domination was to be a powerful factor in inclining many to join the standard of the ecclesiastical reformers, and it was mainly by the zeal of the reformers that effectual resistance was to be made to the ambitious aims of France, until the danger of annexation was removed by the death of Mary's husband, then Francis II.

With the triumph of the Reformation in Scotland a cause of alienation was, however, to be created between the young sovereign and the people. But for her French upbringing, there might have been no religious severance between them, and thus there need not have been any political one. By the decision of Parliament, wrote Knox, Mary was " sold to go to France to the end that in her youth she should drink of that lycour, that should remain with hir all hir lyfetime, for a plague to this realme, and for her final distruction." [1] This is, of course, the language of a bigoted and bitter partisan. Mary's partisans were equally convinced that her final destruction was brought about by the wicked insubordination and intrigues of the Protestants ; and all that we are here concerned to note is that the arrangements for her marriage to the Dauphin, however splendid the prospects it might seem to foreshadow, must be reckoned a chief contributory influence towards her calamitous failure as a Scottish sovereign.

Meantime the child, who had been the occasion of such various and complex intrigues and such bitter and bloody strife, had been spending her infant years in the palace on the isolated rock of Stirling. Tales would probably be told her of the evil deeds of Scotland's " auld enemies," and of the devastations which on one occasion

[1] *Works*, i. 219.

reached to within six miles of Stirling; but the wide
and beautiful prospect which surrounded her rock on all
sides, was for the most part a scene of peace; and her
days passed without any incident, suggestive of the hideous
conflict which had over and over again devastated the
southern parts of the kingdom.

Shortly after her removal to Stirling she was, according
to Sadler, sick of so serious an illness as the small-pox;[1]
but it is rather curious that Sadler should have known what
" neither the governor nor any man here knoweth "; and
we may almost conclude that the malady was nothing worse
than chicken-pox. In March, 1548, shortly after she
went to Dumbarton, a rumour arose that she was dead.
De Selve,[2] who had learned that she had been very ill,
but on March 23rd wrote that she had recovered, does
not state what the malady was; but on the 18th Luttrell
learned that she was alive, and had lately recovered of
" a dyseas that they call here the mawlys or messellys."[3]
In this he is confirmed by La Chapelle,[4] who doubtless
had authentic information; and the statement of Huntly
to Somerset, that she had been " veray sick in the small
pokis,"[5] was most likely a mistake. At a later period
she had small-pox; but we can scarce credit that she
had small-pox three times.

Beyond records of her illnesses we have few particulars
of her early life. From April, 1545, she was entrusted
to the special care of John, fifth Lord Erskine—who had
charge of her father, James V., during his minority—and
Alexander, fifth Lord Livingstone of Callendar. These

---

[1] Sadler's *State Papers*, i. 263.   [2] *Correspondance Politique*, i. 315.
[3] *Scottish Papers*, i. 98.   [4] Teulet, i. 167.
[5] *Scottish Papers*, i. 99.

After a drawing by G. B. Campion.

STIRLING CASTLE.

guardians had under their command a powerful force, made up of the neighbouring lairds and their retainers, who, on account of their duties at Stirling, were, on July 5th, discharged from the necessity of " passing to armyis or raidis aganis our auld inymis of England."[1] Her tutors, or spiritual guardians, were John Erskine, parish priest of Inchmahone, and Alexander Scott, canon of the chapel royal of Stirling and parson of Balmaclellan.

Of her early education we are told nothing ; but her nurses or governesses evidently amused her, occasionally, with ancient tales similar to those which Sir David Lyndsay recited to her father. " I have harde," wrote Randolph to Throckmorton, April 28th, 1561, " ofte tolde for troth, to troble yor L. wth, howe the Quene of Scotland, that nowe is, beinge a verie babe, seinge the cardinall in his dysguised garmentes sodenly entre into the chamber wheare she was, cryed owte for feare, ' Kyll, kyll the Redeaton, he will carrie me awaye.' Whether yt was the wyll of God that his deathe at that tyme sholde be prophesed *in ore infantis et lactantis* because he had that tyme solde her [which he had not] and promysed that she sholde be carried into France or not, I leave to the dyvine judgment of God. Redeaton and Robin good fellowe were brother barnes, nevews to a page." [2]

For playfellows she probably had from an early period the four Marys who accompanied her to France and returned with her to Scotland. They were daughters of the houses of Fleming, Livingstone, Seton, and Beaton of Creich. Mary Fleming, probably a sister of James, fifth

---

[1] *Reg. Privy Council*, i. 111.

[2] MS. Add., British Museum, 35,830 f. 79. The anecdote was first *published* in the *Scottish Historical Review* for January, 1905.

Lord Fleming, and daughter of Lady Fleming, the Queen's aunt—a natural daughter of James IV., and the Queen's governess in France—became in January, 1566-7, the wife of the notable Maitland of Lethington. Mary Livingstone, daughter of the Queen's guardian, generally known, on account of her vigorous habit of body as "the lustie," married John Semple—who, Knox tells us, was surnamed "the dancer"—son of Robert, Lord Semple, and was ancestress of the poetic Semples of Beltrees. Mary Beaton— whose beauty is celebrated by Buchanan in his *Valentiana*, —was the daughter of Sir John Beaton of Creich, keeper of Falkland Palace. In 1566 she espoused Alexander Ogilvie of Boyne, whom Lady Jean Gordon would have preferred to have married, had not the Queen assigned Lady Jean to Bothwell. Mary Beaton's elder sister, Lady Scott of Buccleugh, became in after years a too notorious friend of the Queen. Mary Seton, alone of the four Marys, remained unmarried while Queen Mary was in Scotland, and was sent for to attend on the Queen in England. To Knollys the Queen praised her skill as a "busker" of the hair. In a well-known ballad of doubtful origin, mention is made of the tragedy of Mary Hamilton, one of the Queen's Marys; and, as a matter of fact, amongst the names of the "dames, damoiselles, et femmes de chambre" of the Queen of Scots in France occurs that of "Mademoiselle Hamilton, fille du gouverneur d'Ecosse et Miel Stuart, sa gouvernante."[1]

Among others who attended Mary to France were several young gentlemen, including certain of her half-brothers, the natural children of James V. According to Chalmers,[2]

---

[1] De Ruble, *La Première Jeunesse de Marie Stuart*, p. 282
[2] *Life of Mary*, i. 10.

From the picture in the possession of the Countess Dowager of Seafield, by her kind permission.

MARY LIVINGSTONE.

licences to travel were recorded for three of them —
Robert, commendator of Holyrood, John, commendator
of Coldingham, and Lord James, commendator of
St. Andrews ; and various contemporary writers affirm
that Lord James, whose influence on her destiny was
afterwards to be so great, did accompany her. Henry
Johnes, a servant of Somerset's secretary, reported that both
the " Lords James " declined to go, " for that they could not
have the young gentylman of Fyef with theim " ;[1] but a
refusal to go on such a plea as this would, we must believe,
be deemed a high misdemeanour. Since a licence was made
out for Lord James of St Andrews, he probably went ; but
if he did, he must have returned to Scotland with the Scottish
guardians and tutors.

Even before Parliament had definitely decided that Mary
should be sent to France, preparations were being made for
her departure ; and on June 24th instructions were given that
the galleys to escort her should set sail quietly that night
from the Firth of Forth, a number of soldiers being placed
on board as if their destination was Broughty Ferry, while
their real purpose was to reach the west coast. [2] Statements
of several historians as to their evading English cruisers have
no foundation in fact.

From the time, however, that Mary went to Dumbarton
the English must have had a shrewd guess of an intention
that she would set sail thence to France : and by June 28th
Grey knew that the four galleys had gone to Dumbarton for
this purpose.[3] The intention to send her to France was
necessarily matter of public knowledge from the time of the
meeting of Parliament ; but although the Queen-Dowager

[1] *Hamilton Papers*, ii. 618.   [2] Teulet, i. 170.
[3] *Scottish Papers*, i. 131.

left the camp on July 13 for Dumbarton, no hurry was shown in beginning the momentous voyage, and arrangements could have been made to intercept the French ships. The Queen did not embark until July 28th, and the ships lay at anchor in the frith waiting for an east wind, which did not spring up until August 7th. Making a wide circuit northwards, the galleys—which, in the person of the charming young girl, were supposed to have, in a manner, under their charge the destiny of two and perhaps three nations—then returned southwards by the west coast of Ireland, and, thus eluding the English ships that lay in wait off St. Abb's Head, reached on August 20th the little port of Roscoff, near Brest, where a small chapel has been erected to mark the spot where Mary first set foot on French soil.[1]

[1] Dr. Hay Fleming (*Mary Queen of Scots*, p. 14) follows other writers in giving August 13th as the date of Mary's arrival in France ; but the 20th, as stated by Guiffrey (*Lettres de Dianne de Poytiers*, p. 33), is probably correct. There can also be no doubt as to Roscoff being the port.

CHAPTER II

THE FAVOURITE OF FRANCE

IT was not until October 16th—nearly two months after she landed in France—that Mary arrived at the Château of Carrières Saint-Denis, near St. Germains. The disembarkation near Brest was made for the purpose of avoiding the English cruisers ; and after spending some days at Roscoff she sailed for the mouth of the Loire, and then up the river to Orleans, whence she journeyed by short stages to her destination. The King, who was then at Moulins at the celebration of the marriage of Antoine de Bourbon, left minute directions in regard to the preparation of her rooms ; it was arranged that she and the Princess Elizabeth should stay together, the best suite in the château being selected for them and their attendants.[1]

After his return on November 9th, Henry wrote in enthusiastic terms of the beauty and grace of the child— "le plus parfayt enfant que je vys jamès " ;[2] Catherine de Medici was equally enthusiastic : " This small Queen of Scots," she writes " has only to smile in order to turn all French heads."[3] The early years she had spent in

[1] *Lettres de Dianne de Poytiers*, ed. Guiffrey, p. 33.
[2] Quoted by de Ruble, p. 31.
[3] De la Ferrière, *Lettres de Catherine de Médicis*, p. liv.

Scotland only gave a certain piquancy to her attractiveness : " Even her natural language," says Brantôme,"
" which was very rustic, barbarous and harsh, she spoke
it with such fine grace and formed it in such a manner,
that she made it seem quite beautiful and agreeable in
her, though not in others."[1] No doubt in view of the
fact that Mary was supposed to have brought with her
her kingdom of Scotland as a kind of free gift to France,
every one was disposed to be charmed with her ; but,
making due allowance for a certain idealisation in the
eulogies which she universally evoked, it can hardly be
doubted that she was a peculiarly attractive as well as
quick and clever child. She seems to have had a certain
natural gift of predominance, which, however, she by no
means misused ; she was the most popular child amongst
all her young acquaintances, and throughout life she made
friends easily amongst both men and women ; her cordiality
was open and unstinted ; towards all, high and low, she
was disposed to cherish sincere goodwill, unless provoked
to entertain an opposite sentiment. Proofs of her minute
and generous interest in the welfare of her servants and
attendants are abundant in her letters to her mother, while
she was still a young girl ; and her terrible misfortunes
in later life made her no whit less considerate than before
of her humblest associates. Possessing a strong individuality and a rather emotional temperament, she could be
fully reckoned on either as friend or enemy. A *camaraderie*
of even a somewhat masculine quality was one of her
most marked social gifts ; and her friendship from the
beginning with the sickly Dauphin is strong evidence
both of her tact and sympathy, even although she knew

[1] *Œuvres Complètes*, ed. Buchon, ii. 135.

After an engraving of the drawing by François Clouet, formerly in the possession of the Earl of Carlisle, now in the Musée Condé at Chantilly.

MARY QUEEN OF SCOTS
At the age of 9 years.

that much of the glory of her own future depended upon the friendship.

The effect of Mary's genial and friendly disposition was necessarily enhanced by her personal charms ; no blemish in her appearance intervened to mar the effect of her pleasant intentions ; she could be, in a manner, irresistible whenever she wished to be so. According to universal tradition—dating from her early childhood—she was dowered with a radiant and exquisite attractiveness. Like her mother she became exceedingly tall, and her form was symmetrical and graceful. Her complexion was pale and delicate : with dark brown eyes, she inherited the darkish chestnut hair of her father ; but her features are not remarkable for regularity or fineness. She could hardly be termed pretty, and her portraits do not indicate a beauty or comeliness sufficient to justify the contemporary eulogies. But on such a point, the opinion of contemporaries is the only adequate guide. Much of her charm probably depended on her air and manner ; she possessed a strong and remarkable individuality, with apparently peculiar histrionic gifts. She did not belong to the order of cold, statuesque beauties : it was herself, or what was supposed to be herself, rather than her features that exercised the attraction. Beautiful in the strict sense or not, she was evidently, judging even by her portraits, a person of marked distinction. The earlier portraits represent a personality which, if somewhat obscured or veiled, might well be pleasant and fascinating ; and if in the later portraits the expression is reserved, severe and, in several ways, dubious, her terrible experiences and sorrows must have stamped on her countenance their own impress.

Dowered with whatever personal attractiveness Mary

may have been, her new surroundings and her education and training were well fitted to develop and enhance it. The French court under Henry II. presented the same scene of elaborate splendour and gaiety as under his predecessor Francis I. Never was the art of enjoyment cultivated anywhere with greater assiduity : the enjoyment was of a many-sided character, but it had its root in extreme sociality, sociality in some respects of a very questionable kind, according to modern European notions of propriety, but refined by a peculiar devotion to the humanistic influences of the Renaissance. It is hardly possible for us to realise its exact tone or to strike a proper balance between its excellences and its defects. It is not to be understood if strictly judged by the standards of our more precisely ordered, but coarsely material and stridently utilitarian, age. It belonged, moreover, to a time when the Church, the supposed guardian of social morality, had completely swamped its own rules by the character and multiplicity of its exceptions.

The confusion in regard to social morality prevailing at the French court was a sort of *reductio ad absurdum* of what had come to be the practical tenets of a Church founded on the professed worship of virginity. The Church's original counsels of perfection—which, while ranking marriage as a sacrament, confounded virtue and goodness with mere asceticism—were now quite set at naught, not merely by virtual ecclesiastical tolerance or permission, but even by high and very general ecclesiastical example. Nor did the French court strikingly differ from other courts in its disregard of the ancient conventions. At this time, and both earlier and later, it was a fashionable custom for kings and princes in every court of Europe to choose

From a drawing after François Clouet in the Bibliothèque Nationale, Paris.

Photo by A. Giraudon, Paris.

HENRY II. OF FRANCE.

mistresses whom they publicly delighted to honour ; and in this, as in everything else, they were a pattern to their courtiers. It can hardly be affirmed, therefore, that Mary —who was accompanied to France by the bastard children of her father—was, in this respect, specially unfortunate in her new surroundings. Indeed, the court of Henry II. was much more observant of the proprieties than that of his predecessor, though strangely enough the main originator of a change for the better was the King's own mistress, the remarkable Diana of Poitiers, who was a woman of exceptional resolution as well as tact and discretion, and who—notwithstanding the peculiar position she occupied —having a great regard for the respectabilities, did her utmost to make the King and court conform to them, so far as outward seeming was concerned.[1]

In any case, there can be no question as to the importance attached, at the court of France, to what Mary, at a later period, referred to as "joyusitie." Amusement was not wooed after the somewhat rough and ready, and often quite ineffectual, fashion of the present time. Then, as now, it formed the main vocation of the leisured classes ; but at the French court it was practised with elaborate art. The old chivalric games and contests retained their ancient vogue. Tournaments, with their displays of feats of arms, attracted multitudes of sightseers, at least as completely representative of rank and fashion as those who now throng to the special horse races of the year. Also, archery, tennis, hawking, and the chase were the favourite daily recreations, assisting to supply that variety which is

"The very spice of life,
That gives it its full flavour."

---

[1] See especially De la Ferrière, *Lettres de Catherine de Médicis*, vol. i. p. xlviii.

Mary was thus initiated early in the practice of outdoor
amusements and sports, was instructed in the management
of horses, dogs, falcons, etc., and was led to acquire a
fondness for pet animals and birds.[1]

But a prominent peculiarity of the court was the
importance attached to social intercourse, and the methods
of rendering it enjoyable. In the society of the court,
in the time of Mary, the dance counted for much. Soon
after her arrival in France the King himself took pains
to procure for the Dauphin, Mary, and the other royal
children a teacher of dancing, who, besides being
a special master of the art, was " virtuous and well con-
ditioned." [2]

The art was not acquired by them in a merely amateurish
fashion ; high proficiency was sought after by systematic
and long-continued training ; and the display of individual
skill in dancing by ladies and gentlemen was then quite
common. Moreover, various elaborate varieties of the
dance—ballets, masques, etc.—had lately been introduced
at the court of France by Catherine de Medici.[3]

Mary became specially skilled both as performer and,
so to speak, stage manager, in the more elaborate enter-
tainments ; and it was her indulgence in such long semi-
histrionic performances that called forth against her the
denunciations of Knox, who regarded her proficiency in
them as a certain sign of impiety. Although Sir James
Melville diplomatically flattered Elizabeth by declaring
that Mary " dancit not so hich and disposedly as sche

[1] See especially de Ruble, pp. 68-70.

[2] Letter quoted in Tytler's *History of Scotland*, vol. ii. (1861), p. 382.

[3] For an account of the dances then in vogue at the French court, see
Belleval, *Les Fils de Henry II.* (1898), pp. 316-24.

did," [1] we must suppose that in the art of dancing Elizabeth, compared with Mary, was a mere tyro.

Like many great ladies of her time, Mary was also an excellent musician ; and though it may be that, as Sir James Melville implies, Elizabeth excelled her as a performer on the virginals, we must believe that Mary had the sweeter and more musical voice. According to Brantôme she " sang excellently, accompanying herself on the lute, which she touched deftly with her beautiful white hand and her finely shaped fingers" ; [2] and Conaeus also affirms that she was a proficient performer on the zithern, the harp, and the virginals.[3] Her musical as well as histrionic tendencies were, moreover, attested by her command of all the charming modulations and graces of exquisite French pronunciation. Antoine Fouquelin dedicated to her, as his best pupil, his *Rhétoric Française*, adding in her praise certain lines translated from Ovid :

> "Quand sa bouche céleste eust ouvert ton soucy
> L'on eut dit que les cieux souloient parler, ainsi,
> Et que d'un prince estoit digne telle excellence,
> Tant avoit de douceur ta divine éloquence."

The elocutionary gifts of the royal children were carefully developed by dramatic recitations ; and masquerades— written by their masters—were frequently given by them in presence of the court.[4]

Mary also more than dabbled in poetry. At the French court, as at that of Scotland from the time of James I., poets were held in much honour ; the cultivation of literature was the fashion of the day amongst the most exalted personages ; and native poetry, formerly the work

---

[1] *Memoirs*, p. 125.   [2] *Œuvres Complètes*, ed. Buchon, ii. 134.
[3] Jebb, ii. 15.   [4] See de Ruble, pp. 94-7.

of popular minstrels, gradually developed, under the more
direct patronage of the court, into a more dignified and
elaborate art. The art, as practised by the court poets,
was doubtless modish and artificial ; but if spontaneity was
too much sacrificed to rhetorical and rhymal ingenuity, a
facility and correctness in verse-writing were acquired,
which might well be the envy of modern poetasters.
Mary's tutor in the art was Ronsard, who from his
thirteenth year had been page to her mother, whom he
accompanied to Scotland when she became the wife of
James V.

According to Castelnau, Mary's favourite poets were
Ronsard, Du Bellay and Maisonfleur, who all three, it
need hardly be said, made her charms the subject of graceful
hyperbolical eulogy. As for Mary's own poetical flights,
they were at least aided by some technical accomplishment ;
and though her temperament was not altogether poetic,
she, to borrow Melville's phrase in regard to her playing,
wrote verses "raisonable for a queen." The excellence of
her literary training is also revealed in her letters, which—
as is indeed generally the case with other letters of the royal
and noble dames of the period—are characterised by a
correctness, ease, and elegance of style indicative of a
somewhat high standard of culture.

While dancing, music, and the drama were made to
conduce so much to the pleasantness of social life at the
French court, special enthusiasm was also shown for the
visibly beautiful and the external " embellishments of life."
Great elaboration was displayed in personal adornment—at
which Mary was a great adept, her dresses excelling in their
tasteful splendour that of all the other ladies at the court—
in domestic architecture, in the decoration of rooms, and

After a drawing by J. W. M. Turner, R.A.

THE PALACE AT BLOIS.

in bedecking them with paintings, beautiful furniture, statues and various miscellaneous ornaments ; and if imperfect sanitary arrangements detracted greatly from the comfort of the most splendid dwellings, this is not to be imputed to any lack of taste or civility, but to the backwardness of practical science.

All this goes to prove, not, as is often taken for granted, that the society at the French court—gay, joyous, and smitten also by a peculiar moral laxity—was essentially frivolous, but on the contrary rather, if anything, that frivolity had a subordinate place in its amusements. The worst forms of frivolity—those associated with coarseness, ignorance, and mere giddy inanity—had no place in the polished society of the court of France ; devotion to art in music, painting, and poetry is certainly not frivolity ; and if not a complete cure for it, is at least a check on it.

Moreover, there was at the French court a sincere respect for learning and the more strictly intellectual forms of culture. Margaret, sister of Henry II.—a lady of sufficient erudition to have qualified her for head of a modern young ladies' college in one of the universities—had much to do with the direction of the studies of the young Princesses. They were carefully instructed not only in French literature, but more particularly in geography and history ; and, in addition to a thorough mastery of the chief modern languages—Spanish, English, and Italian—they acquired more than a smattering of Greek and Latin.

The Latin themes of Mary are in nowise remarkable specimens of the art of Latin composition, and the sentiments are exactly what we might expect from an exemplary young princess, trained according to the precepts most appropriate to her station. " The true grandeur and excellence

of a prince, is, my dear sister,"—she is writing to the
Princess Elizabeth—"not in splendour, in gold, in purple,
in jewels, and the pomps of fortune, but in prudence, in
wisdom and in knowledge. And so much as the prince
ought to be different from his people in his habits and
manner of living, so ought he to have nothing to do with
the foolish opinions of the vulgar."

The Latin oration in praise of learned ladies which, in
her thirteenth or fourteenth year, she declaimed with such
success before the French court in the hall of the Louvre,[1]
owed the applause with which it was greeted chiefly, in
all likelihood, to her charming personality and her skilful
elocution. But though she probably never became so accomplished a linguist as her rival, the more coldly
intellectual Elizabeth, she in after life continued her Latin
studies ; and after her return to Scotland prosecuted them
for some time under the direction of George Buchanan.[2]

Nor was the supreme subject, religion—or the something then called by that name—at all neglected : on the
contrary, her uncle, the Cardinal of Lorraine, did what he
could to ensure that she should become a devout, and, if
it may be so expressed, a thoroughly prejudiced Catholic.
If we can hardly accept the rather too comprehensive statement of Father Stevenson,[3] that her " moral and religious
education " was placed in the hands of her maternal grandmother, Antoinette de Bourbon, there can, at least, hardly
be a doubt that abundant use was made by the Cardinal
of the child's devout female relatives in order suitably to
influence her religious sentiments ; for the Guises were

---

[1] Brantôme, *Œuvres Complètes*, ed. Buchon, ii. 135.
[2] *For. Ser.*, 1561-2, No. 985.
[3] *Mary Stuart*, p. 95.

AN DNI 1575
ÆTAT 50

From a contemporary engraving.

THE CARDINAL OF LORRAINE.

anxious to render her the ductile instrument for the accomplishment of their own particular purposes, which
included the entire subservience of Scotland—and even, it
was hoped, England—to France and Catholicism.

As regards the Cardinal's own conceptions of religion,
or as regards the exact character of the dominion of religion
at the French court, it is hardly possible to arrive at
a quite clear and credible conclusion. Like the Scottish
Beaton, the Cardinal of Lorraine was primarily an ecclesiastical politician ; and his type of character is not one
which, with our modern notions of what is fitting, it is easy
to regard with almost any kind of tolerance. While quite
as zealous an ecclesiastic as Beaton, he was more un-
blushingly lax as a moralist, and while an equally subtle, he
was a still more unscrupulous, diplomatist, and he had
apparently a much larger capacity for various kinds of
meannesses.

No more piquant illustration of the prevailing topsy-
turvydom in the moral codes of the time—as well in
social matters as in civil and ecclesiastical politics—could
be given than the employment by the Cardinal, as his
chief agent in consolidating his influence over the King,
of the King's mistress, Diana of Poitiers. And yet Diana
was in every way a better woman than the Cardinal was
a man. The ascendancy of this remarkable person was
utilised by her with a tact, prudence, restraint, and even
benevolence, which import a combination of mental and
moral endowments, rarely to be met with, even in ladies
occupying quite unequivocal positions.

A peculiar indication of Diana's remarkable qualities
was the apparent cordiality and confidence subsisting between
her and the King's lawful consort, Catherine de Medici,

whom she in many ways befriended. It thus came about
that to Diana was intrusted the chief superintendence of
the household—both domestic and educational—of Mary
Stuart and the other royal children.   According to Guilliame
Chrestian, physician-in-ordinary to the King, she exercised
the utmost care " to secure for the young children, not
only vigorous, healthy and well-complexioned wet nurses,
but wise and prudent governesses ; and she likewise caused
them to be instructed by good and learned preceptors,
as well in virtue and wise precepts, as in the love and
fear of God."[1]

There can hardly be a doubt that the influence she
exercised over Mary was a wise and wholesome one, and
not the evil one, which some writers prefer to take for
granted that it must have been.   Mary, in letters to her
mother, refers in very warm terms to Diana's kindnesses ;
and, desirous to manifest her special gratitude to her, she
wished that a marriage might be arranged between the
young Earl of Arran and Diana's daughter, Mademoiselle
de Bouillon.[2]

Notwithstanding the peculiar moral vagaries that had
the open sanction, by example as well as by precept, of
the ecclesiastical authorities, a profound respect was shown
for the ecclesiastical orders and the customary ordinances
of religion.   The belief in a special supernaturalism was in
no way weakened by the prevailing looseness of moral obligations.   Though Huguenotism had gained a considerable
footing among those of a stricter habit of life, scepticism
was still very much at a discount.   Among the bulk of
the upper and lower classes, the Holy Catholic Church

---

[1] Guiffrey, *Lettres inédites de Dianne de Poytiers*, p. 10.
[2] Labanoff, *Lettres*, i. 42.

Diane de Poitiers, 2.ᵉ femme de Louis de Brezé Grand Senechal de
Normandie, criée Duchesse de Valentinois par Henri II en 1548.

LA·GRANT·SENECHALLE

From the drawing after François Clouet in the Bibliothèque Nationale, Paris.

Photo by A. Giraudon, Paris.

DIANA OF POITIERS.

was deemed as essential to a properly constituted civil society as the king and the nobles. "All the clergy of France," wrote Castelnau, "and nearly all the nobility and the people, who held the Roman faith, regarded the Cardinal of Lorraine and the Duke of Guise as *called of God* for the preservation of the Catholic religion, established in France for twelve hundred years ; and it seemed to them not merely impiety to change or alter it in any way, but impossible to do so without the ruin of the state." [1]

Towards the close of September, 1550, Mary was gratified by a visit from her mother. The visit had become possible by reason of the success of the Franco-Scottish forces in delivering Scotland from the peril of subjugation by England, and of the conclusion, in April, of a peace between France and England, in which Scotland was included ; and it now also seemed advisable to make more definite arrangements for rendering French influence in Scotland supreme.

One of the most essential steps towards this consummation was the elevation of the Queen-Dowager to the regency ; and in order to prepare for this she brought with her a large following of the Scottish nobility, whom, Leslie tells us, the French king entertained with such kindness that " he allured thair hairttis in sic sort, that at all tyme the said King Henrie was thocht to be the moist humane and luffing King to Scottis men of ony that had bene mony yeris preceding." [2] Leslie also mentions that earldoms were to be conferred on various noblemen, and he further states that a great number of other gifts and confirmations were made by the King to other noblemen and gentlemen " onder his seill and handwreit oblishing

---

[1] *Mémoires*, ed. Petitot, p. 25.   [2] *Historie of Scotland*, p. 236.

him in *verbo regio*" either to cause the young Queen to ratify them at her majority, or himself " to give them as guid within the realme of France."

As the Venetian ambassador put it, " the King bought them completely, so that in France there is neither Scottish duke, nor lord, nor prelate, nor lady, nor dame, but who is manifestly bribed by the most Christian King." [1]   Arran, to whom was now given the actual possession of the Duchy of Châtelherault, was induced to grant a conditional assent to the proposed arrangements ; but, probably on account of some dissension and discontent amongst the Scottish nobility in France, as reported by Sir John Masone,[2] it was not immediately carried out.

The Queen-Dowager remained in France more than a year, not returning to Scotland until November, 1551. While she was in France, ambassadors arrived from Edward VI. with instructions first to " demand the Queen of Scots in marriage," but, in the event of this being refused, to solicit the hand of the Princess Elizabeth of France.[3]

In acceding to the latter request, Henry II. was no doubt influenced by the desire of securing the support of England against the Emperor ; but, unless as a temporary expedient which could afterwards be dispensed with, the arrangement could not have had the support of the Guises and the more strict Catholics. Not only so ; we must suppose that the Guises regarded it as, to a certain extent, interfering with the political and ecclesiastical possibilities associated with the future of their niece, Mary Stuart. But secretly displeased with the new alliance though the

[1] *Venetian State Papers*, 1534-54, p. 361.
[2] *For. Ser.*, 1547-53, p. 791.   [3] *Ibid.*, p. 109.

Queen-Dowager might be, it was diplomatically fitting that she should, on her return journey, pass through England and pay a ceremonial visit to Edward in London.

According to Bishop Leslie, Edward sought to persuade the Queen-Dowager to propose to the King of France that negotiations should be resumed for his marriage to the Queen of Scotland. Somerset was then lying in the Tower under sentence of execution ; and if the Queen-Dowager, as Leslie states, told the young King that "it was the rigorous perswit maid be fyre and sword be the Protector" [1] that forced the nobility to send the young Queen to France, this part of her answer would, in the particular circumstances, have a peculiar cogency. Conaeus either borrows or corroborates Leslie's story ; [2] and it is not unlikely that Edward referred with regret to the failure of the Scottish marriage proposal ; but if his inexperience led him again to seek to re-open the matter, his counsellors probably convinced him of the futility of his hopes ; and there is no evidence that anything further was done.

While the Queen-Dowager was still in France a curious plot was revealed for poisoning her daughter. Its designer, Robert Stewart, was an ally of the murderers of Cardinal Beaton, and after the capture of St. Andrews Castle had rowed in the French galleys ; but nevertheless he had joined the Scottish Guard in France. Obtaining leave of absence, he went to England and sought to interest the English Council in his scheme, probably in hope of a substantial reward.

According to Bishop Leslie, [3] and the report of M. de

[1] *History*, p. 240.   [2] Jebb, ii. 116.   [3] *History*, p. 240.

Chémault to the King and Constable of France,[1] the plot was revealed to the French Government by a Scotsman, John Henderson, then resident in England. A report about the occurrence by Sir John Masone, English ambassador at Paris,[2] was evidently founded on incorrect hearsay, and the English Council knew much more about the matter than he did. They had already sent Stewart to the Tower ;[3] and but for the communication of Henderson to the French Government, nothing further would probably have been heard of the matter. When France demanded his delivery it was at once granted. He was not, as Leslie states, apprehended " in the towne of Blaise, in France," but was delivered over the frontiers at Calais,[4] and arrived at Angers as a prisoner on June 5th.[5]

According to Leslie, Stewart was hanged and quartered, his likeliest fate. Father Stevenson seeks to identify him with a Robert Stewart, who, after a career of political crime, shot the old Constable Montmorency in the back at the battle St. Denis, November 10th, 1566, and was afterwards executed as a murderer ;[6] but the narrative of this Stewart's career by Francisque-Michel,[7] shows that he was another than the personage who intended the young Queen's assassination.

Another unpleasant discovery for the Queen-Dowager was that Lady Fleming, having been honoured by the special civilities of her royal host, was in what Lady Fleming herself regarded as the distinguished predicament of being, as she said, " enceinte du roi." She was therefore,

---

[1] Teulet, *Relations*, i. 260-70. 　[2] *For. Ser.*, 1547-53, p. 97.
[3] *Journal of Edward VI.* 　　　　[4] Teulet, *Relations*, i. 273.
[5] *For. Ser.*, 1547-53, p. 121. 　[6] *Mary Stuart*, pp. 114-15.
[7] *Les Ecossais en France*, i. 532-6.

in April, 1551, hurriedly sent to Scotland, where shortly afterwards—very little to the joy of the ladies at the French court[1]—she gave birth to a male child, who became famous as the " Bastard of Angoulême."

Whether the intrigue was contrived by the Anti-Guise party to supplant the influence of Diana of Poitiers, or whether, as is most likely, the persons chiefly responsible for it were Lady Fleming and the King, it was utilised by the Guises for the purpose of isolating Mary more completely from Scottish associations.

Before her mother left France, it was arranged that Lady Fleming's place as the child's guardian should be taken by Françoise d'Estamville, Madame de Paroy, a person, to borrow the words of de Ruble, " d'un âge mûr, incapable de donner de l'ombrage à Catherine et à Diane de Poitiers."[2]

What was of equal consequence, Madame de Paroy was a strict Catholic, and, at the time of her appointment, enjoyed the full confidence of the Cardinal of Lorraine, who wrote to his sister that she was fulfilling her duties so well that no better arrangement could be conceived, while she might rest assured " que Dieu est bien servi et à la vieille façon." [3]   But in the end Madame de Paroy failed to be so successful in her office as had been anticipated.   In her earlier years the child was disposed to be submissive enough to her as her governess ; but Madame de Paroy was not a person to whom one of Mary's gay, lively, and generous temperament could become strongly attached, and as Mary approached womanhood their intercourse became more and more strained.   Finally Mary, who had

[1] For. Ser., 1547-53, p. 97.   [2] La Première Jeunesse, p. 87.
[3] Labanoff, i. 16.

a will and temper of her own, accused Madame de Paroy of seeking to bring her into bad grace with her grandmother and the Queen. So much, apparently, was she disquieted by her governess's evil, and, according to her own protestations, quite unjustifiable, accounts of her, that she prayed her mother to supersede her by Madame de Brêne, who was a friend of Diana of Poitiers.[1] Suggested or not by Diana, the proposal had not only the approval of Diana, but of the King and Queen and of Mary's grandmother and uncles. Further evidence of Diana's influence was manifested in the two-fold proposal that Diana's daughter, Mademoiselle de Bouillon, should carry her train in the absence of Madame de Brêne, and that the niece of Madame de Brêne—described by Mary as " une famme veuve bien sage "—was to be her companion in her sleeping-chamber.[2]

Considerable confusion and error are manifested by various biographers of Mary in regard to her places of residence and mode of life previous to her marriage to the Dauphin, some of them allowing themselves to suppose that her days were passed mainly in " the seclusion of a nunnery " —a by no means fit preparation for the onerous worldly duties she would afterwards have to discharge. With greater prudence, Father Stevenson contented himself with the admirably uncircumstantial, but wholly delusive, declaration that " the arrangements which had been made by her mother " [presumably during her visit to France] " for her removal to a healthier moral atmosphere placed her beyond the reach of influences which otherwise might have proved dangerous," [3] his allusion being apparently to the superseding of Lady Fleming by Madame de Paroy.

---

[1] Labanoff, i. 41.   [2] *Ibid.*, i. 43.   [3] *Mary Stuart*, p. 41.

To dispose of the misrepresentations both of Father Stevenson and the maintainers of the nunnery theory, Dr. Hay Fleming has sought to utilise the dates of Mary's Latin themes in order to show " that during that period Mary was travelling with the court from one royal residence to another." [1] Had he been acquainted with the very complete table of removals of Mary and the other royal children from 1550 to 1559 published in de Ruble's volume,[2] he would not have found it needful to pen his careful but imperfect note on the subject ; [3] nor need he have troubled himself at all about the matter had he realised the significance of the change in Mary's position when, on reaching her twelfth year, she took rank at court, and was assigned a separate establishment of her own. Previous to this the royal children were accustomed to change their residence from one royal *château* to another ; but their " removals " were not necessarily consonant with those of the court. So much for Mary's earlier years.

From December 7th, 1553, she took rank at court, and arrangements for her separate establishment were completed by January 1st, 1554, when she celebrated the occasion by entertaining her uncle, the Cardinal, to supper.[4] This new arrangement, Dr. Fleming justly enough remarks, " did not detach her from the court " ; what he fails to recognise is that, on the contrary, it, for the first time, definitely attached her to the court. This is, however, a minor matter. What is more important is that, in this connection, Dr. Fleming homologates a remarkable misreading of the closing paragraphs of the Cardinal's letter

---

[1] *Mary Queen of Scots*, p. 19.
[2] *La Première Jeunesse* (1891)—pp. 253-7.
[3] *Mary Queen of Scots* p. 207.   [4] Labanoff, *Lettres*, i. 18.

of February 25th, 1553.[1]   Here are the Cardinal's words :
" Je n'oublie pas à bien ramantevoir d'estre songneus à
sa bouche, mais, à dire vérité, ylz sont si mal en l'estat qui
sont, que j'ay grand envye la voir mestresse et son cas à
part."   And here is the translation of them on which
Dr. Hay Fleming has permitted himself to place the seal
of his approval : " I forgot not to remind her to keep
a seal on her lips, for really some who are in this court are
so bad in this respect, that I am very anxious for her to be
separated from them, by the forming of an establishment
of her own." [2]

Further, Dr. Fleming supposes that both Father Stevenson
and Sir John Skelton, who quoted the earlier part of the
letter, omitted this " final sentence " on account of its
evil import : [3] his theory being that an important reason
for the formation of a separate establishment for her was
that, by being no longer exposed to the bad example of
the court, she might be enabled to keep—if the expression
may be permitted—" a more decent tongue in her head."
He makes no attempt to explain, in accordance with
this theory, a former observation in the same letter of
the Cardinal : " I must not fail to tell you, madame,
that so much does the King enjoy her society, that he
frequently spends an hour in conversing with her, and
this is a great pleasure to him, for she talks as well and
as sensibly as if she were a woman of five-and-twenty."

To talk thus could hardly imply the indulgence in
what the Cardinal also deemed improper language ; and
further, if we consider that, by the new arrangement,
Mary would really be brought more directly than before

---

[1] Labanoff *Letters*, i. 16.   [2] *Mary Queen of Scots*, p. 18.
[3] *Ibid.*, p. 206.

under the linguistic influences of the court, Dr. Fleming's supposition becomes doubly untenable : indeed Mary does not seem to have been indulging in anything worse than complaints of her treatment by the officials of the royal household.

At the instance of Henry II., the Parliament of Paris took upon it to pass a declaration that, in accordance with French custom, Mary's majority should date from the beginning, and not from the end, of the year of her majority ; and that from the commencement of her twelfth year her kingdom should be governed in her name by the advice and counsel of persons chosen by the French king, who was now her guardian.   The Regent, now Duke of Châtelherault, had been induced to promise the recognition of the regency as soon as the young Queen attained to her so-called majority.   But he had consented to the arrangement unwillingly ; his inconstancy was notorious ; and the Queen-Dowager and Henry II., anxious that their great *coup* should be accomplished as soon as possible, sought to concuss Châtelherault into antedating his resignation by a year.

The attempt was a scandalous interference with Scottish independence ; but every precaution was taken to render it successful, and the discreet activity of the Queen-Dowager triumphed over all difficulties.   She used every means to augment the popularity she had already won by the success of her policy against England.   She did everything she could to settle the controversies which had been nourished amongst the nobility during the time of the wars ; she sought to keep herself as prominently as possible before the public view ; and, accompanying the Regent in his progresses, she made the utmost use,

Leslie tells us, of her opportunities to gain the secret consent of the nobles, both temporal and spiritual, to her virtual usurpation of the regency.[1]

Châtelherault's very proper resolve to retain the regency until the young Queen had at least completed her twelfth year, availed him nothing : it was a foregone conclusion that the convention of the nobles at Stirling should agree, in accordance with the French king's communications, that Mary had now reached her majority; that the appointment of a Regent now lay with her ; and that, by the advice of her curators, she might appoint her mother, or any other person, at their pleasure ; that is at the pleasure of the French king. At first, Châtelherault held aloof from the convention ; but on letters being sent him by Huntly and other nobles, his resolution failed, and he agreed to terms for his resignation. If Sir James Melville[2] is to be believed, his compliance would have been less easy to obtain had his half-brother, the Archbishop of St. Andrews, not then been so ill that, for the time being, he had lost the power of speech ; but at the meeting of Parliament, April 12th, 1554, the Duke gave in his resignation ; and indeed he was no match for an opponent possessing such resources of blandishment and bribery as did the Queen-Dowager.

By obtaining possession of the regency, the Queen-Dowager was now in a commanding position for furthering what she deemed the highest interests of her child and of her relations of Guise, who were bent on the subordination of Scotland to France. Admitting that her task had been lightened by the pusillanimity of the Duke, whom his half-brother, when his speech returned

<hr />

[1] *History*, p. 244.   [2] *Memoirs*, p. 20.

From a drawing in the British Museum.

MARY OF LORRAINE, QUEEN OF JAMES V. AND MOTHER OF
MARY QUEEN OF SCOTS.

to him, characterised as "bot a very beast for geuen ouer of the gouernment,"[1] her success up till now had been sufficiently remarkable. "A croune," says the satiric Knox, was "putt upon hir heade, als seimlye a sight (yf men had eis) as to putt a sadill upoun the back of ane unrewley kow ";[2] but hardly any one but a very ardent, clever, artful, and tactful woman could have managed to have had so completely her own way, as up to this time she had had, with the selfish and turbulent Scottish nobles.

Whether her policy—not a wise or fair one so far as Scotland was concerned—was a wise one, either in her own interests or in those of her child, is another matter; but in any case, like many women, she was more successful in winning power than in knowing how to turn her power to the best account ; and she now manifested the characteristic weaknesses of her sex in a too eager partisanship, and a lack of right calculation as to possibilities.

Whatever truth there may be in Knox's views as to the "monstrosity " of female government, it cannot be doubted that events in Scotland and England were in many ways modified by the almost simultaneous inauguration of a period of female sovereignty in both countries : in England by the recognition as sovereign, in the beginning of April, 1553, of Mary Tudor, and in Scotland by the recognition in April, 1554, of Mary of Lorraine's regency and of her daughter Mary Stuart's majority. In the case of Mary of Lorraine—who was of course also, in many important respects, the mere agent of France and of her brothers of Guise—while it may be granted that even the subtlest of male political intriguers could scarce

---

[1] Sir James Melville's *Memoirs*, p. 21.　　[2] *Works*, i. 242.

have achieved so much for the child, Mary, as she had
already done, on the other hand, a regent of the male
sex could hardly have consented to play the exact part
which she, on behalf of her relatives, was devoted enough
to play; nor is it likely that any one but a woman,
knowing Scotland as Mary of Lorraine ought to have
known it, would have indulged in such an optimistic dream
in regard to Scotland's subjection to France, by the means
she used to effect it.

If Scotland was to be, somehow, deluded into allowing
itself to become the mere appanage of France, it was
incumbent on the Queen-Regent to exercise even greater
caution and circumspection in the future than she had
done in the past, and not to awaken any premature
suspicions as to the purpose she had in view. She could
not have adopted a better method of arousing suspicion
than by inaugurating her rule by such an arrangement
of the principal offices as would enable her to fill some
of the more confidential posts by Frenchmen. Villemore
received the great office of Comptroller; de Binton was
named Governor of the Orkneys; de Rubay, appointed
nominally Vice-Chancellor under Huntly, virtually
superseded him in the practical duties of the office, the
sole charge of the Great Seal being given to the nominally
subordinate official; and to d'Oysell, the French ambassador, was entrusted, without any official position, the
general administration of Scottish affairs. In addition to
this, Frenchmen were more and more promoted to important positions, both temporal and spiritual.

The Scottish nobles had hardly reckoned to pay so
dearly for the rewards and honours, on account of which
they had consented to the hocus-pocus which had secured

for the Queen-Dowager the regency; and we may well believe that, as Leslie states, they were thus made to "conceave sume jolesie against the Queen's government even in the beginning."[1] For a time, however, the conciliatory character of her domestic policy greatly helped her; and at first, also, she strengthened her position by showing a strong desire to be on friendly terms with Mary of England. But the general considerateness and prudence of her rule could not hide that, lurking in the background, there was a dangerous French purpose.

Not only was she garrisoning the principal strongholds with French soldiers, but in 1556 she proposed to raise a tax for the maintenance of a standing army. The avowed aim of the proposal was to guard Scotland against the possible ambitious purposes of England that might follow the marriage of Mary of England to Philip of Spain; but the nobles, almost to a man, resented her suggestion, not so much as a menace to their authority as a slight to their loyalty; and though she at once desisted from pressing it, it helped not inconsiderably to the gradual accumulation of suspicion against her.

Mary Tudor's marriage to Philip of Spain, July 25th, 1554, necessarily changed the attitude to her both of Mary Stuart's relatives and of the King of France. Should the marriage result in an heir to the English crown, not only would Mary Stuart's inheritance of that crown become highly improbable, but her dominion in Scotland might be seriously endangered, while France, besides being faced with the united empire of England and Spain, might also be compelled to loose its grasp of Scotland.

Fate was not destined, in this matter, to be kind either

[1] *History*, p. 257.

to Mary Tudor or to Spain ; but the great vista of
Spanish possibilities, which for a time glimmered before
the eyes of watchful Europe, must have been viewed
with curious and anxious thoughts by the devoted band of
intriguers who had then charge of the fortunes of the
young Queen of Scots. To us also it affords a glimpse
of one of those remarkable might-have-beens which show
how much of a nation's destiny turned, in those days of
supreme sovereignty, on a throw of fortune's dice. And
even although the marriage failed to bring any permanent
advantage to Spain, it had, we may well believe, no small
influence—and not for good—on the fortunes of Mary
Stuart.

The claims of Lady Margaret Douglas, or her son Lord
Darnley, were not then widely recognised : and the chances
are that, but for the marriage, Mary Stuart, and not
Elizabeth, would have succeeded to Mary Tudor's throne.
Personally this would have been Mary Tudor's choice.
She was prevented from interposing against Elizabeth, solely
by the representations of Philip, by whose influence also
it mainly was, that the Catholics raised no objection to
Elizabeth's succession. In doing so great a service to the
Protestant Elizabeth, Philip was partly influenced by the
hope of obtaining her hand, and thus, after all, securing
possession of England for his dynasty ; but, in any case,
it was to him of the highest moment that Mary Stuart, then
Dauphiness of France, should not become Queen of
England.

Meanwhile the temporary alliance between Spain and
England, which had been cemented by the royal marriage,
led to a curious confusion in the ecclesiastical politics of
Europe. While Pope Paul IV., the nominee of Henry II.,

was found supporting France both against Spain, the great traditional bulwark of the Papal power, and against Mary Tudor, who with such conscientious ruthlessness had quelled the resistance to the Papacy in England, Mary of Lorraine, the agent in Scotland of the recognised champions of the Papacy in France, was following a course still more inconsistent with her ecclesiastical preferences.

She had found it expedient to encourage in England the revolutionary schemes of the Protestants against Mary Tudor, and—in order to obtain Protestant support against the Hamiltons and their party—she was also driven to adopt at first so mild an attitude towards heresy, that Protestant refugees were allowed to return to the country. She also desired to involve Scotland in the hostilities which had broken out between England and France; but here her efforts did not meet with their customary success, and the general result of a policy which, from the subtlety of its expediency, had become incoherent was bound in the long run to be disastrous.

But the fortunes of Mary Stuart in France now demand our attention. The involved and uncertain character of European politics made her relatives of Guise more anxious for the consummation of their wishes in her marriage to the Dauphin. The marriage could hardly be deemed a foregone conclusion should Henry II. die before it took place; and even now they had to withstand the perpetual intrigues of the Constable and his party to delay or prevent it. Yet Henry never seems to have given any signs of a desire to resile from his purpose; for we can hardly regard seriously a reported statement of the French ambassador, that should Philip of Spain arrange a marriage-between the Archduke Ferdinand and the Princess Elizabeth of England,

Henry would give Mary Stuart to Lord Courtenay " to prevent the House of Austria establishing itself in that kingdom." [1]

Mary Stuart was not at the French King's disposal for any such match ; nor had he ceased either on personal or political grounds to desire her marriage to the Dauphin. The friendship between the two children had from the time Mary came to France been fostered with the utmost care by Henry : and he viewed it with a sentimentalism verging on the ludicrous, considering the entirely worldly nature of the arrangement and the physical unworthiness of his sickly son to become the mate of the very flower of European princesses. When the two, a few months after Mary's arrival in France, danced together at the marriage of the Duc d' Aumale he was supremely delighted at the spectacle, and still more by the congratulations of his royal relatives regarding the " beautiful match." Later, the good understanding between the two children gave him the liveliest satisfaction ; and there were amongst him and his friends pleasantly humorous asides about the custom of the two youthful lovers " to retire by themselves into a corner of the apartments, in order that they might be able to communicate to each other their small secrets." [2] As she grew towards womanhood Mary became more and more a favourite of the King, and hardly other than imperative political necessities could have caused a change in his views as to her marriage to his son.

At last, on April 8th, 1556, the Cardinal of Lorraine informed his sister of the King's intention that her daughter should be married during the coming winter ; but unless

---

[1] *Venetian State Papers*, vi. No. 552.
[2] Baschet, *La Diplomatie Vénitienne*, p. 486.

she herself paid a visit to France, he was doubtful whether
the King would carry out his intentions so soon, though he
comforted her by an enthusiastic eulogy on the gifts and
graces of her daughter, who, he assured her, "ruled the
King and Queen." [1]

Instead of coming herself, the Queen-Dowager in July
sent her secretary—seemingly Maitland—to make arrangements for the marriage ; but the King was then preoccupied
with fears about the health of his wife, whose confinement
was immediately expected. After her delivery he started on
a provincial tour ; and later the young Queen was attacked
by a " persistent fever "—caused, it was supposed, by the
great heat—from which she did not begin to recover until
October, while about this time the Dauphin also fell ill of
a quartan fever. [2]

In the spring of 1556-7 the Estates of Scotland suggested that the Queen-Dowager should either herself go to
France, or send deputies to complete the arrangements for
the marriage. Finding it inconvenient to go, she wrote to
the King and Constable advising that they should communicate with the Scots. [3] But the war with Spain now
engrossed Henry's attention, and, although negotiations
continued, no definite step was taken by him until after
the defeat and capture of the Constable at St. Quentin
on August 10th. Not only by the defeat was a heavy
blow struck against the opponents of the Guisian influence,
but the Constable's disaster was in striking contrast with
the magnificent successes of the Duke of Guise in Italy
and Picardy. Thus, while the defeat brought home
to Henry the necessity of having Scotland at his

[1] Labanoff, i. 35-6.   [2] *Papal Negotiations*, p. 423.
[3] Teulet, *Relations*, 296.

service against England, he was in a mood, as the Venetian ambassador wrote, to do everything he could for " the gratification of the Duke and Cardinal of Guise, the said Queen's uncles, who by the hastening this marriage chose to secure themselves against any other matrimonial alliance which might be proposed to his most Christian Majesty in some negotiations for peace, the entire establishment of their greatness having to depend on this." [1]

On October 30th Henry therefore addressed a letter to the Scottish Estates, inviting them to send deputies to discuss terms for the marriage.[2] In answer to this and other communications, Parliament, on December 14th, chose nine deputies, representative of each of the three estates and of Protestant as well as Catholic opinion. Every precaution was also taken to obtain adequate guarantees for the preservation of the independence of the country. The young Queen was to bind herself to preserve the ancient freedoms, liberties, and privileges of Scotland ; so long as she remained out of Scotland it was to be governed by a commission of regentrie to the Queen-Dowager ; and the French King and Dauphin were to bind themselves and their successors, in case of Mary's death without issue, to support the succession to the Scottish throne of the nearest heir by blood.

The Commission, which arrived in France in March, found that Henry II. was quite pleased with the terms. The pecuniary details were arranged also without a hitch,

---

[1] *Venetian State Papers*, vi. No. 1079.

[2] Letter in the Advocates' Library printed in Keith's *History*, i. 348-9. Dr. Hay Fleming in a discussion as to the date (*Mary Queen of Scots*, i. 210), in which he favours the 29th, overlooks the actual date in the King's letter, " le trentième jour d'Octobre," which must be regarded as decisive.

and it was further decided that the Dauphin should, after the marriage, bear the title of King of Scotland ; that on his accession to the French throne, the two kingdoms should be united under one crown ; that in the case of the death of her husband, the Queen should have the option either of remaining in France or returning to her kingdom ; that, should there be male issue of the marriage, the eldest surviving son should inherit both crowns ; and that should there be only female issue—which in France was debarred from the succession—the eldest surviving daughter should inherit the throne of Scotland.[1]

The only demand of Henry with which the Scottish Commissioners found it impossible to comply, was that the Scottish crown should be sent to France, in order that the Dauphin should be crowned by it King of Scotland ; but at the Commissioners' request the Estates, in the following November, agreed that the Dauphin should be granted the crown matrimonial, it being understood that the grant was merely "by way of gratification during the marriage, without any manner of prejudice to her highness's self, the succession of her body, or lawful succession of her blood whatsomever." Letters of Naturalization of Scotsmen having been granted by Henry in June and confirmed by the Parliament of Paris on July 8th,[2] the Scottish Estates also, in November, reciprocated the civility by granting Letters of Naturalization to all the subjects of the King of France.

Thus Scotland's old alliance with France was renewed under omens which seemed to promise even happier relations in the future between the two countries than those of the past. Nevertheless, the immediate political horizon of Scotland was not quite free from threatening clouds.

[1] *Acta Parl. Scot.*, ii. 504-19.　　　　[2] Teulet, i. 312-17.

Not to mention more, the manner in which the marriage might affect the relations with England must have given matter for puzzling thought to the more serious of the Scottish politicians.

As before, Scotland had sought alliance with France partly as a protection against England ; but the dynastic question raised by Mary Stuart's near heirship to the English throne promised new complications, the issue of which it was very difficult to forecast. The Guises made, of course, no concealment of their hopes—by no means displeasing to the Scots—that their niece should inherit the English throne. But all this was bound up with the aggrandisement of France ; and to the Scottish Commissioners the marriage would have assumed a quite different aspect, had they been aware of the real character of Henry's purpose.

Before the signing of the public marriage-contract, Mary had already signed secretly three separate deeds by which, so far as she was able, she virtually guaranteed to Henry II. the utmost of his ambitious desires. By the first, in the event of her death without issue, Scotland and all rights Mary might have to the kingdom of England were made over in free gift to the crown of France ; by the second, Scotland with all its revenues was made over to the King of France and his successors, until France should be reimbursed of the money spent in Scotland's defence ; and by the third, while asserting her right to dispose of her kingdom as she thought fit, Mary renounced, by anticipation, any agreement, interfering with these engagements, to which the Scottish Estates might induce her to consent.[1]

These secret articles implied that Henry II. and the

[1] Labanoff, i. 50-55.

From a drawing by François Clouet in the Bibliothèque Nationale, Paris.

Photo by A. Giraudon, Paris.

MARY QUEEN OF SCOTS IN 1559.

Guises were engaged in concert with the Queen-Dowager in an active conspiracy against Scottish independence. Without the certainty beforehand that Scotland could be concussed into annexation to France, the bequest of Mary would be a mere empty form. Mainly through the efforts of the Protestants, the Queen-Dowager was to fail in the task that was assigned her ; but even had she not failed, it is by no means certain that Henry's hopes would have been in the end fulfilled ; for they left out of account the varied possibilities of Mary's future, in case of the death of the Dauphin without issue.

A good deal has been said in condemnation of the part played by the young Queen in this base transaction. Dr. Hay Fleming thinks that she did not fully realise the import of the deeds ;[1] and in a sense this may be true. Their actual significance was indeed too plain to be misunderstood except by the veriest dullard ; but Mary, we must suppose, dreamt of no other future than one in which her fortunes would be permanently linked with those of France. In her youthful inexperience she failed to take into account the uncertainties and strange surprises of life. She could not foresee that having a son—though not by a King of France—she was to feel constrained to will her crown, and her rights to the English throne, away from him. Nor was it revealed to her that, having disowned her Protestant son, she was to choose as his successor no other than Philip II. of Spain, who had been the great rival of Henry II. and still remained the most dangerous foe of France. When she signed the deeds, she, like her mother and her uncles of Guise, was heart and soul with France and Henry II. against this dangerous rival.

[1] *Mary Queen of Scots*, p. 24.

The French and Spanish dynasties were then engaged in what appeared to be a mortal struggle for supremacy in Europe ; and this supremacy seemed to depend mainly on which of the two obtained possession of the two minor kingdoms of England and Scotland.   In the young Queen's eyes, as in those of her mother, Scotland was not of much account as compared with France ; and besides, it was possibly only by the aid of France she could hope to win the crown of England, which Philip II. was threatening to snatch from her.   We cannot understand her situation or standpoint, if we fail to recognise that to the rulers of those days kingdoms were mainly pawns in a great game of ambition.

This consideration tainted the policy of Henry VIII. and Elizabeth of England, as it did that of Henry of France and Philip of Spain : the youthful Mary can hardly be blamed if she was no better than her neighbours and seniors ; indeed she was much more excusable than they, not merely on account of her youth, but because the kingdom of her forefathers was to her almost an alien land.

The marriage was preceded on Tuesday, April 19th, by the ancient ceremony of hand-fasting, at which the Cardinal of Lorraine officiated.   It took place in the grand hall of the new Louvre, the fête ending with a ball at which the King, in company with the young Queen of Scots, led off the first dance.   The marriage itself followed on Sunday, April 24th, in the Cathedral of Nôtre Dame, gorgeously decorated for the occasion à l'antique.   The Bishop of Paris received the young couple at the porch under a royal canopy of fleur de lis and addressed to them a discourse ; but the nuptial ceremony was performed by the Cardinal

Charles de Bourbon, who, we are told, pronounced the sacramental words that united them in marriage, with a reverence and dignity "qu'il est impossible de le dire."

For the French court and for Paris the occasion was of quite exceptional interest, because no Dauphin had been married at home for more than two hundred years. Then the marriage was in reality the celebration of a great triumph of French diplomacy, and seemed to inaugurate a new era of French glory.

The grace and beauty of the bride were also not only fully in harmony with the splendid and brilliant scene, but seemed to add to it its last touch of perfection. "She appeared," writes Brantôme, "a hundred times more beautiful than a goddess of heaven." "So that the universal voice of the court and the great city was that a hundred and a hundred times happy must be the Prince who went to join himself in marriage with this Princess—that if the Kingdom of Scotland was anything of a prize, the Queen was far more precious than it, for even if she had had neither sceptre nor crown, her person alone was worth a kingdom." [1]

But Brantôme is discreetly reticent as to the fitness of the Dauphin to be the mate of such a bride. As, in presence of the brilliant gathering of royalties and nobles, she stood before the altar in the bright freshness of her dawning womanhood—tall, stately, and surpassingly fair in her blue velvet robes, variegated with gems and white embroideries, on her brow a golden coronet sparkling with precious stones, and round her throat a gorgeous necklace of glittering jewels—she must have contrasted so cruelly with the wasted and stunted form of the bright-clad youth—

[1] Œuvres complètes, ed. Buchon, ii. 136.

with the puffed face and unhealthy eyes—who divided with her the chief attention of the notable assembly, as to give almost a touch of burlesque and profanity to the solemn formalities of the holy ceremony.

In the evening the enthusiasm of the people was gratified by a grand royal procession through the principal streets to the *Palais de Justice*, where a great banquet was given to the nobility and royal officials. Through the throng of admiring citizens the Dauphin and Dauphiness rode together in a litter, the King and princes on splendid chargers adorned with cloth of gold flowered with silver, and the ladies on ambling hackneys accoutred with crimson velvet and having trappings of gold. The windows of the palace were left unscreened so that the people might at least feast their eyes on the banquet. It was followed by a ball at which the royal ladies and others, including the Queen of Scots, took part in elaborate dances. There were also masques, mummeries, and other pastimes, including a grand triumphal march after the fashion of the old Roman triumphs.

Finally by an ingenious contrivance six galleons gorgeously adorned with cloth of gold, and having sails of silver cloth artificially extended, came sailing along the ball room with the movements of vessels on a tossing sea. In each of them sat a prince clad in cloth of gold, and masqued ; and as the galleons passed before a marble table, at which sat the principal royal ladies, each of the masqued princes in turn took up one of them to occupy a vacant throne beside him. The ladies selected were the Queen of France, the Dauphiness, the Queen of Navarre, and the Princesses Elizabeth, Margaret, and Claude ; and as they sailed away on their prosperous voyage amidst the gay plaudits of the nobles, the rejoicings of the memorable day came to

From a drawing by François Clouet in the Bibliothèque Nationale, Paris.

Photo by A. Giraudon, Paris.

FRANCIS II. OF FRANCE IN 1560.

a close. For several days the festivities were however prolonged by a splendid series of fêtes and tournaments.[1]

The marriage was swiftly followed by a series of events which brought about astounding changes in the European situation. By the death of Mary Tudor on November 17th, Mary became in her own view and that of her advisers *de jure* Queen of England. By order of Henry II. she was therefore proclaimed in Paris, Queen of Scotland, England and Ireland, and she and the Dauphin assumed the English arms. This has been condemned as a rash and hasty step ; but it was hardly to be expected that Mary, being able with impunity to protest against Elizabeth's accession, should refrain from doing so, unless for very special reasons.

Not to have protested would have even betokened a kind of pusillanimity, although the action of Henry II. was also specially provoked by the intrigues of Spain ; Philip II., in the hope of securing the hand of Elizabeth, having exerted every influence to secure her accession, although, according to Catholic opinion, she could not be reckoned other than a bastard. Mary Stuart's proclamation as Queen of England was mainly a move in the political game that Henry was playing against Spain ; and thus, notwithstanding his hostile proclamation, he not only sent to Elizabeth his congratulations on her accession, but made proposals to her for a secret peace.

It was not by Henry's advances that Elizabeth was induced to decline, as she did, the hand of Philip. It was

---

[1] For accounts of the marriage ceremony and rejoicings see *Discours du Grande et Magnifique Triomphe*, etc. Rouen, 1558, reprinted by the Roxburghe Club, 1818; Teulet's *Relations*, i. 302-11 ; and *Venetian State Papers*, 1557-8, No 1216.

a foregone conclusion that she would decline it ; but, as the result mainly of the changed situation consequent on Mary Tudor's death and of Elizabeth's independent and uncertain attitude towards Spain, the peace of Cateau-Cambrésis was on April 2nd, 1559, signed between the three countries ; and thus, instead of marrying Elizabeth of England, Philip saw himself, by a complete *volte-face*, affianced to the Princess Elizabeth of France.

Mary Stuart could hardly, however, resile from the position she had taken up in regard to the English succession, without at least some definite recognition of her rights as next heir to the English throne after Elizabeth. Such an arrangement was, we now know—Elizabeth being constituted as she was—utterly hopeless on any conditions ; but Mary's knowledge of Elizabeth's peculiarities was not then what it was to be.   In view of events in Scotland —then in the throes of the Reformation—she therefore thought fit to send her, on April 21st, a friendly letter expressing her personal satisfaction at the conclusion of the peace, and the hope that the alliance between her and her "very dear and loved sister and cousin" would be perpetual ; and on May 25th, in reply to a similar communication from Elizabeth, she affirmed that she desired nothing so much as to see an increase in their friendship, which she assured her she would do everything in her power to promote.[1]

The marriage of Philip II. to the Princess Elizabeth of France, June 22nd, 1559, was followed by a grand tournament in honour of the foreign guests who had been deputed to be present at that ceremony and also at the marriage of the Duke of Savoy to Margaret of

[1] Labanoff, i. 62-5.

From Mr. J. J. Foster's " The True Portraiture of Mary Queen of Scots,"
by permission of Messrs. Dickinsons.

MARY QUEEN OF SCOTS AS QUEEN OF FRANCE.
From the bronze bust in the Musée du Louvre, Paris.

France, which was to take place a few days afterwards.
A master in feats of arms, Henry had distinguished himself
in encounters with the Dukes of Savoy and Guise, but
had had to give way before his young captain of the
Guards, the Count of Montgomery, and desired, against
the strong remonstrances both of Catherine de Medici
and Diana of Poitiers, to have his revenge.

At the first shock of the second encounter the lances
of both were broken, but Montgomery's had carried away
the King's visor, and Montgomery being unable with
sufficient quickness to lower his broken lance, the shaft
glanced along the steel breastplate and penetrated deeply
into the King's left temple. An attack of fever followed
which brought about his death on July 10th, and thus
Mary Stuart, in her seventeenth year, became Queen-
Consort of France.

With her elevation to this brilliant position not only,
however, had the fortunes of Mary Stuart reached their
climax : solicitudes and fears immediately began to mingle
with her felicity ; and in France her happy days were
already well-nigh over. Infatuated with the merely
dazzling aspects of their great scheme for the advancement
of their own and their niece's fortunes, the princes of
Guise failed sufficiently to consider the possibility that the
union between her and the heir of France might be but
brief and that there might be no issue by it.

Notwithstanding the unhealthy debility of Francis
from his infancy, they seem to have flattered themselves
that he would become, as he reached manhood, moderately
vigorous, and that he would probably survive at least
sufficiently long to have children by their niece. In cherishing such a hope, they were probably encouraged by the

physicians, who did not properly understand the case. Mr. Swinburne, also not understanding the case, has scoffingly referred to the poor Dauphin as "the eldest and feeblest of the brood," implying, presumably, that the iniquities of the parents or grandparents had fallen on the children. As a matter of fact, however, neither Henry nor Catherine had suffered anything from iniquities of the kind referred to, and the theory of transmission of a disease to grand-children is not now accepted by physicians. In any case the weakness of their eldest child was not due, as is usually supposed, to a syphilitic affection either of a secondary or tertiary kind, but to the previous barrenness of Catherine, the disease being that now known as "végé-tations adénoides du pharynz nasal." [1] But her husband being in such a condition of health, Mary had practically no chance of ever becoming a mother, and the marriage was one only in name.

Meantime, by the sudden death of Henry II., which the Guises may have sincerely lamented, and which un-doubtedly added another element of uncertainty to the future, fortune for the time being appeared in a manner to have favoured them, for they now became the virtual rulers of France. Through their niece—by whom the weakly boy who was her husband was entirely fascinated, and who seems to have managed him with much cleverness and discretion—they were at once taken into the King's special confidence.

Though feverishly ardent in the pursuit of outdoor amusements, Francis was taciturn, obstinate, and morose, and quite incapable not merely of grappling with difficult

---

[1] See Potiquet, *La Maladie et la Mort de François II.* (1893), illus-trated by portraits and diagrams.

After an engraving by Cock.

MARY QUEEN OF SCOTS
As Queen of France.

questions of state policy, but of submitting to the daily
routine of official observances ; and thus he handed over
to the Guises the government of the country. The
Constable of Montmorency, against whom the Guises had
formerly intrigued in vain, was now dismissed from office ;
and to the deputation of the *parlement*, sent to congratulate
him on his accession, Francis intimated that he had assigned
to his uncles of Guise "the management of affairs "—
to the Duke of Guise the charge of the army, and to the
Cardinal of Lorraine the control of finance. It is true
that he continued to bear to his mother the "reverence
and respect " which, according to the Venetian ambassador,
"were extreme at all times," [1] and desired that she should
be consulted on all affairs of importance ; but the initiative
and the authority lay, of necessity, with the brothers of
Guise. This, rather than the vague story that Mary had
sneered at Catherine as "a merchant's daughter," was, we
must suppose, the origin of the enmity with which Catherine
came to regard the lady who had succeeded her as Queen-
Consort.

At first, the satisfaction of the brothers of Guise
with their position must have been complete, for notwithstanding the internal disquiet of the country, they
had every opportunity for consolidating their power and
still further advancing their own and their niece's fortunes.
Could Heaven only vouchsafe to her husband some length
of days, or bless the marriage with male issue, their
most ambitious hopes as to the results of the marriage,
including the succession of their niece to the English
throne, seemed almost certain sooner or later to be fulfilled.
Nor apparently, in their opinion, was there immediate cause

[1] *Venetian State Papers*, 1558-80, No. 85.

for extreme anxiety either as to the King's health or as to the possibility of issue. On the contrary, there began to be an apparent likelihood that the devout petitions of the Cardinal for the birth of an heir might soon be answered.

Mary's health about this time became uncertain and she was troubled with frequent sicknesses, which the matrons at court soon came to regard as symptoms of her interesting condition. Deluded by these opinions and by their own fervent desires, the Guises soon began to whisper the happy secret to their intimates, until it became the general theme of court gossip and was even communicated to Philip of Spain. In her inexperience and her hysterical condition—due partly to anxiety as to the troubled fortunes of her mother in Scotland—Mary also allowed herself to defer to the opinions of the gossips, and, like Mary Tudor, buoyed herself up for a time with utterly groundless imaginations, even adopting the floating tunic then usually worn by ladies in her supposed condition. Towards the end of September, 1560, her delusion vanished, and she resumed her ordinary robes; but the Guises, though profoundly chagrined, sought to hide even from themselves their own dismal foreboding; a king, they said, of sixteen years and a queen of seventeen had still a future before them.[1]

But soon their better judgment must have told the Guises that, except by the very special favour of Heaven, the chance of an heir to the French throne by the marriage on which they had ventured all their hopes was all but gone, and that the tenure of their present supremacy would cease

[1] These particulars were first made known by de Ruble (*La Première Jeunesse*, pp. 187-8).

as soon as the breath departed from the frail body of their
niece's husband.

In a few months *le petit roi*, as he was called by the
people, had become a tall man ; but his rapid growth was
a mere symptom of disease. It meant the beginning of
the end ; and even if no accidental illness befell him, the
physicians, sanguine though they wished to be, could not
predict for him a life of more, at the utmost, than two or
three years. Notwithstanding his imprudent ardour for
the chase and the game of tennis, his health during the
summer and autumn gave no cause for particular anxiety ;
but after a day at the chase on November 16th, near
Orleans, he appeared to have caught a chill, and in the
evening he complained of pains and noises in the head.

The country was then in a condition bordering on civil
war. In dread of the results of a complicated Huguenot
intrigue against them, the Guises had filled Orleans with
soldiers, and the Prince of Condé, who had been enticed
to the court, was thrown into prison. In such a crisis the
sudden dangerous illness of the King must have filled the
Guises with almost overwhelming anxiety, and for a time
they sought to conceal it from the court and from
the foreign ambassadors.

On November 20th Michiel Surian, the Venetian
ambassador, reported from Orleans that the King was
remaining in bed only to allay the anxieties of his mother,
and that had he been a private person he would have been
going about as usual ; on the 22nd he intimated that
" every one feels that His Majesty's illness is not dangerous,"
and that there was no doubt " but that in two or three days
he will have quite recovered " ; but on December 1st he
had other news to tell: " Although," he said, " they

endeavour to conceal the malady more than ever, the Queen-mother cannot suppress the signs of her sorrow, which is increased by the recollection of the predictions made by many astrologers, who all prognosticate his very short life." [1] The malady, the seat of which was in the left ear, had begun to affect the brain, causing attacks of delirium followed by fainting fits ; and from the first the case was quite hopeless.   But those who had him in charge carried reserve and secrecy as to his condition to the utmost limits of possibility.

On December 1st, the gates of the court were closed, no one entering the King's chamber except the two Queens and the three Guises ; and the antechamber, previously crowded, remained empty.   Not even were any servants permitted to attend on him, his deathbed being watched only by his wife, his mother, and the despairing Guises.   Never perhaps was there a royal deathbed scene so wretchedly and grotesquely miserable.   The life that was now ebbing away was that of one who, with all the outward favours heaped on him by fate, was the mere creature of misfortune.   He was quite unfit for the great position he had been called to fill, and his life was of no intrinsic value to France, to the world, or to his relatives.   It is even by no means certain that his mother, in the position of political nullity she now occupied, was anxious that her son should be longer spared to her ; and the other watchers, desiring with all their heart and soul that he might survive, were in reality concerned only about how his death would affect their own fortunes.   The secret enmity cherished by Catherine against her daughter-in-law now also, it is said, manifested itself in bitter disputes in presence of the dying

[1] *Venetian State Papers*, 1558-80, Nos. 207, 209, 211.

King, the Guises being too much concerned about the future to interfere effectively against Catherine.

Maddened by the near prospect of his removal from power, the Duke of Guise overwhelmed the physicians with invectives and reproaches against their science, which could not do more for a king in the flower of his age than for an old miserable mendicant ; and with oaths and blasphemies he even accused them of poisoning the wretched sufferer, and threatened that, in the event of his death, they should be hanged.   On the other hand, the Cardinal of Lorraine placed his faith chiefly in the customary ecclesiastical machinery—prayers, invocations of the saints, processions, masses, and expiatory ceremonies. [1]

" The whole court," wrote the Venetian ambassador, " is now constantly engaged at prayers, and processions are being made in all the churches of the city, which are attended very piously by the brothers and the sister of his most Christian Majesty, by the King of Navarre and many other personages." [2]   In presence of crowded audiences of ecclesiastics the preachers asked from Heaven the favour that the life of the sickly King might be spared, until the heresy now threatening them should be extirpated ; and, infected with the ecclesiastical ardour of the Cardinal of Lorraine, the King, in his half-conscious moments, is said to have murmured menaces against the Calvinists.

But, apart from miraculous intervention, his death was merely a question of a few days.   On December 2nd, he was somewhat relieved by copious evacuations ; but the revived spirits of the miserable company at his deathbed were almost immediately crushed by an aggravation of his

[1] See especially de Ruble, pp. 202-6.
[2] *Venetian State Papers,* 1558-80, No 213.

illness during the night.   It now became manifest to every
one that his case was beyond hope ; and on the evening
of December 5th, 1560, the sufferer—whose sudden illness
had interrupted so inopportunely the dire projects of the
Catholics against the enemies of their faith, and whose life
was also so dear to Mary Stuart and the Guises, for their
own sake as well as that of Catholicism—ceased to be an
object of almost any further thought either to the world or
to his relatives.

CHAPTER III

THE WIDOWED QUEEN

TO Mary Stuart the death of her husband was, by the circumstances in which it placed her, an almost overwhelming stroke of ill-fortune. In her verses on her bereavement she refers in very proper terms to the personal character of her loss :

> "Si en quelque séjour,
>   Soit en bois et en prée,
>   Soit sur l'aube du jour,
>   Ou soit sur la vesprée,
>   Sans cesse mon coeur sent
>   Le regret d'un absent."

But though her feelings towards the poor sickly Francis appear always to have been kindly, it was not, in such a case, to be expected that regret for the dead should overpower all other considerations. The loss of her husband had been preceded, on June 10th, by the death of her mother, which she seems to have felt far more acutely : she was rumoured to have " loved her incredibly and far more than daughters usually love their mothers." Then succeeded, on July 6th, the treaty of Edinburgh, which provided for the removal of French troops from Scotland. Scotland was therefore now in the hands of the Protestants, and under the special protection of

[1] *Venetian State Papers*, 1558-80, No 175.

Elizabeth, so that before Mary had ceased to be Queen-Consort of France, it had become doubtful whether over Scotland she would ever possess any real sovereignty.

Nor could Mary immediately obtain much sympathy in her misfortunes from those who had lately sat in company with her around the deathbed of the dying King. Catherine de Medici, according to Sir James Melville[1]— who was sent to carry condolences to France, and who, on account of his previous service with the Constable, had a thorough knowledge of French political parties— was even " blyeth of the death of K. Francis hir sone, because sche had na gyding of him, but only the Duc of Guise and Cardinall his brother " ; and Mary's uncles of Guise were too much occupied in saving all that they could from the wreck of their own fortunes, to give much immediate consideration to anything else. " Every one," wrote Michiel Surian on December 8th, " will forget the death of the late King, except the young Queen, his widow, who, being no less noble-minded than beautiful and graceful in appearance, the thought of widowhood, at so early an age, and of the loss of a consort who was so great a King, and who so dearly loved her, and also that she is dispossessed of the crown of France with little hope of recovering that of Scotland, which is her sole patrimony and dower, so afflict her that she will not receive any consolation, but brooding over her disaster with constant tears, and passionate and doleful lamentations, she universally inspires great pity." [2]

This is, probably, a pretty accurate account of Mary's miserable condition. She herself wrote to Philip of Spain that, without the aid of Heaven, her misfortunes would

[1] *Memoirs*, p. 86.   [2] *Venetian State Papers*, 1558-80, No. 215.

From a drawing after François Clouet in the Bibliothèque Nationale, Paris.

Photo by A. Giraudon, Paris.

MARY QUEEN OF SCOTS IN 1560,
As a widow, wearing her "deuil blanc."

be unsupportable.[1] Trained, though she had been, to master her feelings, and to subordinate the present to the future, and the realities of life to its outward pomp and glitter, her nature was too strong and passionate not to assert itself in great extremities. When, therefore, she entered upon her forty days' seclusion as a widow, her mood must have been quite in keeping with the ceremonial gloom of her position.

There is really no ground for the prejudiced statement of Froude that Mary, " who had watched dutifully by the sick bed of her husband was speculating, before the body was cold, on her next choice."[2] She had been trained to look for political guidance mainly to others ; and in her new and dark situation, she would be disposed to trust mainly to the speculations of her uncles, in whose wisdom and goodwill she had entire confidence, but who were too absorbingly occupied in despairing efforts to preserve the King in life, to give much thought to anything else. But of course there was bound to be speculation by outsiders, even some days before the King's death. To no one was the question as to who should be Mary's next husband a matter of intenser interest than to Elizabeth ; and naturally Throckmorton, the English ambassador, was very curious to know all that was to be known ; but the statement in his letter to Cecil of December 6th—quoted by Froude— that " so far as he could learn," she " more esteemed the continuance of her honours and to marry one that might uphold her to be great, than she passed to serve and please her fancy," cannot be founded, as Dr. Hay Fleming, supporting Froude's rash conclusion, seems to suppose,[3] on

---

[1] Labanoff, i. 91.   [2] *History*, cab. ed., vi. 443.
[3] *Mary Queen of Scots*, p. 227.

any definite statement, made during her husband's illness or immediately after his death. Such a premature utterance of her intentions is really inconceivable, even if it were not the undoubted fact that for several days after the death she declined, seemingly from utter prostration, to see any one.

Ultimately she was persuaded to receive the young King, the King of Navarre, and her uncles of Guise ; and some time afterwards she granted interviews to those who were her special friends, and received in audience the foreign ambassadors [1] ; but the probability rather is that offers of marriage had begun to be pressed upon her, before she had done much speculation of her own.

It was soon manifest that Mary would have no lack of suitors. Among the earliest to let their aspirations be known were Frederick II. of Denmark, and the ill-fated Eric XIV. of Sweden, while one of the two sons of the Emperor Ferdinand was then, as later, thought to stand a very good chance. The young Earl of Arran, who seems to have been in love with Mary from boyhood, and had just been rejected by Elizabeth, was also, in a few weeks, eagerly pressing his claims, through the mediation of the King of Navarre and the Constable ; and Lady Lennox had already begun to " be of good hope " as to the chances of her son, Lord Darnley. Mary herself would perhaps have been quite content to have waited for the young King of France, Charles IX. ; but to the attainment of this supremely desirable consummation was the insuperable obstacle of Catherine de Medici. Failing the French match, that which most fascinated the imagination of Mary was the Spanish one, although by reason of the peculiar personality

[1] See especially de Ruble (p. 208), who quotes letter of Surian, January 9th, 1561, not calendared in *Venetian State Papers*.

of Don Carlos, the marriage, from the point of view of
personal desirability, would have been an even more
miserable alliance than had been that with the poor dead
Francis II.

At first there seemed every likelihood that the marriage
to Don Carlos would be Mary's destiny. To Philip II. the
fate of the young widow, lately the hope of France, was
bound to be a subject of keen political interest. Though
he was now married to Mary's favourite friend, Elizabeth
of France, we must believe that his interest in Mary's fate
was more political than personal. Her husband's death
was undoubtedly a remarkable stroke of good fortune for
Spain. It had rendered, abortive the ambitious designs of
France as to Scotland and England : and Philip had now a
chance of utilising the young Queen of Scots for similar
designs of his own. Very shortly, therefore, after the death
of Francis II. the Cardinal of Lorraine and he had begun to
bargain about the Cardinal's niece ; and for a time it seemed
that the Cardinal's efforts on his niece's behalf would be
sufficient to remove all obstacles in the way of procuring for
her a second marriage, both as grand and as deplorable as
her previous one.

The main interests which Philip and the Cardinal had
in common, were the interests of Catholicism, which, so far
at least as they were represented by the Cardinal, now
appeared in France to be in supreme danger. Had it
been possible, the Cardinal would have preferred the French
marriage : in furthering the Spanish match he was, in a
sense, acting directly against the interests of France ; but
he had to consider primarily its spiritual or ecclesiastical
interests, and this for the very good reason that they were
bound up with his own future.

As for Mary, the thought of separating herself from France and the scenes of her former social triumphs was very far from a pleasant one ; but so soon as she recovered from the shock of her calamity, the ambitious hopes which had been nourished in her were certain to revive ; and in having regard mainly to the political aspects of her next marriage, she was acting more in accordance with royal traditions than the skittish and unmanageable Elizabeth. "It does not appear," says Dr. Hay Fleming, "that Mary's thoughts of another marriage lowered her in Throckmorton's eyes."[1] This is doubtless true, for instead of lowering her, they raised her in his eyes. His high opinion of Mary's "behaviour" and of her "wisdom and kingly modesty," rested on the fact that she "thinketh herself not too wise, but is contented to be ruled by good counsel and wise men."[2]

Before the expiry of Mary's period of seclusion, Philip II. had instructed Perrenot de Channtonay, his ambassador in France, to appeal to the interests of the House of Guise as a reason for advising their niece to accept the hand of Don Carlos ; but it is unlikely that the subject was even remotely alluded to in the interview between Mary and the Spanish ambassador, when he went to offer her his condolences. We can hardly suppose that even the jealously watchful Throckmorton imagined that marriage-proposals were the direct subject of their colloquy. Mary had been on specially friendly terms with Philip since his marriage to her old companion, Elizabeth of France ; and topics for a genial and friendly conversation with his ambassador would not be wanting. Mary may have wished to show herself as complaisant as possible ;

[1] *Mary Queen of Scots*, p. 34.   [2] *For. Ser.*, iii, No. 833.

but it is unlikely that negotiations took a definite shape before the arrival, towards the end of January, of Don Juan Manrique, who, after paying court to the young French king, "went," says the Venetian ambassador, "to visit the Queen of Scotland, with whom, in the presence of the Duke of Guise and the Cardinal of Lorraine, he held very confidential communications, and, I am assured that, besides his other concerns, Don Juan is also empowered to treat a marriage between her Majesty and the Prince of Spain." [1]

The suspicion that such negotiations were in progress was bound to create a deep sensation both in England and France. As Throckmorton remarked to the Venetian ambassador, if the marriage took place, "the friendship subsisting between the Queen his mistress, and the King Catholic, would be converted into a no less enmity." [2] Until now, Philip had given Elizabeth the benefit of his influence with the English Catholics, so that she might be unhampered by domestic difficulties, while assisting the Scots against the efforts of the French for the annexation of Scotland. Such a policy was, however, dictated only by what he deemed a peculiar emergency. It must have been adopted with reluctance ; from a purely Catholic point of view it was difficult to justify it ; with the death of Francis II. all reason for its continuance appeared to cease ; and, even before this, its disadvantages had become only too obvious.

On July 25th 1560, de Quadra reported to Philip that "the Catholics here complain that your Majesty should sustain this Queen in her dominions and so cause heresy to strike its roots in this realm," and on August 4th he even

---

[1] *Venetian State Papers*, 1558-80, No. 233. [2] *Ibid.*

wrote that it was no longer possible for him to do anything for Philip's service in England.[1] Thus, before the death of Francis II., relations between Elizabeth and Philip had already become strained ; and, by the time Philip had commenced negotiations for the Scottish marriage, the reputation of Elizabeth had become seriously compromised by the mysterious death of Dudley's wife, Amy Robsart, and by the open favour she was showing to the widower.

So much was this so, that on January 22nd de Quadra assured Philip that he could, if he would, easily turn her out of her kingdom by means of her own subjects, and suggested that, in view of possibilities, some step should be taken, in his interests, towards declaring her successor.[2] Following this came, through de Quadra, on February 22nd, a request from Dudley for the influence of Philip on behalf of his marriage to Elizabeth, on the promise of his becoming a supporter of Catholicism.[3]

While putting but little faith in the intentions of Dudley or Elizabeth, Philip thereupon instructed his ambassador to do all that he could to inveigle them into the marriage,[4] for the simple reason that it would inevitably ensure Elizabeth's ruin. Had they proceeded in their path of folly to the end, the advisability of the marriage of Don Carlos to her rival would have been unquestionable. But it was almost impossible, in any given case, to predict what Elizabeth might or might not do ; and it may have been that, being fully aware of Philip's aims, she was mainly endeavouring to beguile him. At any rate, she meanwhile had sent Bedford to Paris to form an alliance

---

[1] *Spanish State Papers*, 1558-67, pp. 171, 174.
[2] *Ibid.*, p. 180.   [3] *Ibid.*, p. 180-4.
[4] *Ibid.*, pp. 184-5.

CATHERINE DE MEDICI IN 1561.

with the Huguenots, and to do his utmost to prevent the marriage of the Queen of Scots to a foreign prince.

But Philip was also failing to take into sufficient account the alarm which the marriage scheme was bound to arouse in France, not only among the Protestants but among many Catholics. More especially was he astray as to the character of the opposition that might be expected from Catherine de Medici, the peculiarities of whose strong and exceptional personality were only beginning to manifest themselves. To Catherine the proposed marriage was entirely detestable, alike on public grounds and for her own private reasons. But of course the private reasons were here the supreme consideration. Had the future of France been her main care, she could at once have stopped the Spanish negotiations by offering Mary the hand of Charles IX. A dispensation for such a marriage could have been obtained without difficulty, and, in promoting it, Catherine would only have been helping to give effect to the long-cherished purposes of her late husband, and would have been credited, at least by Catholic opinion, with rendering an inestimable service to France. But such a marriage would mean in the end the reinstatement of the Guises in power, and, as before, her own political annihilation.

In her own view also she had no option but to do her best to prevent Mary making an alliance that would add to the prestige of Mary and Mary's uncles ; and for this reason alone she was prepared to go any length in her opposition to the Spanish marriage. She had, besides, hopes of securing the hand of Don Carlos for her youngest daughter Margaret, whom Henry II. had designed for Henri de Béarn, afterwards Henry IV. ; and she now, through her daughter-in-law, sought to bring the claims of Margaret before the attention of Philip.

Not only so, but she even promised—for the bafflement of her rivals was dear to her almost beyond price—to place the young King under Philip's guardianship and to cause the King of Navarre to renounce his pretensions to that country, if only Philip would depart from a scheme which promised to restore her rivals to more than their old influence. Finding her offers and promises at first of no avail, she had recourse to warnings and even vowed, rather than that Philip's purpose towards Mary should have effect, to ally herself with the heretics and with Elizabeth.

Threatened with a combination against him of two women so formidable and, both politically and religiously, so apparently unscrupulous, Philip's heart began to fail him, and he shrank from facing the possibilities which Catherine's menaces conjured up. As the affianced bride of Don Carlos, Mary could hardly have gained possession of her Scottish throne without the armed assistance of Spain ; and since Elizabeth had apparently dropped her intention of immediately marrying Dudley, the hope of a Catholic rising in England had become remote. Moreover, Philip, as a sincere Catholic, dreaded to be the occasion, even indirectly, of strengthening the Huguenot cause in France. Towards the end of April, therefore, Catherine was gladdened by the announcement from her daughter that the scheme of the Guises—in regard to which she had no official information, either from the Guises or Philip—had failed, and that the negotiations for the marriage would not proceed further.[1]

[1] Paris, *Négociations sous François* II., p. 847. See also especially Cheruel, *Marie Stuart et Catherine de Médicis*; and de Ruble, *La Première Jeunesse.*

From a drawing by François Clouet in the Bibliothèque Nationale, Paris.

Photo by A. Giraudon, Paris.

MARGARET OF VALOIS,

According to Brantôme, Mary "desired a hundred times more to remain in France a simple dowager, and content herself with Touraine and Poictou for her dowry than to go to reign in her savage country : but messieurs her uncles, at least some if not all of them, counselled her to go." [1] In this statement there is no doubt a great deal of truth. She would not have returned to Scotland could she have well avoided it ; but (1) it was her best chance of winning Don Carlos, and (2) her uncles would have had no peace from Catherine until they had sent their niece out of the country. On account of Mary's letters patent to the Scottish Parliament, formally announcing the death of her husband,[2] Dr. Hay Fleming supposes that for some time after the death of Francis II. Mary was " on good terms with her mother-in-law " ;[3] but the situation was rather that of an armed truce. Nominally she and her uncles had compromised matters with Catherine : but the real character of the terms on which they stood to her was shown by the removal of the Guises from power, and by the story of the Spanish match.

There was thus left for Mary no other choice than the great venture of a return to Scotland. But from the first she had contemplated the alternative of a return without any form of foreign help, and had been doing her utmost to secure for herself a favourable welcome from her Scottish subjects. There was of course the almost insuperable difficulty of the question of religion, which had done so much to drive her mother from power ; but Mary had probably, as yet, but an imperfect knowledge of its formidable character, and she

---

[1] Œuvres, ed. Buchon, ii. 136.   [2] Labanoff, i. 80-4.
[3] Mary Queen of Scots, p. 34.

had resolved to adopt meanwhile a temporising policy. This she would be better able to do than had her mother, for the reason that she would be unhampered by the necessity of securing French dominance in Scotland, the grand project for the annexation of Scotland to France having collapsed with the death of Francis II.

As soon also as the Scots came to know that they had not to dread any French entanglement, her sovereignty would become more acceptable to them. Could she now succeed in identifying herself, as her Scottish ancestors had done, primarily with the interests of the Scottish nation, all, notwithstanding the nation's internal divisions, might possibly be well with her. The main question was whether with her foreign upbringing, her special ecclesiastical bias, and her peculiar ambitions, she could properly understand the nature of the Scottish political situation, as, for example, Elizabeth understood the political situation in England.

Some time before her mother's death her mother's authority had been over, and her own sovereignty had virtually, if not formally, lapsed. The government was now in the victorious hands of the lords of the Congregation, headed nominally by the Duke of Châtelherault, who was now gratified by the definite declaration of Parliament as to his right of heir-apparency to the crown, and again found himself, by one of the strange revenges which the whirligig of time sometimes brings round, in substantially the same high position that he had occupied during Mary's infancy. As before, however, he was but a figure-head—the mere puppet of more determined, if not more ambitious, personalities than himself. As before, also, the country was virtually under the dominance of

the ecclesiastics : not however, represented by those of
the faith of Cardinal Beaton—now long gone to his account
—or of Beaton's successor, the Duke's scandalous half-
brother, John Hamilton, but by the party whom Beaton
had so sternly and cruelly persecuted, the party of the
redoubtable John Knox and of his political henchman,
Lord James Stewart, who had the honour to be, though
by left-handed descent, half-brother of the absent Queen.

The Duke, after his weak and dull manner, had no
doubt continued to bear a grudge against the Queen-
Dowager for his deprivation of the regency and the
failure of his scheme, countenanced by Beaton, for the
marriage of his son to her daughter ; and he was now
enticed, as he had been enticed before, to make a profession
of Protestantism, in the hope, as before, that his heirs
should inherit the Scottish throne. The proposal, however,
by which he had now been beguiled was that Elizabeth—
as long ago had been suggested by Henry VIII.—should
marry his son. But even had Elizabeth not then been,
as she was, in the most enamoured stage of the Dudley
flirtation, and had she not been disinclined to marry
either Dudley or any one else, she would not have chosen
Arran.

The aim of the Protestant Scots was to unite the
two kingdoms under Arran and Elizabath; but this aim was
kept in a manner in the background. Indeed the Estates
had intimated to Francis II. their purpose of sanctioning
the marriage, and had had the audacity to " request him
to direct his ambassador in England to assist theirs herein."[1]
Elizabeth, however, would not have accepted the Scottish
crown, either with or without Arran. The political

[1] *Scottish Papers*, i. 476.

complications created by it would have been too perilous ; and, besides, Elizabeth never manifested any special interest, either in the permanent union of the two kingdoms or in the future of Protestantism in Britain. What she was mainly anxious for was to be let alone to govern her own kingdom in peace ; what might be its fate—far less the fate of Scotland—after she was done with it, troubled her but little.

The failure of the proposal was evidently anticipated both by Lord James and Maitland ; but had Francis II. survived, and Mary been formally deposed, it is hardly likely that the crown—Elizabeth having rejected Arran— would have been settled on the Hamiltons. The chances are that it would have lighted on the head of Lord James Stewart, who was yet unmarried. Doubtless there were difficulties in the way of such a consummation, but in the end the stronger and abler man was bound—in such a position of affairs as then prevailed in Scotland—to win. Châtelherault and Arran, being the mere puppets that they were, would have been put aside after they had ceased to serve the purpose of Lord James and Maitland. The existing form of government could not have been permanent had Francis II. survived ; and it was only by electing Lord James as king that the Scots could have put their house fully in order.

Without the summons of Mary, the Scottish Parliament —or rather a Protestant and packed convention bearing that name—had met in August, 1560, and, without intimating to her their purpose, had formally adopted, on the 17th, as the nation's " Confession," a complete system of Protestant doctrine : and on the 25th it passed three important Acts, the first abolishing the authority of the

Pope and the Catholic prelates ; the second condemning all doctrine contrary to the newly accepted Confession ; and the third forbidding, under severe punishment—death being that for the third offence—the celebration, or attendance at the celebration, of the Mass. This could only be meant as a mere preliminary to the formal deposition of their Catholic Queen. Yet Acts which she and her husband were bound, as Catholics, to regard with mere abhorrence the Scots had had the assurance to send to them, by Sir John Sandilands of Calder, for ratification. They could not expect that their ratification would ever be granted ; but should Elizabeth accept the Arran proposal they would be in a position to defy their nominal sovereigns, and should she not, they intended, we must believe, to defy them all the same.[1]

The reply of Francis to the Scottish communication was that he was " greatly displeased with their proceedings," and that he would send " two good and notable personages as his deputies to assemble Parliament legitimately—and see that they come to their reasonable ' debvoir.' "[2]

But the processes which were determining Mary's life towards its tragic close seemed ever to go on with the regularity of clockwork. Before the dispute could come to an issue, Francis II. lay adying at Orleans ; and after his death, but before she knew of its occurrence, Elizabeth handed to the Scottish Commissioners in London her reply to the Arran marriage-proposal. It was to the effect that she was not disposed presently to marry ; and it seemed to recommend that matters in Scotland should remain in statu quo, Arran—whose amour propre she sought to solace by the declaration that he was " a noble gentleman

---

[1] Acta Parl., Scot, ii. 525-35. [2] Scottish Papers, i. 492.

of great worthiness "—being recommended to choose a
partner according to his own will.[1]

Such an indefinite arrangement as that which Elizabeth
seemed to recommend could not long have been continued,
had not the apparently impending crisis been, by the death
of Francis, succeeded by one of a totally different character.
That death closed the door on another of the remarkable
might-have-beens in the history of Scotland and the life of
Mary, and quite transformed the immediate political outlook both for Scotland and her. But for it, Mary might
never again have set foot on Scottish soil except by armed
aid. The sudden crisis found, however, the Scottish
political leaders with their plans incomplete, and very much
at a loss as to how to cope with it. If it did not spread
amongst them a feeling of actual consternation, it almost
dumfoundered them with perplexity and doubt.

The outstanding Scottish Protestant personalities at this
time, those on whom the fate of Mary and, in a sense, of
Scotland seemed to depend, were Knox, Maitland, and
Lord James Stewart. In some respects Knox was the most
remarkable, if not the cleverest, of the three. He was
the evangelical successor of the martyred Wishart, before
whom he had, in his younger days, carried a protective
drawn sword ; and if not the equal of his ecclesiastical
father in personal modesty or mere emotional fervour, he
probably far excelled him in that combination of qualities
which constitutes what is termed force of character.

A fundamental element in force of character is, of
course, a certain measure of self-assurance, and in Knox
self-assurance ultimately came to be inordinately large.
Had it been combined with weak intellectual capacity, he

[1] Keith, ii. 9-10; *For. Ser.*, iii. No. 786; *Scottish Papers*, i. 495.

From the engraving in Beza's "Icones."

JOHN KNOX.

might have developed into a type of religionist represented by the modern fanatic revivalist, or had it represented mainly narrow-minded conviction, he might have degenerated into a mere sectarian faddist ; but though he had a certain affinity to both these types, Knox owed his success as Protestant reformer not merely to his inordinate self-assurance but to a varied combination of gifts and graces. His vivid eloquence, declamatory and extravagant though it may have been, was tempered by a strong infusion of common sense, and much insight into the idiosyncrasies both of men and women and the practical needs of his time.

The cleverness of his ridicule was on a par with the weight and fervour of his denunciation ; and as an orator of the racy, forceful and assertive type he can have been surpassed by few of any time or country. His striking oratorical gifts secured him almost unbounded influence over a large percentage of the townsmen, both the better class burgesses and their dependents the " rascal multitude " ; for if he found it a hard task to bring the latter under the strict discipline of the Protestant Kirk, he owed to them not a little of the success of his crusade against " the monuments of idolatry."

But Knox was also something more than a mere popular ecclesiastical orator : he was, like the great Catholic ecclesiastics of his time, a shrewd man of the world. Whatever he might pretend to himself, he by no means acted as if he believed, with St. Paul, that " not many mighty, not many noble are called," or that the things in this world that are strong could be put to shame by those that are weak.

On the contrary, he seems to have supposed that a

preliminary to any lasting success in his crusade against the Papacy, was to secure the support of the nobility and gentry.   Therefore, in 1555, he suggested to such of them as were already inclined to the Protestant doctrines, to invite the " principal men of the country " to what would now be termed a house party, where Knox could converse with them familiarly, as well as exercise on them his great gifts of public persuasion.   His round of visits to the country houses began in the north-east district, where Erskine of Dun was the host; after which he proceeded to Calder House, in West Lothian, the seat of Sir James Sandilands, where he had the remarkable good fortune to win such recruits as John, fifth Lord Erskine, Archibald Lord Lorne, afterwards fifth Earl of Argyll, and Lord James Stewart, then Prior of St. Andrews.

After a winter spent in Edinburgh, and devoted mainly to similar tactics, he made a tour, under " noble and distinguished patronage," in the west of Scotland, officiating chiefly in the houses of the gentry, including, besides several houses of the lower barons, Ochiltree, the seat of the lord of that name, and Finlaystone, the residence of the Earl of Glencairn, where he " ministered at the Lordis Table," after what he deemed the non-idolatrous fashion.

Returning by Calder, where many persons of mark from Edinburgh and the " country about " were induced to meet him " for the rycht use of the Lordis Table," he went a second time to Dun, where he administered the " Table of the Lord Jesus " unto the " most parte of the gentilmen of the Merse " ; and before his audacious crusade against the Mass compelled him again to return to Geneva, he taught in Edinburgh, in the Bishop of Dunkeld's " great lodging," to a greater audience than he had ever done before.

In the sixteenth century what was termed the Gospel of Christ had ceased, be it remembered, to be altogether a gospel of persuasion and peace. Knox had necessarily, in the first instance, to appeal to persuasion; but he found it desirable above all things to persuade the mighty, because he intended that, ultimately, compulsion should be added to persuasion. Protestantism had no chance, then, of permanently succeeding, or even of openly surviving, in any country unless it very speedily secured a preponderance of the armed forces : the absolute " truth of God " was then supposed to be within the reach of human knowledge ; but, apparently, for any particular country, what it was, could be determined, not even by the count of heads, but, in the end, only by the compulsion of the civil magistrate, inspired by the spiritual fear of the divinely guided ecclesiastic. The primary aim of Knox had therefore been to secure for his doctrine the support of the pains and penalties that were at the civil magistrate's disposal, and the short cut to this consummation was to gain to his side the support of the nobility and gentry with their armed followers.

Mere persuasion could not have created the swift and startling ecclesiastical revolution of 1560. It was effected by the sword, and by the external help of England ; and, moreover, its most influential supporters were not all impelled mainly by religious or ecclesiastical motives. The nobles listened to Knox because they had special worldly grievances against the Catholic clergy ; many of the gentry, as well as the people, supported the Reformation from dread of French domination ; and much of the fervour displayed against the " monuments of idolatry " represented the merely destructive passion of a democratic mob.

As regards Knox himself, it would be unjust to affirm that his motives were essentially personal and selfish. That even in his regenerate condition he was quite uninfluenced by mere personal ambition and love of predominance can hardly be maintained ; but yet of the honesty of his beliefs, the fervour of his ecclesiastical zeal, and his high devotion to what he deemed a great cause there can, in the century that now is, hardly be a question.

Still, he was primarily, of course, an ecclesiastic—an ecclesiastic of the sixteenth century ; and he could not leap away from his shadow. With his zeal and force of character he dominated the new ecclesiastical situation in Scotland, and under his guidance the Reformation there was bound to assume a more intolerant and ambitious character than it had done in England, where ecclesiastical excesses and pretensions were on the whole admirably held in check by the secular-minded and self-devoted Elizabeth.

But it is as idle to denounce the narrow intolerance and unlimited ecclesiastical ambition of Knox as it is absurd to belaud them, or to affirm that the Scot was practically not the Scot until Knox created him. The contribution of any single individual to the formation of what is called national character can in the long run be but infinitesimal, however much he may be able to con- tribute to a nation's temporary eccentricities. There could, for example, be no greater misrepresentation of the legacy Knox left to Scotland, than to affirm that it owes to him its intellectual freedom, such as it is. Intellectual freedom cannot be gained at a bound ; and not only so, but the intellectual freedom which many now deem an indispensable element of their manhood, was not then supposed to be a proper possession for any one, and Knox—an ecclesiastic to the marrow of his bones—had he met it in any one, would have been almost petrified with horror.

The mission of Knox, according to his own view, was to make known what he deemed the "truth of God," the truth which he supposed to have been set down, by direct communication from Heaven, in a supernatural book, of which, by virtue of his office, he was the divinely appointed interpreter. How a supernatural book should require any merely human interpretation to make its meaning clearer, and how the divinely appointed interpreter of it was to be known, are doubtless bewildering puzzles to merely natural human reason ; but once admit the direct interference of supernaturalism, and all such difficulties dissolve like snow before the summer sun.

What therefore Knox, in effect, aspired to be, and what in effect he largely, though—by the mercy of Heaven and the peculiarly stubborn waywardness of Scottish human nature—not altogether, succeeded in becoming, was the Reformation Pope of Scotland. Of the almost boundless character of his ecclesiastical assertiveness we have a piquant example in a letter of his to Elizabeth, which, be it remembered, he meant to be conciliatory, but in which he spontaneously offered to her his advice, or rather command, as to how she should demean herself as sovereign, warning her that "if she refused the counsel of the faithfull" [that is, of Knox], "appear it never so sharpe," she would do so to her own "perdition." [1]

Knox's influence in England was indirect and limited ; but in Scotland it was direct, and he was determined that it should be as unlimited as possible. He could therefore be prepared to welcome Mary's return to Scotland only

[1] Knox, *Works*, vi. 47-51.

on condition of the probability that she would place herself under his direction, in even a more absolute sense than her mother had placed herself under the direction of Beaton ; and as matter of fact the main political problem of Scotland for the next few years was, in effect, whether Knox or Mary should be its sovereign.

Knox, indeed, affirms that the death of Francis II., which almost necessitated Mary's return, was the "cause of joy to us in Scotland,"[1] and it may be granted that Knox never had any scruple in rejoicing at the death of his enemies ; but in this particular case a little anxiety, if not some trembling, must have mingled with his mirth. True, he was comforted by the expectation—though when the news reached him of the death of Francis he could not be quite certain of this—that the "faithful" in France would be delivered by it ; and there was also the prospect of temporary relief in Scotland from what Randolph, the English ambassador, describes as the "schurge" that was "hangyne over yt," by the apparent threat of a second French invasion.[2] All this was very well so far as it went, and had Mary died also, Knox's cup of thanksgiving would have been running over ; but since she was alive, the death of her husband might prove, as, for a time at least, it did, the reverse of a blessing to the "faithful in Scotland." Randolph's—or Maitland's —anticipations were to be in the end fully justified : "I beleve here wylbe a madde worlde ! Our exacteness and singularitie in religion will never concurre with her judgemente. I thynk that she wyll hardeley be broughte under the rule of our discipline, of the which we can remytte nothynge to anye estate or persone."[3]

---

[1] *Works*, ii. 32   [2] *Scottish Papers*, i. 498.   [3] *Ibid.*, i. 520.

From the picture in the possession of the Earl of Lauderdale.

MAITLAND OF LETHINGTON.

The character and real intentions both of Maitland and Lord James Stewart are harder to read than those of Knox. The latter are written large in Knox's own account of himself and his contemporaries, and in the features of his remarkable handiwork, the Scottish Reformation. Though he exercised much secret influence over the Lords of the Congregation, and could also do some intriguing on his own account, without their knowledge, his general political aims were never matter of doubt : when he sought to conceal, or made pretence to modify his real opinions—as in the case of female sovereignty, so far as it concerned Elizabeth—he showed that he was a mere tyro in the art of humbug. If meddlesome, he was candid. Few who have sought to busy themselves with the great practical problems of politics have ever been more open and above board; and we must believe that he fully deserved the epitaph uttered by Morton at the side of his grave : " He nather fearit nor flatterit any fleche."

On the other hand, Maitland, while perfectly honest in his main political aims, was essentially a diplomatist, a diplomatist in an age when diplomacy had reached the height of its unscrupulous subtlety ; and again in Lord James we are presented with the problem of a statesman who, by reason of the peculiarity of his birth and his relationship to the sovereign, was placed in a position of exceptional delicacy and difficulty. The fact that he was in a peculiar way equal to it, in some sense deepens the mystery that attaches to him. Which of the two, Maitland or Moray, was in reality the cleverer may be a moot point, but it can hardly be doubted that Maitland was the more thorough politician.

Generally known as Maitland the younger, of Lethington,

William Maitland was the eldest son of the famous lawyer and poet, Sir Richard Maitland, Lord Lethington, who long survived him. The family, of ancient Norman descent, was settled in Berwickshire as early as the twelfth century; but none of its members was ever ennobled, and they belonged to that class of gentry whose fortunes depended greatly on success at court. On this account Maitland received a very thorough education, which was completed abroad; and like his father he, early in life, entered the royal service. It was no doubt his father's influence that secured him, about 1554, a position in the household of the Queen-Dowager, to whom his great discretion and ability must soon have been evident, and who, after employing him on several important diplomatic missions, conferred on him, on December 4th, the high office of Secretary of State. Yet almost from the time that he entered her service he had seemingly ceased to be a convinced Catholic.

While at supper, in 1555, along with other promising young men whom the laird of Dun had invited to meet Knox, Maitland had, it would appear, a sharp bout of argument as to attendance on the Mass, nothing being omitted by him that "mycht mak for the temporisar"; but in the end he greatly gratified the self-sufficiency of Knox by saying, "I see perfytlye that our schiftis will serve nothing befoir God, seeing that thei stand us in so small stead befoir man." It was on this occasion that Knox, being evidently very hard pressed by the "sharp wit" of Maitland, found it needful to express his disbelief that "James' command-ment, or Paul's obedience," in a certain matter, "proceeded from the Holy Ghost." [1] Plainly if Knox knew better

---

[1] Knox, *Works*, i. 248.

than either James or Paul, it was vain for Maitland to argue further with him ; but it may be that Maitland, even thus early, as later, did not quite accept Knox at his own valuation, though he was too prudent to say so.

Whether Maitland, notwithstanding this remarkable discussion, continued his conformance to Catholic observances we are not informed. In accordance with the advice of her brother, the Cardinal of Lorraine, the Queen-Dowager was then dealing "in Scotland in a spirit of conciliation." She had not taken any definite action against the Protestants until some time after Maitland had become her secretary ; and it was only after this, also, that her real designs as to French annexation would become manifest to him.

As, in some disputes with the Doctors of the Sorbonne, Maitland had made it evident that he was at least by no means an orthodox Catholic, his position had become highly dangerous. But a formal resignation of such an office was not then possible ; it would have meant his imprisonment, if not his death. It is therefore nothing to his discredit, that for some time after he was fully aware of her treacherous purpose, he continued nominally in her service, and waited a favourable opportunity to desert to the Lords of the Congregation. This occurred after they occupied Edinburgh, on October 18th, 1559. Next day Maitland made his escape from Leith, in which the Queen-Regent had fortified herself ; and, after delivering himself up to Kirkcaldy of Grange, he advised that the Queen-Regent should be opposed to the uttermost, affirming that there was nothing in her but " craft and deceit." [1]

Henceforth Maitland showed himself an irreconcilable

[1] Knox, *Works*, i. 464.

opponent of any French alliance. Since he had so completely burned his boats he had, of course, for the time
being, no other choice; but he burned them, we must
suppose, because of the special knowledge he had acquired
of the French designs. His desertion was thus an almost
irreparable calamity to the Queen-Regent, whose specious
pretences could now deceive nobody; and it was probably
in consequence of his revelations that the Council, on the
22nd, resolved to suspend her from the office of Regent.
The transfer of his unique talents as diplomatist to the
cause of the Lords had also much to do with the final
triumph of their cause. Apart from his peculiar gift of
persuasion, he could bring special influence to bear on the
nobles and barons, to whom the mere triumph of Protestantism counted for nothing.

By his skilful baits Maitland finally, after many evasions,
won over to the Lords even the shifty Earl of Huntly—the
"wily young man" of Henry VIII.'s time—whose jealousy
had been aroused by his virtual supersession in the
Chancellorship by de Rubay, but whose Catholicism and
selfish caution had hitherto kept him aloof from the
Protestant party. On April 28th, 1560, Huntly was
prevailed upon to sign the Lords' bond for the defence of
the Reformed doctrines and the expulsion of the French,
though he did so secretly in the presence of Lord Ruthven,
Maitland, and Randolph, requiring them "to keep it secret
for two or three days." [1]

The neutral nobles such as Morton—then, on account
of the minority of Angus, the acting head of the Douglases
—Hume, and others of the south of Scotland, whose interest
in the quarrel came to be only personal or political, were

---

[1] *Scottish Papers*, i. 386.

also won, mainly by Maitland's handling of them. On
May 6th Morton, Borthwick, Douglas of Drumlanrig,
the Kers of Ferniehurst and Cessfurd, and twenty-three
others over whom Morton had special influence, signed
the common band ; and there was thus laid the foundation
of the Morton-Maitland alliance, which, broken and
renewed more than once, was to have much to do with
the wild occurrences of subsequent years.

Thus we may almost say that, in securing the triumph
of the Lords of the Congregation, Maitland is entitled to
rank alongside of Knox. Though he had nothing to do
with the original opposition to the Queen-Dowager, he set
that opposition on a much firmer basis, rallying around
it many supporters whose interest in the religious question
was but secondary. For a time his political influence
became as supreme as the ecclesiastical influence of Knox,
and he held the Scottish nobility in the hollow of his hand.
"I find Lethington," wrote Cecil, "disposed to work
the nobility to allow whatever your Majesty determine ;
he is of most credit for his wit, and almost sustains the
whole burden of foresight." [1]

Great as was the work done by Maitland in the organi-
sation of a political opposition in Scotland against the
Queen-Dowager, he rendered the Protestants a service quite
as invaluable as this in securing for them the armed aid
of Elizabeth. That only some three weeks after he had
gone over to the Lords, he should have been chosen to
go on so cardinal a mission, is testimony sufficient to
the astounding growth of his influence ; but the choice
of him was more than justified by results. The revelations
he was able to make as to " the French devices to the

[1] *Scottish Papers*, i. 427.

prejudice of England "[1] doubtless greatly commended him to Elizabeth and Cecil ; but in whatever company he was, Maitland always wielded great personal ascendancy. More truly of him than of Mary, it may be said that he was in possession of a " magic whereby men are bewitched," for his witchery was exercised over persons who were in great part proof against the womanly charms of Mary. No one had ever a better grasp of the realities of a political situation ; no one could read more unerringly the motives of his opponents ; no one could mystify and bewilder them with such cunning subtlety. And, while he had an almost unequalled gift of plausibility, he had also the advantage of entire sincerity in his main political aims ; and in any cause on which his heart was bent, he could bring to the aid of his acute intellect a very real emotional eloquence.

In his first mission to Elizabeth, Maitland also appeared to the very best advantage, for he was able to convey the perfectly true impression that his intentions were absolutely sincere, and that he had at heart the interests of England, because he was convinced that its interests were inseparably bound up with those of Scotland. His aim was not to tempt Elizabeth to deliver the Scots out of a merely temporary difficulty, or even to assure the triumph of Protestantism in Scotland, but to promote permanent goodwill between the two countries.

That Elizabeth was profoundly impressed with his sincerity and ability, was shown by her in a letter to Norfolk, requiring him to take precaution that Maitland's life was not endangered by the French on his way north, and referring to Maitland as " one in whom ye shall find

[1] Instructions in Sadler's *State Papers*, i. 604-8.

much understanding and knowledge of the state of Scotland, and, as we trust, a plain earnest affection to have
his country free from conquest or oppression." [1] Besides
being the main agent in securing the treaty of Berwick,
February 27th, 1559-60, by which armed aid was obtained
for the Protestant Lords, it was mainly by his management
that the Scots agreed to the treaty of Edinburgh, July 6th,
1560, which, on certain conditions, provided for the disuse
of the English title and arms by Francis and Mary ;
Cecil, in a letter to Norfolk, June 25th, while the negotiations were proceeding, affirmed that, but for him, the
folly of others " would hazard all." [2]

Maitland's attitude towards the proposed Elizabeth-
Arran marriage was a little ambiguous, but this is hardly
surprising. He told Cecil that he had agreed to join the
deputation only in order not to give offence to the Duke
and Arran, who had earnestly pressed him to go ; and,
in a later letter, he informed him that the general wish
for the marriage was so earnest that it seemed to be " the
only meanes to joyne us in ane indissoluble union." [3]
He did not dare to do more against the project than
advise delay, in order that it might the better succeed ;
and he acted towards Elizabeth as if he knew nothing of
her preferences : he wished " no pleasour to any my
countrymen, joyned with her Majestie's displesour." [4] And
had he been as anxious for the completion of the arrangement as were, seemingly, the majority of the Scots, the
reception which Elizabeth gave the proposal showed that
his caution was fully justified.

By the death of Francis, two days before Elizabeth

---

[1] *Scottish Papers*, i. 316.   [2] *Hatfield MSS.*, i. p. 241.
[3] *Ibid.*, i. 461, 464.   [4] *Ibid.*, i. 484.

had handed in her dubious declinature to the Scottish Commissioners, the unwise haste of their proposal was still further made manifest. Froude[1] supposes that her refusal was the result of the news of the death of Francis; and Mr. Lang puts the case thus, "Elizabeth now, out of fear, declined to marry Arran."[2] According to Mr. Lang's punctuation, the meaning of his sentence would be that Elizabeth, in declining to marry Arran, was actuated by fear; but, from the context, the meaning which Mr. Lang intends to convey is that she declined to marry Arran because by the death of Francis she was delivered from fear of a French alliance against her. As matter of fact, however, when Elizabeth handed in her declinature, the last news that had reached her from Throckmorton was that "now the physicians mistrust no danger of his life";[3] and Throckmorton's letter announcing his death she did not receive until December 13th, as she was penning a letter of instructions to Throckmorton on the supposition that Francis was alive.[4]

That what was in reality a revolutionary proposal had been made to Elizabeth was more than awkward both for Maitland and Lord James, even although neither may have had any real desire for the Arran marriage; but, before he left London, Maitland did his best to remedy the situation by writing to Cecil a proposal that Mary, on agreeing to recognise the legitimacy of Elizabeth's rights, should be acknowledged as next heir. Elizabeth's "doubtful" answer involved, he saw, the return of the Scottish Queen, though he promised to do his utmost to keep the nation in touch with England, as indeed was imperative for

---

[1] *History*, cab. ed., vi. 442.   [2] *History*, ii. 95.
[3] *For Ser.*, iii. No. 758.   [4] *Ibid.*, No. 796.

his own as well as his country's sake.[1] Meanwhile he was
much concerned as to how the change would affect the
relations of Scotland with France. The situation there,
he understood but imperfectly ; and the announcement
that de Noailles was on his way to propose a renewal of
the French alliance gave him cause for special anxiety.
He dared not rejoice, as others were already rejoicing, for
he thought that the late security against French influence
had " lulled most men asleep." He thought Mary would
be bound to follow her uncles' advice, and so could not
forget what hitherto had been done contrary to her pleasure :
he " feared many simple men should be caryd away with
vayne hope, and broght abed with fayre words." If Lord
James, whom the Protestants proposed to send to " grope
her mind," could persuade her to trust her own subjects
he would take courage ; if not, he saw " the perell "—of
French annexation—" large, greater than ever it was " ;[2]
and of course that would mean also his own ruin. With
more definite information on the French situation he was,
however, by February 26th, disposed to take a more hopeful
view, and he evidently included himself among those who
favoured her return, provided she neither brought " force
nor counsel of strangers."[3] But much of course at the
same time depended on Elizabeth's attitude ; and unless
Mary and Elizabeth should come to some working arrangement, he knew that his " familiarity with England " would
be his undoing. But being mainly a politician and averse
to the extreme character of the Scottish Protestantism, he
had no cause, provided Mary cherished no bad intentions

---

[1] *Scottish Papers*, i. 511, 518; *Hardwicke Papers*, i. 174; and especially,
Spanish State Papers, 1558-67, p. 306.
[2] *Scottish Papers*, i. 510.   [3] *Ibid.*, i. 516.

towards him personally, to be so despondent about the consequences of her return as was Knox. On the contrary he felt, as an unmatched diplomatist, a peculiar professional interest in the political problem, the character of which was being gradually unfolded to him ; and, could he secure the trust of his sovereign, he did not despair of a solution of it which would be of the highest benefit to both countries.

The attitude of Lord James Stewart towards his sister's return differed considerably both from that of Knox and that of Maitland. Though a " precise Protestant," like Knox, his high worldly interests, on which he plainly set some store, might be greatly affected by the policy he might adopt ; and, while the ambitious hopes of Maitland could not range so high as those of Lord James, the latter's range of action was more strictly limited by his Protestant convictions. As the half-brother, though by left-handed descent, of the nominal Queen of Scots, Lord James was deemed by many a far from ineligible successor to her. Undoubtedly, could Knox have brought it about, this semi-royal personage, who was so much after his own heart, would have been chosen king, even long before the death of Francis II. Indeed Knox had even cherished a hope that Elizabeth might be induced to marry him, for he desired that Arran might be sent and secretly kept in England " till wise men considered what was in him, if misliked the Prior of St. Andrews second " : [1] and in a " memorial for the Queen " it is suggested by the Council to " explore the very truth, whether the Lord James enterprises towards the crown for himself or no, and if he do, and the Duke be cold in his own cause, it may not

---

[1] *Scottish Papers*, i. 236.

From the picture at Holyrood Palace.

JAMES STEWART, EARL OF MORAY.

be amiss to let Lord James follow his own device, without interference." [1]

Since Châtelherault was induced for "his own cause" to join the Reformers, the chance of Lord James had meanwhile to be at least postponed ; but even as late as June 19th Cecil refers to him as "not unlyke either in person or qualities to be a king soon." Once the Estates had voted for the Arran marriage, Lord James had no other option than to show himself "mervilous erneste" for it ; but the fevered Duke and Arran suspected that his designs were hostile, though Randolph believed that "there was no man wyllnger" it should come to pass than he. Yet he took no conspicuous part in pressing the proposal on Elizabeth. In his letters to Cecil—who did not favour the proposal—he makes no reference to it of any kind, and while asking him to credit Maitland as himself in all cases, he expresses, in merely general terms, his confidence in Cecil's devotion to the common cause.

To suppose that the Lord James was really anxious for the Elizabeth-Arran marriage would be to credit him with both an unnatural disinterestedness, and a meekness quite alien to his latent force of character. The desperate figure all along cut by the Duke in Scottish politics must have awakened his amused contempt ; his estimate of Arran's fitness, notwithstanding his bravery as a soldier and his persuadedness in religion, to supplant himself as the possible sovereign of Scotland, could not have been high ; and the unconcealed eagerness of both father and son to get hold of the Scottish crown, could hardly have evoked his sympathy. Apart from the question of religion, we must also credit Lord James with kindly feelings towards his

[1] *Scottish Papers*, 241.

sister, of whose childhood he must have had none but pleasant memories ; and he was well aware that for her late attitude towards himself and Scotland, others, rather than she herself, were responsible.

When he learnt of the death of Francis II., Lord James, as was customary with him, seemed to place himself entirely in the hands of others, and at the disposal of his country. We have no evidence that, at first, he uttered any distinct wish, or opinion, or hope, or fear of his own ; but he seems to have immediately discerned, as had Maitland, that her return was well-nigh inevitable. The illstarred Arran marriage-proposal, followed by Elizabeth's rejection of it, had necessarily turned the thoughts of the majority of the Scots towards the daughter of the royal house who was their sovereign *de jure*, or, as Maitland put it, made " many enter in new discourses." [1]   On the other hand, the Arran proposal caused Mary to entertain a more favourable opinion of Lord James than, perhaps, she might otherwise have done. It was to his credit that he had made no attempt to snatch supreme authority for himself, and she had discernment enough to see that he was not responsible for the proposal. As early, there-fore, as December 31st, Throckmorton was able to report that " she holds herself sure of the Lord James, and of all the Stewarts. She mistrusts none but the Duke of Châtelherault and his party." [2]

By the Convention of January–February, 1560-1, it was decided that Lord James should make the experiment of a visit to Mary ; but no definite instructions were given him—except by the irrepressible Knox. According to Knox's own account, Knox " plainlie premonisshed " him

[1] *Scottish Papers*, i. 506.   [2] *For. Ser.*, iii. No. 833 (5).

" that yf ever he condiscended that sche should have Messe publictlie or privatlie within the Realme of Scotland, that then betrayed he the caus of God, and exponed the religioun evin to the uttermoist danger that he could do." To this Lord James replied that he would never consent that she should have Mass publicly ; but, his Protestant zeal being tempered by some worldly discretion, he added that it would be impossible to prevent her having Mass in her own chamber.[1]

According to Maitland the "somme" of the legation of Lord James was to know his sister's mind, and whether she would repose confidence in her subjects or not ; and he was of opinion that for this Lord James was meetest in many respects, being "zelous in religion, and one of the precise Protestantes, knowen to be trew and constant, honest and not able to be corrupted, besides that nature must move her hyghnes to beare him some good will, and it is lyke that she will rather trust him than any other." [2]

Meanwhile, Mary herself was doubtless as perplexed about Scotland as the Scottish Protestants were perplexed about her ; and she, or her advisers, felt that immediate interference with the crisis was imperative, whether she designed immediately to return to Scotland or not. Sometime, therefore, before the expiry of her period of seclusion, on January 15th, she had been making arrangements for sending to Scotland a Special Commission of four Scotsmen. Its original purpose, according to Throckmorton, writing on January 18th, was to "labour the Estates" to remove the clause in her late covenant of marriage by which she could again marry only with their consent, and

[1] Knox, *Works*, ii. 142-3.   [2] *Scottish Papers*, i. 510

to "suspend further proceedings in matters of religion."[1]
A Convention of Estates, be it remembered, was then
busy taking order for "establishing religion" [that is,
Protestantism] "universally"—"something more vehement,"
wrote Maitland to Cecil, "than I, for my opinion, at
ane other tyme wold have allowed."[2]

On January 22nd, Throckmorton, however, reported
to Cecil that Mary had changed her determination in
treating with her subjects concerning her marriage and
the state of religion in her realm,[3] and next day he explained to Elizabeth that she had changed her mind, "upon
occasion of letters out of Scotland."[4] Although Throckmorton clearly implies that Mary's change of mind
happened after he wrote his letter of the 18th, Dr. Hay
Fleming—by an unaccountable slip—accepts Throckmorton's
statements of the 22nd and 23rd, as explaining why Mary's
instructions to the deputies, dated as early as January 12th,
"contain no reference to the second marriage."[5] Throckmorton must somehow have been misinformed, and the
most likely supposition is that he was mistaken in his
earlier information; indeed much of his information was
necessarily unreliable—he was clever and indefatigable, but
not quite infallible.

In his letter of the 23rd he further informed Elizabeth
that Mary had written "severally and kindly to them all,
and amongst the rest to Lethington, Balnaves, and Grange,
promising oblivion of things past." This again was probably only half correct, for Mary's letter to Maitland is
dated the 25th; but that her Commissioners carried private

[1] *For. Ser.*, iii. No. 889.   [2] *Scottish Papers*, i. 509.
[3] *For., Ser.* iii. No. 915.   [4] *Ibid.*, No. 919.
[5] *Mary Queen of Scots*, p. 227.

letters to many noblemen and gentlemen is corroborated by a reference of Maitland, to Cecil, February 26th, to the "sede of sedition" in the private letters,[1] and by the report of Randolph, that they brought "well nere" three hundred letters "with credit as theie lyste to frame yt," etc.

The truth was that Mary was manifesting in her public communications—and doubtless still more in her private ones—a discretion, and something more, so great and so unexpected as quite to baffle and bewilder the extreme Protestants and to cause deep disappointment and chagrin to Elizabeth.

The most important points in Mary's public communications, sent primarily to the chief representatives of the different parties—the Duke, the Archbishop of St. Andrews, Huntly, Atholl, Argyll, Bothwell, and Lord James—were that before the King's death she had been striving with him for their reconciliation to him ; that she wished to bury all offences in oblivion ; that she hoped for a renewal of the league with France, in regard to which M. Noailles had been sent ambassador ; that she desired a deputation of the Estates to be sent to inform her of their deliberations ; and that she intended to return to Scotland as soon as she had settled her affairs.

The only thing in Mary's message likely to cause anxiety was the proposal for the renewal of the French league. That head, Maitland described as "difficil," and he affirmed that, if it took place, there would ensue with time that which neither Scotland nor England would like.[2] Happily the French league, on account of the changed circumstances of Mary, soon became a vain dream. When she wrote, her marriage to Charles IX. was

---

[1] *Scottish Papers*, i. 517.   [2] *Ibid.*, i. 517.

not deemed an utter impossibility, though events were rapidly dissolving her former interest in the fortunes of France. By the time the Scottish Parliament met in May, communications from Lord James, then in France, had greatly lessened Scottish anxiety as to French intentions. If Knox's account of the answer given to the French ambassador [1] be accepted, the proposal was rejected in terms wantonly insulting ; but the letter of the Scottish Council to Charles IX., shows that the Estates were not so lacking in diplomatic amenity as Knox would represent. The proposal was rather evaded than directly rejected, the Council thanking him for his letters " as to the renewal of the old friendship between the realms, for which they will not be ungrateful, consistent with their duty to their sovereign." [2]

Immediately after the expiry of her period of seclusion, which had been spent in the sole company of her grandmother, Antoinette de Bourbon,[3] Mary went with her grandmother to a private château about seven miles from Orleans. When, however, the court left for Fontainebleau, she accompanied it, though solely to have an interview with the English Commissioner, Bedford. On account of Throckmorton's illness, Bedford's visit was delayed until the 16th, when both arrived together, and had interviews the same day with the King and Catherine de Medici, who, on their stating that they had also a message to the Scottish Queen, directed the Duke of Guise to conduct them to Mary in her own apartment, where he found her in the company of the Bishop of Amiens, divers other French bishops, and many ladies and gentlemen.

To their condolences she replied in specially friendly

---

[1] *Works*, ii. 166.   [2] *Scottish Papers*, i. 534.   [3] De Ruble, p. 210.

FONTAINEBLEAU.

From an old print.

terms, stating that "Considering that the Queen now showed her the part of a good sister, whereof she was in great need, she will endeavour to be even with her in good-will." On their mentioning that, at a more convenient time, they had something else to say to her, she prayed them to advertise the Duke of Guise when they desired to repair to her—a significant indication of the footing on which she stood with Catherine de Medici.

The long detailed account by Bedford and Throckmorton of their various interviews with Catherine, the King of Navarre, and the Queen of Scots is full of interest, though their diplomacy was plainly hampered by their imperfect knowledge of the French political situation. Elizabeth's main aim, in relation to Scotland, was to obtain from France and Mary the ratification of the treaty of Edinburgh, and specially of the clause acknowledging her title to the English crown ; but Throckmorton had failed to discern how distinct were becoming the interests of Mary from those of France. Not only had the King of France no power now to ratify a treaty which primarily concerned Scotland, but his ratification of it, in the changed relations between France and Mary, was really not a matter about which Elizabeth needed to concern herself.

As for Mary, if the attitude she took up was evasive, this was not unjustified by the peculiarities of her changed circumstances. She replied that she could not ratify the treaty until she had the advice of her nobles ; but she took care to assure the English ambassador that she was not averse to the ratification, and was not desirous to shift the matter : " For if her Council were here she would give such an answer as would satisfy him." She further wished that she and Elizabeth " might speak together, and then she trusts that they would satisfy each other much better than they can do by messages and ministers."

If Mary was to acknowledge Elizabeth's title to the English throne, it was only fair that Elizabeth should take measures for annulling the offensive arrangement of the baffled Henry VIII., which debarred Mary, now next heir by descent, from the English succession. Whether there was danger to Elizabeth in doing so was another matter. Much depended on the characteristics of the two ladies ; but, without the mutual arrangement, it was certain that Mary could never cease to plot against Elizabeth, while there was at least the possibility that concessions which would be mutually gratifying might issue in permanent cordiality.

That Mary became sanguine of effecting an understanding may be inferred from letters of the Papal Nuncio shortly after Mary left for Scotland. On August 21st he wrote that the Cardinal of Lorraine gave him hopes that Mary and the Queen of England " will henceforth maintain concord and union," and that he had heard " that the Queen of Scotland cedes to the Queen of England her rights to that kingdom, and that the Queen of England declares the Queen of Scotland her heir if she dies without children " ; and on the 30th he intimated, on the authority of the Duke of Guise, that the affair was "a settled thing, though not finally sanctioned." [1]

Behind all this there was of course the question of religion ; but while the Protestants hoped for Mary's conversion, the Catholics had not yet given up hope of Elizabeth's return to the old faith ; indeed the idea in France then was, that she was "not resolved of what religion"

[1] *Papal Negotiations*, ed. Pollen, pp. 62-3.

she "should be." In any case, throughout the protracted negotiations that were to follow between the two queens, Mary always seemed to have the diplomatic advantage, little good though it did her ; and Elizabeth, though politically she triumphed over Mary, always had the appearance of being in the wrong, and never more so than when she succeeded finally in ridding herself of her rival for ever.

With this question of mutual recognition the question of Mary's marriage had of course an intimate connection, and it was already a subject of keen interest to Elizabeth. In answer to Throckmorton's enquiries, the Protestant King of Navarre expressed his opinion that the favoured suitor was the Archduke. He promised to do his best to hinder it ; but he added, " I told you, M. l'Ambassador, a remedy against this mischief, whereunto you make me none answer : you know what I mean."[1] Dr. Hay Fleming[2] supposes that the King may have referred to a suit of his own for Mary's hand ; but even if we could suppose him capable of alluding in such familiar fashion to his own chances, or that Throckmorton in such a case would have made him no answer, the remedy most within the power of Elizabeth was to marry the Archduke, as Cecil earnestly desired she should.

Mary, whose stay at the court had been prolonged by Bedford's visit, left it for Rheims about March 18th, her journey being broken at Paris on the 20th, that she might inspect " her robes and jewels."[3] At Rheims, where she arrived on the 26th, she was privileged to be present at the first properly appointed family council, since the change in the family's fortunes and outlook by the death

---

[1] For. Ser., iii. No. 1030 (23).   [2] Mary Queen of Scots, p. 232.
[3] For. Ser., iv. No. 77 (1).

of her husband, there being present the Cardinals of
Lorraine and Guise, the Duke d'Aumale, the Marquis
d'Elboeuf, and her grandmother the old Duchess of Guise.[1]
Perhaps no family council had ever more important or
critical matters to discuss—their future position and policy
in France, the marriage of their niece, the problem of
her return to Scotland, her future relations with Elizabeth,
and the answers to be given to the rival Scottish deputies,
Leslie and Lord James, whose coming was expected shortly.

While on her way to her grandmother at Joinville,
Mary was met at Vitry on the 14th by John Leslie,
then parson of Oyne, Aberdeenshire, and afterwards Bishop
of Ross, commissioned by Huntly and other Catholics of
the north to invite her to return to Edinburgh by Aberdeen,
where they promised to have ready for her a force of twenty
thousand Catholics, to enable her to mount the throne of
Scotland as a Catholic sovereign.[2] Though the fortunes
of Leslie and Mary were afterwards to be very closely
linked, she at present declined to commit her future in
Scotland to Catholic keeping ; but she invited Leslie to
remain, meanwhile, in attendance on her. One sufficient
objection to Leslie's proposal was that it would place her
at the mercy of Huntly, who had betrayed her mother,
and whom Randolph described as " him, of whom man
never was at any time assured " ; and at any rate the
scheme of Leslie was premature until the Spanish marriage
question was decided.

Next day Mary was overtaken at St. Dizier by the
emissary of the Protestants, her half-brother and her friend
of old days, Lord James Stewart, whose political career,
since last she saw him, seemed to have raised an almost

---

[1] *For. Ser.*, No. 77 (9).   [2] Leslie, *De Origine*, p. 575.

insuperable barrier against her confidence and affection. The meeting must have been painful and agitating to both, but it was sufficiently satisfactory to Lord James from an inquisitive point of view. It is hardly likely, either, that on the one hand, as current rumour surmised[1] and Leslie asserts, Lord James made overtures for a grant to him of the earldom of Moray,[2] or that, as Throckmorton anticipated, she made him an offer of a cardinal's hat,[3] for Lord James made no mention of this to Throckmorton ; but we must suppose that, in some way, she remonstrated with him as to his Protestantism.

Nor, apparently, did Mary whisper to Lord James a syllable about the Spanish negotiations, of the forwardness of which Throckmorton was at this time advertised by other means ;[4] but Lord James had seemingly no difficulty in discovering those of her intentions which he communicated to Throckmorton. The more important points were (1) that in the ratification of the treaty she would be guided by the advice of her Estates ; (2) that she "was not glad of the kindness between England and Scotland," though whether she wished, as the prejudiced Throckmorton supposed, to "provide that there should be no traffic" between them is another matter ; (3) that she would endeavour to gain the consent of the Estates to her marriage to a foreign prince ; and (4) that she was as careless of the amity of France as she was of that of England.

The question as to whether Lord James in revealing to Throckmorton and Elizabeth the nature of his sister's communication to him, betrayed her, turns wholly on the

---

[1] Randolph to Throckmorton MSS. Add. (B.M.), 35,830 f. 79.
[2] *De Origine*, p. 577. [3] *For. Ser.*, v. No. 77 (6).
[4] *Ibid.*, iv. 151 (21).

question of his intentions. He came under no obligation
not to reveal what she told him, and she did not make
of him a special confidant. If, however, while pretending
to desire her return on condition that she agreed to the
toleration of Protestantism, he at the same time did what
he could to induce Elizabeth to prevent her return, then,
if he had perfect confidence in her sincerity, he betrayed
her. But the aim both of Lord James and Maitland seems
to have been to induce Elizabeth to adopt a conciliatory
attitude: their difficulty was that Elizabeth would not do
so, and unless she did so, they had good reason to fear
danger to the best welfare of Scotland, as well as to
themselves, through Mary's return.

But, for a time, Lord James was impressed with the
conviction that Mary was but partially revealing her real
intentions; and he was perfectly right in supposing, when
she would not allow him to accompany her to Nancy,
that there was "something there in hand that she would
be loath he should be privy to." The something, we
must suppose, was the Spanish negotiations, which she
probably fondly hoped might then be concluded.

Mr. Lang, led astray by M. Philippson—who boldly
asserts that Lord James did accompany Mary to Nancy,
and regards it as " prouvé par une lettre de Marie Stuart à
Throgmorton, datée de ' Nancy ce 22 avril 1561,' et dans
laquelle elle dit: 'Quant à Lord James, qui est devers moi'"[1]
—has presented Scottish students with a new historical puzzle,
which he supposes deeply concerns the reputation either
of Lord James or Mary.

" Why," asks Mr. Lang, " did Mary say he was with
her, if he was not? Why, if he was with her at Nancy,

---

[1] *Marie Stuart*, i. 296.

did Lord James deny the fact to Throckmorton, and
throw suspicion on his sister ? It is on questions like
this that we expect light from the minute researches of
Dr. Hay Fleming." [1]

But the light that Mr. Lang seems to despair of obtaining was easily accessible to him. Writing to Cecil on
April 23rd, Throckmorton actually makes mention of the
arrival that day of Lord James at Paris,[2] so that the
surmise that Lord James may have been lying, and lying
for purposes entirely base, becomes untenable. M.
Philippson supposes that Lord James arrived on the 29th ;
but Throckmorton had his interview with Lord James not
on the day he wrote, but, as the letter shows, on the 24th.
So much for Lord James. As for Mary, since she must
have known that Lord James would be in Paris and probably
in Throckmorton's company by the time she was penning
her letter, we cannot suppose that she intended to practise
deceit on Throckmorton. Her letter was in reply to
one of Throckmorton's, who had apparently hinted that
by the arrival of Lord James she would obtain the counsel
necessary to enable her to decide as to the ratification of the
treaty. To this Mary answered, " Quant à Lord James, qui
est devers moy " [as Throckmorton had stated], " il y est
venue pour son devoir, comme devers sa souveraine Dame,
que je sois, sans charge ou commission qui concerne autre
chose que son droit." [3] The intention of Mary was not to
convey to Throckmorton the information that Lord James
was then actually with her at Nancy, but that his visit
to her in France was not of an official character. Thus,
instead of a puzzling mystery or a delightful case of

---

[1] *History*, ii. 103. [2] *For. Ser.*, iv. No. 133.
[3] Labanoff, i. 94.

deliberate fabrication, all that Mr. Lang has supplied us with is a disappointing mare's nest.

Lord James did not leave Paris until May 4th, being detained by the expectation of letters from Mary with a Commission under her seal to have charge of the government until her return to Scotland. He received letters, the purport of which he did not tell Throckmorton, but no Commission. Mary may have been merely detaining him until she had definite news as to the Spanish marriage negotiations. Had they terminated favourably, she might have desired another interview with him; but the evil tidings awaiting her at Nancy made it needless to detain him longer.

After doing his utmost to satisfy Elizabeth's curiosity as to Mary's marriage prospects, Throckmorton was able to report, as late as June 23rd, that he had learned from a great person at court—the King of Navarre, most likely —that "the King of Spain has said that he would be loath to marry his son to a process, but that if her matters were clear, he knew no party that he would more gladly match his son with"[1]; and it may well have been in some such terms as these that the King, towards the end of April, made known his decision to the Cardinal of Lorraine.

By May 9th Throckmorton learned that Mary was sick of an ague at Nancy; but the illness may have had connection with the shock caused by the termination of the marriage negotiations. Throckmorton supposed she might be feigning sickness, " to avoid the answer for the ratification," which he wished to obtain from her at Rheims, where the French king was to be

[1] *For. Ser.*, iv. No. 265 (6).

After an engraving by Thos. De Leu.

MARY QUEEN OF SCOTS,
In widow's dress, as Queen of France.

crowned on the 15th.[1] But, sick or well, Mary had
more serious things to think of than her answer to
Throckmorton: that, suffering from such an overwhelming
disappointment—for which she had mainly to thank
Catherine de Medici—she could imperturbably appear at a
great public ceremony, was hardly to be expected in the
case of one so sensitive and passionate. She therefore
did not journey beyond her grandmother's château of
Joinville, where it was reported she admitted " no man
(especially of her own nation) to her speech, saving
physicians."[2] She remained at Joinville until after the
departure of the court from Rheims, but had reached
Rheims by May 28th.[3]

The Spanish negotiations being meanwhile at an end,
Mary made up her mind to return to Scotland as soon
as she conveniently could ; and with the view of com-
pleting her arrangements for this, she arrived on June
10th at Paris, joining the French court at the Louvre,
where she was welcomed with the ceremony due to her
rank as a sovereign.[4] On the touching, yet charming,
appearance of the fair and pale young widow " en ses
habits de son grand deuil blanc," Brantôme enlarges in
his superlatively sentimental fashion ; [5] and he affirms that
the young King was so enraptured with her beauty, as
greatly to increase the anxiety of Catherine for her speedy
departure.

At the Louvre, Throckmorton, on June 18th, had his
long-deferred interview with Mary, whom he found quite
ready, as she had always been, with her answer about

---

[1] *For. Ser.*, iv. No. 189, 198.   [2] *Ibid.*, No. 208 (1); 214 (1).
[3] Labanoff, i. 98.   [4] *For. Ser.*, iv. No. 265.
                    [5] *Œuvres*, ed. Buchon, ii. 135.

the ratification ; she would not say yes or no until "she had the advice of the Estates"; but she added "that she meant to retire all the French out of Scotland, so that she would leave nothing undone to satisfy all parties."[1] She was also quite frank about the burning question of religion : "She was none of those who would change her religion every year; she did not mean to constrain any of her subjects, but trusted they would have no support at the Queen's hands to constrain her."[2] She also said that she was sending M. d'Oysell to Elizabeth to declare what she trusted would satisfy Elizabeth. Throckmorton mistakenly supposed that d'Oysell, who was commissioned also to go to Scotland, would, besides demanding a safe-conduct for Mary, "labour by all possible means to dissolve the league between the Scots and England, and to tie them to the French";[3] and apparently Elizabeth was also possessed with this idea. Her reply, sent by d'Oysell— whom, still haunted, it would appear, by her dread of a French alliance, she would not permit to proceed to Scotland—was that once Mary had ratified the treaty, Elizabeth, besides granting a full passport, would "give order for a friendly meeting for corroboration and per-fection of their amity."[4]

Mr. Lang, strange to say, on this cardinal matter sides with the English Queen. "Mary," he says, "threw away this admirable chance of settling the feud."[5] But is this not to imply that Elizabeth was absolutely in the right, and Mary entirely in the wrong? For how was the feud to be settled? Would Elizabeth agree to recognise

---

[1] *For. Ser.*, iv. 265 (3).   [2] *Ibid.*, 265 (4).
[3] *Ibid.*, 280 (1).   [4] *Scottish Papers*, i. 540.
[5] *History*, ii. 98.

Mary as next in succession to her, or could Mary reasonably be satisfied with anything less than this? " Many a time later," adds Mr. Lang, "was she [Mary] to pray for a meeting that was never granted." But what was the value of any such meeting to Mary, unless Elizabeth recognised her claim, which Elizabeth never intended to do? While Mary would have committed herself to everything, Elizabeth would have committed herself to nothing. This Mr. Lang not only discerns, but seems to approve : " The day she acknowledged Mary as heir might," he says, " be a day near her own death by assassination." But has he not here been entrapped by a too deferential regard to Froude, who [1] supposes that Elizabeth declined to acknowledge Mary from dread of immediate assassination? This possibility was, in fact, always before Elizabeth's eyes ; it was not achieved from lack of conspiracies ; and whether Elizabeth's reasons for declining, as she did, to recognise Mary or her son, or any one else, as heir to her crown were good or bad, or private or public, we must absolve her from being actuated in this by any motive akin to personal cowardice.

Mary's policy on this matter was bound to appeal strongly to the patriotism and self-respect of the majority of the Scots. To Elizabeth's attempt to concuss the Estates to deal with it before Mary's arrival, the Council replied courteously, but a little enigmatically : " Your Majestie may be weill assured that in us salbe noted no blame, gif that peace be nott ratified to your Majesteis contentment," etc.[2] Maitland's hint to Cecil, on learning of the death of Francis II., was also meanwhile giving promise of bearing fruit. As early as July 14th, Cecil wrote to Throckmorton :

[1] *History*, cab. ed., vi. 502. [2] Knox, *Works*, ii. 179.

" There is a matter secretly thought of, which he will dare communicate. That if an accord can be made between her and the Scottish Queen, the latter should surrender to her all manner of claim, and to her heirs, and in consideration thereof, the Scottish Queen shall be acknowledged in default of heirs of the English Queen." [1] Cecil added that Elizabeth knew of this, and he apparently thought the arrangement feasible, though he hoped that she would herself marry and have a son.

Unless Mary had some hope of effecting a working arrangement with Elizabeth, Maitland saw that her coming might " cause wonderful tragedies." He must have mentioned his scheme to Lord James ; and the beginnings of the policy thus initiated are discernible in the conciliatory letter of Lord James, of June 10, to his sister, which virtually embodied an invitation from the Protestant Lords that she should return to Scotland.[2] Maitland's letter to her of the same date has not been recovered, but from her reply of June 29th we gather that he promised to employ himself in her service and to " do the utmost to promote her interest." [3] Possibly in reply to the letter of Mary, who stated that, if he had the will, he had the " knowledge and skill " to do much for her, and that she wished to live in " amity and good neighbourhood with the Queen of England," he indicated his views on the subject of an arrangement with Elizabeth, for before she left for France Mary's friends appear, as we have seen, to have been more than sanguine that such an arrangement would be effected. At any rate, Lord James had, before Mary's arrival in

---

[1] *For. Ser.*, iv. 187 (*note*).
[2] Philippson's *Marie Stuart*, vol. iii. Appendix.
[3] Tytler's *History*, iii. (1862), 399.

Scotland, broached the matter in his usual deprecatory fashion to Elizabeth.

" The mater," wrote Lord James, " is hyghar then my capacite is hable to compas, yett, upon my simple ouverture, your hyghnes can lay a more large fundation. What yff your Majesties titill did remain ontouched, als wele for your self as thissue of your body ? Inconvenient wer it to provyde that to the Quene my souveraine, her own place were reserved in the succession of the Crown of England ? Which your Majestie will pardon me, if I take to be next, by the law of all nations, as she that is next in lawful descent of the ryght lyne of King Hendry the sevint your grandfather." [1]

Being convinced that it was only by some such arrangement, that " wonderful tragedies " could be prevented, it may easily be conceived with what consternation Maitland would contemplate the peremptory and even hostile attitude of Elizabeth towards Mary. Lord James took advantage of Mary's agreement to recognise the *statu quo* in religion—or, as he put it, " the declarateur of my souerains mynd," to proceed to the putting down of the Mass " throughout all partis and execution to pass upon contumaris and all maynteynayris conforme to ane act made in the last parliament ",[2] and on August 10th Maitland informed Cecil that he and Lord James had been for forty days in the north " advancing the religion and the common cause." [3]

Maitland's hope was still that it might be compassed that " the Queen's Majesty and her Highness might be as near friends as they were tender cousins " ; but in view

---

[1] *Scottish Papers*, i. 541.   [2] MSS. Add. (B.M.), 35,830 f. 121.
[3] Keith, iii. 211-16.

of other possibilities—on account of Elizabeth's attitude
to Mary—it was needful to take every precaution ; and
he further suggested that instead of irritating Mary by
insisting on the ratification of the league with England,
Elizabeth's purpose might be better served by including
Scotland with England in a general Protestant league.

It was also only natural that Maitland and Lord James
should agree with Cecil that, unless Mary and Elizabeth
were on more cordial terms than they yet were, it would
be well that Mary's arrival should be delayed ; but they
could hardly have approved of the policy of the English
Privy Council as stated to Throckmorton : " The longer
the Scottysshe Quenes affayres rest vncertayne the better
shall the Quenes Majeste's affayres prosper, especially as
long as she thus forbearith to confirme the treatie.   And
although it may be she will both stay the ratification and
adventure to passe by seas without selveconduct from
hence : yet coulde we not think it good counsell to offer
suche gentlenes as might intice hir to passe thither.   On
thother part if she shall doo that she is bounde to doo
in ratefying the treaty, we shall think it mete to advise
our soveraigne lady, as she is disposed of herself, to answer
her with all courtesy." [1]

On the contrary, Maitland and Lord James had no
desire that Mary should sign the treaty, and Maitland was
doing his utmost to impress on Cecil the advisability of
conciliating Mary.   When he learned that Elizabeth had
declared to d'Oysell that she " would provide to keep her
from passing home," [2] he had some reason to suspect that
the " wonderful tragedies " he dreaded might be near at
hand ; and well might he deem his own wit insufficient

---

[1] MSS. Add. (B.M.), 35,830 f. 146.   [2] *For. Ser.*, iv. No. 337 (5).

" to give advice in so dangerous a cast." What he wished Elizabeth—with whom of course he had to keep on good terms as well as with Mary—to recognise, was the necessity of saying and doing " yea " or " nay." He much preferred that, in accordance with his early hint to Cecil about the succession, Elizabeth should say and do " yea " ; but he was by no means certain that both to say and do " nay " was not better than to say " nay " and virtually do " yea," for Mary was neither to be stopped nor delayed, as the Council seemed to hope, by mere threats. " If two galleys," he wrote, " may quietly pass " [and they might do so, swift as they were, notwithstanding any attempts of Elizabeth to prevent them], " I wish the passport had been liberally granted. To what purpose should you open your pack, and sell none of your wares, or declare you enemies to those whom you cannot offend." [1]

There is some evidence of an actual intention of Elizabeth to stop Mary on her voyage, or at least to prevent her passing through any part of England ; but happily, much perturbed though Elizabeth was by the prospects of Mary's arrival in Scotland, her vagaries and fickleness were usually in the end conquered by her strong common sense. When contemptuously defied by Mary, she began to discern the folly of her vapouring. The suggestive letters of Maitland were also, so far, beginning to tell on her ; and the recommendations of Throckmorton—who did not hesitate to express to Cecil his astonishment at Elizabeth's refusal of the passport [2]—must also have had its effect. It so happened, also, that on August 8th Mary

---

[1] Letter, August 15th, in Tytler's *History*, ed. 1862, vol. iii. p. 400.

[2] *For. Ser.*, iv. No. 337 (2). This has a vital bearing on the attitude of Lord James, who had been in close consultation with Throckmorton,

thought good to write to Elizabeth a conciliatory letter—
the purport of which can be gathered only from Elizabeth's
reply—which she sent with St. Colme, who was empowered
to explain further Mary's attitude to the treaty.[1]

Though Elizabeth expressed dissatisfaction with St.
Colme's explanations, the letter supplied her with a chance
of backing out of her awkward position. In her reply
of August 15th—of which only the draft in Cecil's hand
survives [2]—she therefore declared that since Mary proposed
to be guided by the opinion of her Council, she had suspended her "concept of all unkindness." With the
letter she even sent a passport; [3] but before Elizabeth
wrote, Mary had set sail for Scotland. The threatened
crisis was, however, averted; and while the sequel proved
that Mary would in any case have escaped Elizabeth's ships,
the letter paved the way for the reconciliation policy of
Maitland, which for a time was to "hold the field."

In an interview with Throckmorton, July 21st, Mary
expressed the hope " that the wind would be so favourable
that she would not need to touch on the coast of England."
Should it not, however, she would venture to place herself
in Elizabeth's " hands to do her will with her " ; "and
if," added she, with mocking, yet serious badinage, " she
was so hard-hearted as to desire her end, she might then
do her pleasure and make sacrifice of her." [4] That same
evening, Mary proceeded to the court at St. Germains, where
a grand farewell fête, which lasted four days, was held in
her honour ; [5] and on the 25th, attended by her six uncles
and other friends, she set out towards the coast. Writing

[1] Labanoff, i. 99-102.   [2] For Ser., iv. p. 250 (note).
[3] Scottish Papers, i. 545.   [4] For Ser., iv. No. 455.
[5] De Ruble, pp. 242-4.

on July 26th, Throckmorton says, " She has sent her train straight to Havre de Grace, and herself holdeth such a way between both, as she will be at her choice to go to Newhaven [Havre-le-Grace] or to Calice." [1] Havre-le-Grace was the most suitable port for the western route, by which, when a child, she had sailed for France : if she went to Calais, her intention would be to go by the eastern route to Leith.

Chantonnay thought that Elizabeth's design in keeping a fleet in the North Sea, as she was known to be doing, was to compel Mary to choose the western route towards the country " where the Earl of Arran lies." [2] Unless she had no other choice, it was inadvisable that she should take this route and return, as she had set out, by Dumbarton ; and notwithstanding the risk from Elizabeth's ships she chose the eastern route. Indeed, before she set out from St. Germains, it had been arranged that two rowing-galleys belonging to her uncle, the Grand Prior, should be in readiness at Calais. [3] They were commanded by Villegaignon and Octavian Bosso, two of the ablest mariners of France ; and the one to which the fortunes of Mary were to be committed was specially celebrated for its speed.

On August 3rd, Mary was, however, still at Beauvais, waiting, according to Throckmorton, the return of the secretary of the King of Navarre, who had been sent to England. [4] As regards the news the secretary might bring, we have no information ; but, whether influenced by it or by other considerations, she now resolved to send St. Colme with a special message to Elizabeth, and on that

[1] Keith, ii. 53.   [2] Teulet, ii. 171.
[3] Castelnau, ed. Petitot, p. 124,   [4] For Ser., iv. 324 (2).

account asked Throckmorton to attend on her at Abbeville, which he did on the 8th. That same evening she continued her journey to Calais; and after dispatching St. Colme she finally, on the 14th, committed herself to her perilous adventure : for Throckmorton's servant, coming on that day by Calais, "saw the Queen of Scotland, haling out of that haven, about noon, with two galleys and two great ships." [1]

[1] *For Ser.*, iv. No. 421 (5).

CHAPTER IV

SCOTLAND AND ELIZABETH

MARY was accompanied on her voyage by three of
her uncles, the Duke d'Aumale, the Grand Prior,
and the Duke d'Elboeuf, and, besides a large company of
French and Scottish gentlemen—including Bishop Leslie,
Brantôme, Castelnau and Châtelard—the four Scottish
Marys who as children had accompanied her to France.
The capsizing of a boat in the harbour with all hands
caused her to exclaim, "What augury is this!" for her
mood was in no way hopeful. So consumed did she
appear to be with grief, as to be indifferent to possible
adventures on the voyage, and almost devoid alike of
hopes and fears. So long as the shores of France remained
in view, she riveted her gaze on them, repeating, half
hysterically, "Adieu, France!" and as they gradually
faded from her sight, she redoubled her lament, "Adieu,
France! C'en est fait! Adieu, France, je pense ne vous
revoir jamais plus!" The forebodement proved only
too true, though it was not for some years that Elizabeth
was to be in a position to say to her, "Thus far shalt
thou go, and no further!"

As we now know, Mary had no cause to dread
capture, though the rumour that Elizabeth had fitted out
a large fleet can hardly, as Dr. Hay Fleming supposes,[1]

---

[1] *Mary Queen of Scots*, p. 250.

be attributed to the rash speech of d'Oysell. That there was a considerable fleet in the North Sea is pretty certain ; and also had Mary landed anywhere in England she might, owing to Elizabeth's original orders, have been put to some inconvenience. Rutland, Lord President of the North, had directions from Cecil to keep watch on French and Scottish ships passing along the coast, and to detain all suspicious persons who might land at any of the harbours. The orders sent him were not countermanded by Elizabeth, for on August 17th he sent to Cecil a report that, at three o'clock that morning, his outlooks had seen two galleys off Flamborough Head, as if making for the shore ; and he gave such orders as " he doubted not but Cecil would hear good news of their stay." [1] The galleys —the large one all white, and the other coloured red and having a " blue flag with the arms of France, and in her stern another white flag, glistening like silver "— did not, however, enter any harbour, but, after taking soundings, proceeded on their journey. There also, according to Rutland's outlooks, " appeared, at a good distance from the galleys, thirty-two sail of tall ships, and shortly after, further off, twenty sail, all which, for lack of wind, tried the seas, making no haste away." [2]

Dr. Hay Fleming thinks that this numerous fleet may have been the convoy of Mary ; [3] but nothing is known of any such convoy ; it was seen neither before nor afterwards, and the speed of the galleys would not allow of a convoy of vessels with round keels. We must suppose that the outlooks, in their excitement, exaggerated the number of vessels ; but the likelihood is that the ships,

---

[1] *For. Ser.*, iv. No. 418.   [2] *Ibid.*, No. 419.
[3] *Mary Queen of Scots*, p. 249.

After a drawing by Gordon of Rothiemay.

HOLYROOD PALACE, EDINBURGH.

of which they had but a distant view, were Elizabeth's own fleet ; for the story is curiously corroborated by Castelnau, who states that when they were about half-way on their voyage, the English fleet hove in sight, but were unable to overtake them on account of the swiftness of their galleys.[1] It is unlikely that Elizabeth had no more ships in the North Sea than the two or three barks to which she and Cecil referred. Before July 23rd, de Quadra heard that they were fitting out eight vessels, and he understood that their now apparent zeal against the pirates—after they had treated former requests of his so curtly—was caused by their "intention to take this pirate affair as a pretext for arming against the Queen of Scotland."[2]

In any case, Elizabeth's preparations caused Mary no inconvenience, and after a very prosperous voyage she arrived without adventure at Leith. From the statements of Leslie and Brantôme we gather that the weather had been rather hazy all through the voyage ; and when opposite Berwick the fog became so thick that they had to lie at anchor until the evening of the 18th ; but by nightfall it had so far lifted that they were able to continue the voyage up the frith, so as to reach Leith early in the morning. From the superstitious nonsense written by Knox about the "dolorous face of the hevins," foreshadowing the "sorrow, dolour, darkness and all impietie"[3] that this fair and pleasant young lady was to bring into Scotland, we might suppose that, instead of easterly "haars" being one of the choice features of the Edinburgh summer,

---

[1] *Mémoires*, ed. Labourier, iii. Chap. I.
[2] *Spanish Papers*, 1558-67, p. 210.
[3] *Works*, ii. 264.

the fog that greeted Mary's arrival was almost as un-common there as an eclipse.

Yet the gloom of the weather must have intensified to Mary the rather cheerless character of her adventure ; and the unpreparedness of Scotland for her arrival prevented the exhibition of a national welcome that might have done much to brighten her spirits. The summons for the nobility and magistrates of Scotland to be in Edinburgh, with " their honourable companies," to welcome her, indicated that she was not expected before the end of the month ; and even her special messenger, who arrived in Edinburgh on the 14th, stated that she need not be expected before the 26th. She thus stepped ashore at Leith in the presence of a mere miscellaneous crowd of the common people ; and for temporary shelter she went to the house of Andro Lambie, a Leith trader, who seems to have been known to her mother.   There certain of the nobles visited her, the Duke arriving first, next Lord James, and then Arran.[1]

Preparations for her occupation of Holyrood not being complete, she did not set out for it until evening. Brantôme, after his lively fashion, expresses his shocked amusement at the sorry appearance of the rough and rudely caparisoned Scottish nags that now appeared for the conveyance of her and her cortège to her ancestral palace, [2] whither, besides her curiously assorted French following, she was accompanied by " sundrie nobell men and the town of Edinburgh." [3]

Mary's arrival was celebrated by bonfires on the neighbouring heights of Salisbury Crags and the Calton Hill ; and according to Knox " a company of the most honest, with

---

[1] *Scottish Papers*, i. 501.   [2] *Œuvres*, ed. Buchon, ii.
[3] Leslie's *History*, p. 244.

instrumentis of musick, and with musitians, gave thair salutationis at her chalmer wyndo." [1] Knox's "company of the most honest," Brantôme represents as "five or six hundred *marauds*," who, to the accompaniment of perverse violins and small rebecs—a common stringed instrument of the time—chanted doleful psalms, in amazing discord with the instruments and with one another.

Mary, however, with her usual good nature, affirmed, says Knox, "that the melody lyked her weill; and sche willed the same to be continued some nightis after." As the grieving Knox puts it, nothing was "understude but myrth and quyetness till the next Sunday, which was the xxiii of August." Apart from edifying serenading, the manifestations of joy were probably more evident among Catholics than Protestants; but the Protestants, after all, were patriots. Mary, the daughter of their ancient royal house, had resolved, braving the threats and intrigues of Elizabeth, to trust herself, all defenceless, to the loyalty of her people : and her youth, her personal charm, her frank goodwill to every one, secured her an almost instant popularity.

But the understanding on which Mary had returned— that she was to have the free exercise of her own religion— was not, of course, generally known; and when preparations began for holding Mass in her chapel, this, according to Knox, "pierced the hearts of all," that is, of all who thought as did Knox : the stalwart and rough Master of Lindsay— afterwards sixth Lord Lindsay—of whose implacability Mary was yet to have darker experience, representing the "all" in heading a mob who shouted in the close for the execution of the "idolatre Priest"; [2] but Lord James, who had virtually

[1] *Works*, ii. 270.   [2] *Ibid.*, 272-3.

pledged his word that his sister should have the exercise of her religion, himself remained on guard at the chapel door ; and after the celebration was over, the trembling ecclesiastic was escorted to his chamber under the protection of Lord John and Lord Robert.

The Protestant concern was, however, somewhat allayed by a proclamation on Monday, forbidding every one, until a meeting of the Estates, privately or publicly to make alteration or innovation of the state of religion which the Queen had found " publictlie and universallie standing at her Majestie's arryvell in this her Realme, under the pane of death," all the lieges being at the same time commanded not to molest or trouble, " in wourd, deed or countenance," any of the Queen's French servants or others in her train.[1] Yet the proclamation committed the Queen to nothing ; indeed, it even transformed the supposed establishment of Protestantism into a merely temporary and abnormal arrangement, effected by an irregular convention when the country was practically in a state of revolution. Its effect was virtually to postpone the settlement of the religious dispute until Mary's dispute with Elizabeth was settled, Mary, as sovereign, claiming meanwhile the right to determine what religion she herself should profess.

It need hardly be stated that the real origin of the *impasse* was the belief in the possibility of an infallible Church, on the part of Knox and the Protestants, as well as on the part of Mary and the Catholics. In England, Protestantism had come to imply a certain amount of religious liberty, because the innate and inevitable intolerance of the ecclesiastics of those days was greatly held

[1] Knox, *Works*, ii. 272-3.

in check by the secularity and self-interest of the sovereign. In Scotland it was also being partly held in check by the worldly ambition of the nobility and their ancient jealousy of the ecclesiastics ; but the Scottish sovereign had never attained such prestige and ascendancy as the sovereign had won in England ; and the country had practically revolted from the sovereign's control during Mary's absence in France.

Above all, Mary was now confronted by the stupendous personality of Knox, stupendous even more by virtue of his defects than by reason of his merits ; for his practical sagacity, his righteousness, his strident eloquence, his incomparable assurance, his unbending integrity would not alone have won him his great predominance. To effect this, they had to be conjoined with a curious intellectual superficiality and narrowness, which designed him to be a demagogic genius rather than a thinker, and begat in him an ecclesiastical fervour by which he fell a prey to the strong delusion that the infallibility supposed for many generations to belong to what was deemed the Church of God, had been transferred in a manner to himself, as the Heaven-appointed prophet and guide of the Scottish Reformation. In him Mary had thus to deal with an ecclesiastic who, while professing to be one of her subjects, virtually claimed, as the possessor of an ecclesiastical authority more stringent than that wielded by the successors of St. Peter, a right of direction in politics and religion, that, if conceded, would have robbed her of every vestige of her sovereignty.

Of the quality of Knox, Mary was to have a taste in an interview with him about a fortnight after her arrival in Scotland. The points of view of the two disputants belong

to another age than ours ; but from Knox's records of their
conference, one-sided though we must suppose it to be, we
obtain a better insight into the peculiar standpoints of both
than any amount of bare definition can supply.[1] Mary
sought the interview, owing to a violent attack by Knox on
the Mass, one celebration of which—since it meant the
national tolerance of " idolatry "—" was," he said, " more
fearful to him than gif ten thousand armed enemyes were
landed in any pairte of the Realme, of purpose to suppress
the haill religioun."

Writing of this sermon to Cecil, the Elizabethan
Randolph assured him that " the voyce of one man is
hable in one hower to put more lyf in us than 500
trompettes contynually blusteringe in our eares."[2] But
the " guydaris of the court "—that is, Lord James and
Maitland, probably—thought the sermon, according to Knox,
" a verray untymelie admonition " ; and hence Mary's
interview with him on the Thursday following,[3] in the
presence only of Lord James, who appears to have remained, characteristically, in the background and to have
said nothing. There was, between Mary and Knox, the
primary question as to whether Mary, as a woman, had
any right of sovereignty ; but provided Mary did as he
desired, and on the supposition that " the Realme fyndis
no inconvenience frome the regiment [government] of a
woman, that which thei approve shall I not," in grim
condescension, replied Knox, " farther disallow than
within my awin breast ? "

---

[1] See Knox, *Works*, ii. 277-286.

[2] *Scottish Papers*, i. 551.

[3] Thursday, September 4th (*Scottish Papers*, i. 551). Dr. Hay Fleming
(*Mary Queen of Scots*, p. 50) says a "week after her arrival " ; but he
erroneously supposes it (p. 260) to have been on Tuesday.

After the picture by Mytens at St. James's Palace.

MARY QUEEN OF SCOTS.

But unhappily their ecclesiastical positions were poles asunder; and, even from Knox's own account, we gather that Mary maintained her position with a dexterity and skill, which were quite a match for Knox's assertiveness. " Conscience, Madam," [said he] " requyris knowledge, and, I fear, rycht knowledge ye have none." "But" [said she] "I have bayth heard and red." Mary and Knox thus each, in a sense, claimed the right of private judgment ; but it was a judgment the exercise of which was virtually suspended, when confronted by the two rival apparitions of infallibility, an infallible Book and an infallible Church ; and they took refuge in separate forms of superstition, from which neither, by any exercise of reason, could be ousted.

As to the impressions the one gathered of the other's character and intentions, Mary, admiring, though she probably did, the native courage and grit of Knox, could not be blind to the real character of his aspirations. " Weall then," said she, with characteristic directness, " I perceave that my subjectis shall obey you, and not me ; and shall do what thei list, and nott what I command : and so man I be subject to thame and nott thei to me." Knox assured her that " this subjection unto God, and unto his troubled Churche, is the greatest dignitie that flesche can get upoun the face of the earth, for it shall carry thame to everlasting glorie." "Yea, (quod sche), but ye are not the Kirk that I will nureiss. I will defend the Kirk of Rome, for, I think, it is the treu Kirk of God." After this Knox had no difficulty in making up his mind what to think of Mary : " Yf thair be not in hir" [said he] " a proud mynd, a crafty witt, and ane indurrate hearte against God and his treuth, my judgment faileth me " ; but by " God and his treuth " Knox merely,

if unconsciously, meant Knox himself and his own version
of God's truth.

So far, however, the victory, if not in argument, yet
in immediate effects, remained rather with Mary than
with Knox. The result meanwhile was that Knox was
induced to be as " weall content "—this was his unblushing
comparison—" to lyve under your Grace, as Paul was to
lyve under Nero " : " so long as that ye defyle not your
handis in the blood of the sanctis of God." Of this
resolve, though he cited apostolic example for it, Knox,
with characteristic disregard of that example when he
found it not to accord with his own opinion, afterwards
bitterly repented. God, he tells us, had not only given
him " knowledge, and toung to maik the impietie of that
idoll known unto this Realme," but also influence with
many who, had he but said the word, would " have put
in executioun Goddis judgementis " ; but so careful was
he of the common tranquillity, and so loath to offend
Lord James and others, that he had dissuaded them against
this. " Whairintill," he says, " I unfeanedlie acknowledge
my selff to have done most wickedlie ; and, from the bottom
of my hart, askis of my God grace and pardon, for
that I did not what in me lay to have suppressed that idoll
in the beginning." [1]

Still, if Knox refrained from taking measures to deny
his sovereign the exercise of her religion, he hardly kept
the conditions on which she gave him " libertie to speake
frelye hys conscience " : that he should " gyve unto her
such reverence as becomethe the mynisteris of God unto
the superior powers." Refraining from attacking her in
his sermons, he yet in public communicated to God his own

[1] *Works*, ii. 277.

opinion of her. " Hys prayer," wrote Randolph, "is dayley for her, that God wyll torne her obstinate harte agaynst God and his trothe, or, yf his holly wyl be otherwyse, to strengthen the harte and hand of his chosen and electe, stowtly to withstonde the rage of al tyrantes, or in words terrible inoughe."

But notwithstanding the "terrible enough" words of Knox, the general attitude towards Mary was that of friendliness. The rascal multitude of Edinburgh was quite inclined to enjoy itself in baiting Papal officials ; and the Bishops of St. Andrews and Dunkeld, who had imprudently arrived to pay court to their Catholic Sovereign, in "longe grownes and typettis with hattes upon their heddes," did hardly "dare put their noses owte of their doores for feare of after clappes"; but the Queen herself met with no personal discourtesy from any one. The truth was that each religious party was almost in equal hope of obtaining her open support ; and while the Protestants were assertive enough in the manifestation of their desires, the Catholics were probably quietly confident of final triumph.

On the evening of that very Sunday that Knox "thundered out of the pulpit" against the idolatry of the Mass, Mary—the Edinburgh sabbath of later times had yet to dawn—was entertained by the provost and magistrates—"for the plesour of our Souerane and obteyning of hir hienes favouris—at ane honorable banquet maid to the princes hir graces cousingis." Preparations of an exceptionally elaborate and costly character were also in progress for her official entry into the city, on Tuesday, September 2nd ;[1] or, as Knox, in his dog-in-the-manger manner, put it, "in ferses, in maskings and in other

[1] *Burgh Records of Edinburgh*, 1551-71, pp. 119-21.

prodigalities, faine wold fooles have counterfooted France." [1]

Yet, even on such an occasion, Protestant anxiety regarding the Queen's religion manifested itself with an obtrusiveness which, if well meant, was hardly mannerly. In the forenoon of the " triumph," she set out from Holyrood along the northern outskirts of the city to the Castle, where she dined at twelve o'clock. In the afternoon she made her formal progress through the city, down the Castle Hill and High Street to her palace, a pall of fine purple velvet being borne over her head by twelve representatives of the magistrates, who were followed by a procession of burgesses in gaudy apparel of one pattern, specially made to grace the occasion. As she neared the " Butter Tron," the sound reached her of " certane barnis," singing " in the maist hevenlie wyis," and on her passing through the " painted port " erected there, " ane bony barne discendit doun, as it had bene ane angell, and deliveritt to hir Hienes the Keyis of the toun, togidder with ane Bybill and ane Psalme Buik coverit with fyne purpouril velvet." [2]   Knox, who was probably there, regarding with austere curiosity her reception of the heavenly gifts, thus grimly comments on her demeanour : " The verses of her awin praise sche heard and smyled. But when the Bible was presented and the praise thairof declared, sche began to frown : for schame sche could not refuse it. But sche did no better, for immediatlie, sche gave it to the most pestilent Papist within the Realme, to wit to Arthoure Erskyn." [3]   Of course, she did only what was proper in handing the gifts to her Captain of the Guard ; but Knox, we must suppose, would have been

[1] *Works*, ii. 288.   [2] *Diurnal*, p. 67.   [3] *Works*, ii. 288.

satisfied with nothing less than her renunciation of Catholicism on the spot.

So much for the counterfeit angelic vision. If it failed to charm her from her faith, it was hardly likely that she would be much drawn towards Protestantism by what Randolph terms "the terrible sygnifications of the vengeance of God upon idolaters" which met her at the "Salt Tron," where "Coron, Nathan and Abiron were burnt" [for her edification] "in the time of the sacrifice," and where "the shape of a priest in his ornaments reddy to say Mass" would have been burnt at "the altar at the elevation" had not Huntly "stayed that pageant."[1]

Not content with these symbolic exhortations and menaces, the magisterial wiseacres arranged that before the Queen entered her palace gates, certain children should make to her "some speeche concerning the putting away of the mass." How she accepted the advice of the children, Knox was not there to record; but all ended pleasantly enough, in the presentation of the city's gift, a beautiful cupboard, "double owrgilt," which had cost 2,000 marks, or about one-half of the whole sum expended on the banquet and triumph.

On September 6th the Queen chose for her Privy Council the principal nobles of the kingdom, irrespective of their political or religious leanings, six of whom were to be in constant residence with her to guide her in the dispatch of routine business;[2] but this custom was soon discontinued, the real direction of affairs remaining as before in the hands of Lord James and Maitland.

On the day of the civic banquet the Duke d'Aumale had set sail with the two galleys for France; but the

[1] *Scottish Papers*, i. 552. [2] *Register of the Privy Council*, i. 157.

Queen's other two uncles remained for some time longer with her ; and they accompanied her when, attended also by a number of Scottish noblemen and ladies, she set out to visit her palaces and some of her principal towns. Leaving Holyrood on September 11th after dinner, she in the evening reached Linlithgow Palace, of unique interest to her as the place of her birth in the mournful December of 1542. Thence she set out on the 13th for Stirling Castle, of her early days in which her memory could have been but dim. There, on Sunday the 14th, an attempt of her chaplains to sing High Mass in the Chapel Royal caused a scene of which the only account is the hearsay one of Randolph, who says that "Argyll and Lord James so disturbed the quyere that some, both priests and clerks, left their places with broken heads and bloody ears."

In Stirling also Mary, according to Randolph, barely escaped a serious calamity : "While asleep in bed, a candle burning by her, the curtains and tester took fire, and was like to have smored her as she lay." [1] From Stirling she proceeded on Monday, 15th, towards Perth, where she must have viewed with feelings of at least inward bitterness the melancholy spectacle of the ruined monasteries. Though as courteously received there as elsewhere, and presented, as a "propine," with a heart of gold filled with gold, her visit, in fact, gave her more pain than pleasure.

The memories of the sad last days of her mother, awakened by the sight of the ruined monasteries, combined with the too Protestant character of the pageants, were probably the cause of a sudden illness that overtook her as she rode up the street, and made it necessary to bear her to her lodging, which happily was not far off. [2]

[1] *Scottish Papers*, i. 555.   [2] *Ibid.*, i. 555.

From an old print.

FALKLAND PALACE.

From Perth she passed to Dundee, and, crossing the Tay, proceeded to St. Andrews, where again the evidence of Reformation zeal was borne witness to by the tumbled ruins of the splendid cathedral. Randolph heard, though he hardly credited the story, that on Sunday a priest had been slain there ; but at any rate, either during the journey or at St. Andrews, Huntly and Lord James had a violent quarrel about the Mass, Huntly saying that if the Queen commanded, he would set up the Mass in three shires. The Queen, however, did not command. From St. Andrews she journeyed to Falkland, the favourite hunting seat of her ancestors, at the foot of the Lomond Hills, whither her father had retired to die after Solway. Adjoining it was an immense hunting forest ; but Mary's visit was a mere passing one, and she arrived in Edinburgh on September 29th.

It may be that Mary's progress had been arranged by Lord James, partly as an object-lesson to shake her constancy to her faith ; but, if so, it had no such effect. "She hath beene," wrote the mordant Knox to Mrs. Anna Lock, "in her progresse and hath considered the mindes of the people for the most part to be repugnant to her devilish opinioun ; and yitt in her appeareth no amendment, but an obstinat proceeding from evill to worse." [1] Yet Mary evidently desired to act as prudently, as was consistent with the maintenance of her title to observe the rites of her own religion. Nor was she at all blameable for an unpleasant conflict with the magistrates of Edinburgh, originated by a proclamation of theirs on the very day that Knox was penning his letter. The justification of the

[1] *Works*, ii. 130.

action Mary felt compelled to take, is amply contained in the tenor of the proclamation. Here it is:

"2d October 1561.

"The prouest baillies, counsale and hale dekynnis, persaving the preistis, monkis, freris, and vtheris of the wikit rable of the antechrist the paip, to resort to this toun, incontrair the tenour of the proclamatioun maid in the contrair, thairfor ordanis the said proclamatioun to be proclaimyt of new, chargeing all monkis, freris, preistis, nonnys, adulteraris, fornucatouris, and all sic filthy personis, to remove thamselffis of this toun and boundis thairof within XXIIII. houris, vnder the pane of carting throuch the toun, byrning on the cheik, and banessing the samyn for euir."[1]

Nominally a renewal of a proclamation of March, 1561,[2] this one was not only more insulting, but stricter in its conditions. In the earlier proclamation forty-eight hours of grace was granted ; in the later only twenty-four, with the threat of severe penalties. Moreover the earlier proclamation had been issued "in our Soverane Ladie's name" [she was then absent in France] "and in name and behalf of the lords of the secreit counsale" ; and in pretending to reissue this proclamation now, the magistrates were making the Queen responsible for a public insult, and worse, to the officials of her own religion. No sovereign, of the least self-respect, could have failed to take notice of such indecent insolence.

On October 5th, the Queen therefore sent a macer to command the Council and community to assemble within

---

[1] *Records*, 1557-71, p. 125.　　　　[2] *Ibid.*, p. 101.

the Tolbooth, and deprive the Provost and baillies of their offices, which they accordingly did on the 8th ; and she further caused proclamation to be made that the town should be "patent to all lieges." By Knox—who may have had something to do with the magistrates' proclamation—the Queen's prompt action was ascribed to mere "pride and maliciousness" : [1] it was but further proof, if proof were needed, "that the Cardinalles lessons ar so deaplie prented in hir heart, that the substance and the qualitie are liek to perische together." [2] That she had the support of Lord James and Maitland was a still further bitter pill for Knox. "The whole blame," wrote he, "lycht upon the necks of the two fornamed, be reason of thare bearing."

From Randolph's letters, we learn that the question of Mary's resiling from her faith had been mooted to her, not only, in the language of infallibility and menace, by Knox, but by the English ambassador, Randolph, who showed his anxiety for at least her political welfare, by presenting her with certain pamphlets on the subject of the Mass. This led to conversations with Lord James, the Queen, woman-like, replying, "She could not reasone, but she knew what she ought to believe." She however expressed to Randolph the hope that Elizabeth would not "tayke the werce" with her if she was "not resolved in conscience in those matters" . . . "seinge yt is nether of wyll, nor obstinacie agaynst God and his worde" : from which we may at least gather that Mary had made some progress in mastering the terminology of the precise Protestants. Lord James, Randolph also informs us, continued to deal with her "rudelye, homeleye and bluntly,"

---

[1] *Works*, ii. 290.   [2] *Ibid.*, vi. 132.

and Lethington " more delicatlye and fynelye," while Mary herself was " patient to here and bearethe myche." [1]

It was apparently these private disputes—of which he was probably informed by Lord James—that suggested to Knox to seek the counsel of Calvin in a letter of October 24th.[2] " The latter " [those who " still agree with us in doctrine "] " have," he writes, " this to say in defence of their indulgences, that the Queen, namely, affirms that all the ministers of the Word (and yourself also) are of opinion that it is not lawful for us to prohibit her from openly professing her own religion " ; and Knox, though convinced that Calvin could not hold such reasonable opinions, wished to have a line from him to say that he did not.

Knox's notions of legality were confused, for Protestantism was then devoid of full legal sanction in Scotland, the Parliament by which it had been nominally established being neither properly called, nor its proceedings ratified by the sovereign, whose religious conduct he was proposing to call in question.   True, the extreme continental Protestants held that all rulers ought to be " reformed or deprived by them by whom they were chosen " ; but in Scotland neither the sovereign nor the nobility were " chosen " ; and Knox virtually assumed the existence of a commonwealth, where commonwealth there was none.

About a week after the letter had been dispatched, an event happened which led to a conference, doubtless at the instance of Knox, in the house of James Makgill, the Clerk Registrar, on the question raised in it.   On All Hallows day —1st November—the Queen had a song Mass in her chapel,

---

[1] *Scottish Papers*, i. pp. 392-3.   [2] *Works*, vi. 133-5 ; Teulet, ii. 172-3.

and, according to Randolph, one of her priests was beaten by a servant of Lord Robert. The musical celebration caused a new ferment amongst the Protestant clergy, and it was now, Randolph tells us, called in question whether " the princesse being an idolatre, may be obeyde in all civil and pollitique actions." [1]

At a conference on the subject between the Council and the Protestant leaders, Knox, who, as we have seen, had already written to Calvin on the point to be discussed, spontaneously offered—while concealing that he had already so written—to write " to Geneva for the resolutione of that Churche," whereupon Maitland—who very justly remarked that there " stood mekle in the information," or manner of stating the case—suggested that he himself had better write. Though Knox—who never quite understood Maitland's sense of humour—afterwards professed to have taken this as a serious proposal, it was evidently only intended to quash Knox's offer ; and it was there and then decided, without consulting Calvin, " that the Quene should have hir religioun free in hir awin chapell to do, sche and her household, what thei list." [2]

So far, the conduct of Knox about the letter is perhaps excusable, though not quite above board, but when, in connection with a similar discussion in 1564, the Clerk Registrar stated that during the former debate he thought it was understood that Knox should write to Calvin, " Nay," said Mr. Knox, " my lord Secretary wuld nocht consent that I sould write." [3] In defence of Knox against the accusation of Joseph Robertson, Dr. Hay Fleming [4] affirms that " Knox does not say that Lethington prevented him

---

[1] *Scottish Papers*, i. 569. [2] Knox, *Works*, ii. 292.
[3] *Ibid.*, 459. [4] *Mary Queen of Scots*, p. 263.

from writing, but only that he prevented the others from appointing him to write."

This is literally true, but it is not the whole truth of the case ; and it in no degree explains the mysterious attitude of Knox towards his own letter.   For (1) Knox in this reply conveyed, and intended to convey, the false impression that he had not written to Calvin ; (2) when now asked to write to Calvin, he declined to do so; (3) he must have possessed a reply from Calvin ; (4) he could have no reason for withholding it except that Calvin, who regarded Knox as headstrong, had advised him against any rash action; and (5) if he had Calvin's reply, his proposal that instead of asking the opinion of Calvin on the particular point, they should complain of the general character of his teaching to Calvin and see what Calvin would say, must have been a mere endeavour to ride off on a false issue.

Lord James had, precise Protestant though he was, given his word to Mary about the Mass ; and while recognising all the inconvenience and dangers of the arrangement, he sought to persuade himself that it would be only temporary; the hope of him and Maitland being that a solution both of the religious and political problem was to be found in a cordial understanding with Elizabeth.   The beginning of this had happily been laid by Elizabeth, just as Mary was setting out for Scotland.   Had Elizabeth not written to Mary that letter of August 16th, and had she neglected to send her a passport by St. Colme, the situation on Mary's arrival in Scotland would have been one of great awkwardness. Having returned to Scotland in the face of Elizabeth's menaces, Mary was debarred from making friendly approaches to her ; while had Elizabeth not altered her tone until Mary, in defiance of her menaces, had arrived in Scotland, she could not now have done so, without a sense of humiliation. For some days after Mary's arrival, the private reflections of Lord James and Maitland must therefore have been sombre in the extreme.

That Mary at first actually contemplated breaking off diplomatic relations with England, we learn from Randolph. The second day after her arrival she asked, said Randolph, " what I made here, and when I dyd departe." But Mary's tone to him changed at once, when she knew of Elizabeth's eleventh-hour repentance. " Now," wrote Randolph, " we stand on better terms than before—especially since the Lord of St. Colme's arrival with her safe-conduct, four days after she was landed." [1]

Though Lord James had received no answer, either from Elizabeth or Cecil, to his remarkable overture of August 6th, Mary, on September 1st, sent Maitland formally to announce her prosperous journey and safe arrival, and her desire for the continuance and increase of the friendship between the two countries. The object of Maitland's visit is only partially disclosed in the mutilated copy of his instructions,[2] but it is fully revealed in the general tenor of his conferences with Elizabeth, as detailed in his " Relation," first published, from the MS. in the British Museum, in Philippson's *Marie Stuart.*[3] Though only instructed by Mary in very general terms, the real aim of his embassy, which was largely on his own account, was to set forward the scheme first mooted by him, on his own initiative, to Cecil immediately after the death of Francis II.

As regards the ratification of the treaty, which was

---

[1] *Scottish Papers*, i. 547.   [2] Keith, ii. 72-4 ; Labanoff, i. 104.
[3] III. 444-52.

giving Elizabeth such concern, he stated that he had no instructions, for the simple reason that Mary had not as yet been able to enter into " the manyment of ony effairis. This was perfectly true, for the Privy Council had not then been chosen, and was not chosen until September 6th ; but Maitland's aim evidently was to " grope " Elizabeth's mind as to the recognition of Mary's title, before any answer should be given as to the ratification of the treaty.

In her earlier interviews Elizabeth fenced very cleverly against Maitland's contentions : after Mary had obliged her in regard to the ratification, then would be the time " to do hir any plesour," but before that, she could not " with honour gratifie her in any thing." Her aim was to induce Mary to ratify the treaty by promises, which might be interpreted as meaning much, but which in reality committed her to nothing ; but she was falling into the fatal mistake of Henry VIII., that of seeking to treat with Scotland, not on terms of equality but of lofty patronage. Maitland therefore sought to reveal to her how little reason she had for the assumption of such superior airs. He had no authority, he said, to speak for Mary, but if Elizabeth desired his own opinion, " I will," he said, " frielie speik it, that I think that treaty so preiudiciale to hir maiestie, that sche will neuir confirme it, and in sik forme consauit as hir maiestie is not in honour bund to do it."

More than this : discerning Elizabeth's absorbing anxiety for its ratification, he did not scruple to point out to her the immensity of the favour she was asking Mary to confer on her. In the eyes of the world, the position occupied by Elizabeth was more than equivocal : " It is trew," so Maitland bluntly put it, " that althought your hienes takis your self to be lauch full, yit ar ye not alwayis so

After the picture by Zucchero in the collection of the Marquis of Salisbury.

QUEEN ELIZABETH.

takin abrod in the warld " ; whereas, for Mary's title :
" alswa your hienes wpone your conscience, nore the wyesest
of your subjects can na wise disallow it." The moral
of his tale was that Elizabeth had as good, and probably
better, reasons for coming to an understanding with Mary,
as Mary had for coming to an understanding with her.

He presumed, however, to speak only as the friend
of both countries and of both queens, and disclaimed any
direct knowledge of Mary's own opinions or intentions.
He could not tell whether Mary looked at the matter as
he did : " nor yit speak I ony thing thairof as from hir
maiestie, bot rather to lat your hienes understand that the
noble men hes reassone to desyir your maiestie to cum to
sum qualeficacioun."

Logically, of course, Maitland's case was unanswerable ;
but neither logic nor justice has a vital connection with
questions of international politics, and in that age they
had even less to do with them than they have now. In
this particular case, also, the question of expediency was
unusually complicated. The course advised by Maitland
was perhaps the more expedient for both, provided each
could be sure of the other's good faith ; but however
much the interests of both might have been served by
an amicable understanding, this was found to be impossible.
Had the sovereigns been of the other sex, it might not
have proved so ; but there was now to be considered,
not merely the more incalculable element of feminine
idiosyncrasies, but the predominant question of marriage.

For Elizabeth, it can hardly be said that she was asked
to risk more than Mary. By recognising Elizabeth's title
Mary would, in a manner, tie her own hands. Yet should
Mary marry Don Carlos, England would be greatly at

the mercy of Scotland and Spain. As to the religious
question, it did not greatly concern Elizabeth, except so
far as it bore on the legitimacy of her title, and the safety
of her position in England. Apart from it, she had good
reason to pause before agreeing to Maitland's far-reaching
suggestion; but the attitude she took up from the beginning
—however she might seek in a manner to veil it—was
that of an absolute *non possumus*.

Froude and others justify Elizabeth's obstinacy, on the
supposition that the recognition of Mary's rights would
have been but the signal for Elizabeth's assassination, or
a Catholic rising in England on Mary's behalf. The
assassination possibility may be left out of account, since
it was always there; but as to a Catholic rising, this
would depend upon whether Mary remained a Catholic,
and whether she could be trusted to keep faith with
Elizabeth, questions as to which Elizabeth was as yet but
imperfectly informed; but if Elizabeth did not marry—
and we must believe that she had resolved not to do so
—there was little likelihood that Mary would seek to
disturb her, once she were assured of her right of succession,
or that of her children, to the English throne.

The fact, however, was that Elizabeth's determination was
fixed and unalterable from the beginning, and for reasons
entirely personal and peculiar to herself. So long as the
question of a successor to her remained uncertain, her importance would remain undiminished, and she would have
no rival in the nation's affection; once the succession were
definitely fixed, there was the possibility that the thoughts
and hopes of the nation might be more and more turned
towards their future sovereign. This, in great part, morbid
apprehension of Elizabeth applied to any successor, Mary

or another, whether the succession would be to England's advantage or not.

Froude's mistake as to the character of Elizabeth's apprehension has been transmitted not only, as we have seen, to Mr. Lang, but also to Dr. Hay Fleming. "To agree to his" [Maitland's] "proposal, would," so he writes, "she insisted, be simply to prepare her own winding-sheet and make her grave ready." These are not Elizabeth's words, but a paraphrase of them. She, however, merely meant that she declined to have her own attention and that of her subjects continually directed in this manner to her own decease. It applied to every possible successor ; and it is absurd to suppose that she dreaded that, as soon as her successor should be named, whoever that successor might be, steps would immediately be taken for her assassination. She spoke entirely in figure, her successor being likened to her winding-sheet. "Think you," she said to Maitland, "yat I culd luif my awin windiescheit, princes cannot like their awin children," etc. Maitland could, and did afterwards, reply that Mary was precluded by the will of Henry VIII. from inheriting, and that all the Scots desired was the removal of the disqualification ; but Elizabeth desired this retained, simply because the ambiguity added to her personal importance. In her determination to do nothing to clear up the ambiguity, she was influenced neither by weak dread of assassination nor by high consideration for the welfare of England, but by a mere adamantine self-regard.[1]

Mary's attitude towards Elizabeth is much more difficult

[1] Since this was written, I find that my interpretation of the "winding-sheet" phrase agrees with that of Father Pollen. See his excellent note in *A Letter from Mary Queen of Scots* (Scottish History Society, 1904, p. xviii).

to determine ; for while Elizabeth was hard and cold, Mary was passionate and emotional. Mary's ambition was also wider than that of Elizabeth. Elizabeth had practically reached the summit of hers. As she stated to Maitland, she was married to the realm of England. She had apparently no desire for any wider sovereignty : she showed no similar desire to that of her father to obtain personal dominion over Scotland ; and it was a matter of minor concern to her whether, after her death, the crowns of Scotland and England became united or not. Her main concern and ambition were to rule England successfully —to defend it, because it was now hers, against external foes ; and to preserve it, because it was now hers, from the dangers of revolution. Her own fortunes being bound up with England's greatness and glory, she was prepared to do her utmost to maintain them intact so long as she lived ; what might afterwards become of England was not of prime consequence to her, for the simple reason that it would be no longer hers. Mary, on the other hand, was in the position of one whose ambition had been thwarted, who had to retrieve her fallen fortunes, whose future was peculiarly uncertain, and whose aims and hopes regarding it were largely a matter of conjecture : the most that was certain was that she would not be permanently content either with the present condition of her sovereignty in Scotland, or with her present relations to the English succession.

With the question of Mary's future was of course intimately bound up the question of her religious policy. In accordance with her statement to Throckmorton before she set out for Scotland, she would have desired to have at least begun with a policy of general toleration ; but she soon discovered that this was meanwhile impossible, and with difficulty obtained even a kind of half-toleration for herself.

Had it been possible for her, consistent with her political purposes, to have restored Catholicism, Mary would of course have done so : but this does not bind us to infer that her primary aim, as Froude supposed, was to restore Catholicism—that she threw herself, as he states, amongst " the most turbulent people in Europe " in order " to use her charms as a spell to win them back to the Catholic Church, to weave the fibres of a conspiracy from the Orkneys to the Land's End, prepared to wait, to control herself, to hide her purpose till the moment came to strike : yet with a purpose resolutely formed to trample down the Reformation and to seat herself on Elizabeth's throne."[1] That about the time of her arrival in Scotland she cherished any such firm purpose is clearly refuted by her letter to the Duke of Guise of January 5th, 1561-2,[2] which, as Father Pollen states, " affords the clearest evidence that she then looked forward to an intimate alliance with the Queen of England, and was not weighed down by her responsibilities as a Catholic sovereign."[3]

Mary, when she arrived in Scotland, was a convinced and strongly biased Catholic ; but devotion to the Catholic religion was not, as in the case of Mary of England, either the supreme influence in her life, or its advancement the main aim of her politics. When she left France, her ruling motive, like that of her relatives of Guise, was political ambition cloaked by an artificial religiosity. However desirous she may have been, therefore, for the

---

[1] *History*, cab. ed., vi. 510-11. [2] *Papal Negotiations*, pp. 435-40,
[3] *Ibid.*, pp. xlix-l.

restoration of Catholicism in Britain, it can hardly be
affirmed that she set out for Scotland with "a purpose
fixed as the stars to undo the Reformation." Her main
immediate purpose was to establish herself firmly on the
Scottish throne and obtain the recognition of her rights
to the English succession ; and her ultimate hope was
to obtain the hand of Don Carlos. This hope necessitated constancy to the Catholic religion ; and she certainly
desired to have it believed both by the King of Spain
and the Pope that she was resolved on the restoration
of Catholicism ; but this restoration she would not meanwhile engage in, lest she should endanger her political
ambitions.

With every respect to the value on such a question
of the opinion of Father Pollen, the Pope's letter of
December 3rd, 1561, does seem to imply that Mary had
given a promise to do all that was possible for the
advancement of Catholicism in Scotland ; but her ideas
of what was possible were, at the same time, regulated by
a very constant regard to her own personal interests.
The Pope, well aware of her difficulties and temptations,
and remembering that her mother had lost Scotland to
Catholicism by a too exclusive zeal for the interests of
France, had very special reasons for exhorting her to
constancy. He wished her to take for her model, in this
respect, Queen Mary of England, of "pious memory,"
who "surely did not defend the cause of God timidly,
nor hesitate in withstanding the foes of the Christian
religion" ; and she was to allow no danger to scare
her from the "defence of the holy faith." He, however, was somewhat astray as to her character and aims.
She was quite as courageous as Mary of England. She

was not to be scared by any possible danger from anything on which her heart was set ; but however she might deceive herself, the restoration of Catholicism was never more to her than a secondary consideration.

Mary's future relation to Catholicism in Scotland could not be certainly inferred from her past relation to it in France. Up till her arrival in Scotland her career had been determined for her mainly by others. As yet her character, even if at all definitely formed, had hardly had an opportunity to reveal itself : queen-consort though she had been, neither she nor her husband had had much to say in the determination of French policy. Hitherto she had occupied almost the position of a *jeune fille* ; and in all matters of supreme moment she had been accustomed to feel and think and act as her uncles of Guise had prescribed. Her old affection and respect for them remained ; she was still disposed to trust, so far, to their political guidance ; but the old ascendancy over her and the unity of her interests with theirs were already beginning to dissolve. Her new situation was, moreover, one of the most exceptional and bewildering that any sovereign was ever placed in. So widely different in character were her new environment and prospects from her preceding experiences, that her past life hardly afforded any certain clue to the policy she might pursue ; and while the strength of her devotion to Catholicism might easily be overrated, it might also turn out that the character of her sovereign ambition would be modified by a variety of considerations of whose strength there might at first be no definite sign.

Most female sovereigns have cordially, and even passionately, loved the exercise of sovereignty, and in Mary the passion for sovereignty, invigorated rather than enfeebled

by repression, became inordinately strong ; but what limit
is to be placed on her definite hopes, desires and intentions,
when she arrived in Scotland, and how much she
was prepared to sacrifice in the attainment of her ends,
is another matter.   Unlike Elizabeth, she had a genius
for friendship ; and love, passion, and revenge were all
to play an important part in the decision of her future—
ultimately a more important part than either religion or
ambition.   But, besides all this, her aims were so controlled
and frustrated by the designs of others, that her fate may
be said to have been determined for her rather than by her.

The only definite result of Maitland's interview with
Elizabeth was the dispatch by her, on September 17th,
of Sir Peter Mewtas to demand the ratification of the
treaty of Edinburgh ; but, in consequence of Maitland's
visit, the tone which Mewtas was instructed to adopt
was of a more friendly character than would otherwise
have been possible.   To any appearance of friendliness
Mary was always ready to respond, and whether she
believed in the possibility of true friendship with Elizabeth
or not, the way was now open for at least the assumption
of cordiality.   To Randolph she expressed her great satisfaction with her interview with Mewtas.   She was, she
said, greatly beholden to Elizabeth for sending to visit
her "so good and anciente a gentleman " ; and by him
she understood "farre other wyse of the reportes of
thinges " than hitherto ;[1] and Randolph summed up the
tenor of her professions as to the effect "that what she
may do with honour, fit for a princess occupying her
place, shall be performed to the uttermost."

Mewtas set out on his return on October 7th, bearing

[1] *Scottish Papers*, i. 559.

From the picture attributed to Marc Gheeraedts in the National Portrait Gallery.
Photo by Emery Walker.

WILLIAM CECIL, FIRST BARON BURGHLEY, K.G.

with him a memorandum of Mary on the subject of the treaty, in which she offered to nominate certain Commissioners who should confer with those nominated by Elizabeth, in order to determine what portion of the treaty it would now be advisable to ratify.[1] With Mewtas, Maitland sent a remarkable letter to Cecil, in which he pointed out that if Elizabeth's father, Henry VIII., intended to bar Mary from the succession, her grandfather, Henry VII., could hardly have intended such a slur on his possible descendants, when he gave his eldest daughter in marriage to James IV. While also affirming that he found in his "Queen a good disposition to quietness," there was, he added, "therewith joined, a careful regard to her own state, and a courage such as will be loth to forgo her right"; and he reminded him that England, by falling in with the proposed arrangement, "has a great advantage present, Scotland only by future contingency."[2]

The letter of Maitland was supplemented in characteristically solemn and elusive fashion by Moray, who devoted himself to that aspect of the question of which he and Cecil were accustomed to make so much in their correspondence—the advancement of "true religion in this whole Isle." He was in good hope that the obedience of Mary's subjects, "professouris of the treu religion," would have its effect in inducing his sister "to allow the doctrine of the Evangell," and he was also convinced "touching the matter mentioned by Lethington"; but he was content to leave the matter to the perspicacity of Cecil. Compared with the incisiveness of Maitland, the letter of Lord James was mere "milk-and-water."

Not so, however, a third letter carried by Mewtas, that

---

[1] Labanoff, i. 115-16.   [2] Haynes, *State Papers*, p. 373.

of the very fully persuaded Knox—persuaded, however, in an entirely opposite way from Maitland. Like Lord James, the matter that Knox was mainly concerned about was the conversion of the Queen ; but while his interest in this was not affected by worldly ambition, he was by no means so sanguine as her not unworldly brother professed to be. On the contrary, he wrote, " I wold be glaid to be deceived, but I fear I shall not. In communication with her I spyed such craft as I have not found in such aige—since hath the court been dead to me and I to it." [1] But of course, in seeking to thwart the negotiation by sending such a letter to Cecil, Knox was guilty of an interference with the matters of his sovereign that bordered on treason.

Meanwhile Throckmorton, in Paris, had been holding a singular conference with another famous personage, as keenly interested in the result of the negotiation as any of the three remarkable Scotsmen. This was Mary's uncle, the Duke of Guise. He and the Cardinal of Lorraine, devoted as ever to the advancement of their niece's fortunes, so far as this did not prejudice their own, were, at this particular juncture, also specially desirous to commend themselves to Elizabeth. Their interference—for the Duke represented also his brother—was apparently not due to direct prompting from Mary. It was occasioned by a request of Queen Elizabeth for the suppression of a book by Gabriel de Sacconey, in which Anne Boleyn was compared to the heathen wives of Solomon. Guise wished to impress on Throckmorton that he and his brother desired to do their utmost to bring about an understanding between Elizabeth and their niece on the basis of Maitland's

[1] *Works*, vi. 137.

overture. After entering very fully into genealogical details, he affirmed that Maitland's overture seemed to him the only possible method of providing for the "quietness of the two Queens."

Mary, the Duke further said, was by nature one of the "meekest and best-natured Princes in the world," if she were dealt with fairly. If she married a puissant prince, it would be dangerous for England to leave the matter at large ; but if, on the contrary, Maitland's overture were accepted, "the Queen, her nobles, and subjects, may be assured that the Queen of Scots will never, in marriage or in anything of consequence, proceed without the advice of the Queen and her realm ; and they, her kinsmen, would never give her any other advice." [1]

On Throckmorton the Duke's representations produced a deep effect—so deep that, in a letter to Cecil he expressed the conviction that not to deal with the succession was more dangerous than dealing with it, and prayed that God and the Council would so inspire Elizabeth that they might not be left at her death "to the rage of factions and the mercy of others." [2]

Maitland learned from Randolph of this remarkable interview, and in a letter of October 25th he hoped soon to learn of Elizabeth's determination, and wished him in his next to write amply his opinion. [3] But Cecil was evidently as much puzzled about the problem as Elizabeth, and even more so, for he was puzzled about Elizabeth as well as Mary. Writing to Throckmorton on November 4th he reported that Elizabeth had not yet agreed to a Commission for the revision of the treaty, although

---

[1] *For. Ser.*, iv. No. 592 (1).   [2] *Ibid.*, 596 (1).
[3] *Scottish Papers*, i. 565.

several of the Council were in favour of it, and that
he did not " dare to be busy therein for fear of wrong
construction." [1]

Neither Elizabeth nor Cecil would be rendered more
willing to fall in with the proposal by a letter of Randolph
of October 27th.   By this time Randolph had come to
realise that the old sway hitherto exercised by him over
the Scots, either by bribery or persuasion, was now gone,
and that there was like to be no effect of his " travail " ;
and necessarily he felt keenly his now comparative im-
potence.   How to " use " them with whom he formerly
" had to do " and " govern " himself " amongst them "
was, he now found, beyond his art to determine.   " This
trade," he laments, " is now cleane cut of from me ; I
have to trafique nowe with other kynde of marchants
than before.   Theie knowe the value of their ware, and in
all places howe the marquet goethe."   Some had even
hinted that he himself might " honestlye inoughe tayke
a quiete pencion of thys Quene, as Ledington dothe yerlye
of my mestres."

What Elizabeth and the English had no scruple in
practising, Randolph apparently deemed unspeakable
wickedness on the part of Mary and d'Elboeuf.   That
the " whole state of thys realme sholde be altered by
one heade or two, by a woman and ane man," " semethe
wonder," he said, " unto many."   Those who thought
Mary was without " excellent wisdoms " did, he said, but
" abuse themselves, for what so mever pollicie is in all
the cheaf and best practysede heades in France, what so
mever crafte, falced or deceayte ys in all the subtle
braynes of Scotlande, is either freshe in thys onlie

[1] *For. Ser.*, iv. No. 648.

woman's memorie, or she can fette yt with a wette fynger." [1]

This outburst was due to a special fit of depression : it was that of a diplomatist who, accustomed formerly to have very much his own way, now found himself entirely puzzled and baffled. Yet it must have made Elizabeth and Cecil more dubious than ever as to how to receive Mary's advances. A reply had, however, already been deferred too long, and further procrastination could have no better effect than to reinforce Mary's confidence in the weakness of Elizabeth's case. Logically, indeed, Elizabeth had no case at all ; and since she had determined not to marry, she was, in a sense, almost at Mary's mercy. What she really wished to do was both to avoid naming Mary as her successor and to prevent Mary marrying at all, or, if this could not be prevented, marrying otherwise than she approved—not only a preposterously dishonest programme, but one which could not be carried out.

The case was thus one which, Elizabeth seemed to think, called for a quite exceptional exercise of her powers of procrastination and crooked pretence. Maitland endeavoured to assist the progress of the negotiation by a letter to Dudley on November 13th, in which he exhorted him to do what he could to " be a meane to joyne in perfyte amity soche a couple off ladyes, as I think the world did neuer see the lyke in our age—so richely endowed with all perfection off body and spreit, besydes the gyftes off fortune." And he further stated that in his mistress he had found a "a reciproque goodwill doubly more and more increased, which off late hath taken so deape roote y^t her Majesty doth now wishe nothing more earnestly than y^t she may ones have occasion to see her good sister," etc. [1]

It may therefore have been owing to the representations of Leicester that Elizabeth now proposed that she and Mary should enter into a private correspondence on the matter, without the intervention of ambassadors. Mary was to state her reason to Elizabeth for delaying the ratification, and " gif the same be to be allowed unto zow in reason, zow sall wele persave we will require nothing bot that quhilk honour, justice and reason sall allow us to ask, and that quhilk in like honour, justice and reason yow ought to grant." [2] It all seemed admirably simple, for how could two so intelligent sovereigns, both actuated by such exceptional motives, fail to arrive at an understanding ?

The letter was presented to Mary on December 12th by Randolph, who wrote on the 17th that after a second interview Mary, while telling him that she purposed to use Elizabeth's letter " most secretly," said that she had delayed to answer it, partly owing to a meeting of the Convention, partly because she was expecting a reply from Elizabeth to her last letter.[3]

This letter of Mary's was one in reference to a visit of the French ambassador, de Foix, which was due to a new rupture between Catherine and the Guises, the Duke de Nemours having been lately apprehended on the charge of conspiring to abduct the Duke d'Anjou, eldest brother of the King of France. De Foix, while he wished to secure the support of Elizabeth and the Scottish Protestants

---

[1] Add. MSS. (B.M.), 35,125 f. 8.　　[2] Keith, ii. 133.
[3] *Scottish Papers*, i. 579.

against the Guises, privately advised Mary against coming to an agreement with Elizabeth.[1] Mary had, however, no desire that Catherine should be helped, and she had therefore sought to disabuse Elizabeth of any bad impressions created by de Foix's insinuations against her uncles : she assured her that not only were they perfectly loyal to their king, but specially desirous of promoting friendly relations betwixt all the three countries.[2] A visit to her, about the same time, of de Morette, she also explained, had reference merely to the birth of a child to her uncle and aunt the Duke and Duchess of Savoy. This was hardly true, because he was also entrusted by the Cardinal with an invitation to Mary to send representatives to the Council of Trent ; but since Mary, no more than Elizabeth, intended to respond to the invitation, Elizabeth was not substantially wronged by Mary's explanation.

Mary had thus a pretty good excuse for delay in answering Elizabeth's proposal ; and it was also deemed advisable to discover what had led Elizabeth, after so long delay, to come to such an exceptional resolution, how far she was acting with or without the advice of her councillors, and how far her views as to the treaty coincided with theirs. On the 15th Maitland therefore wrote to Cecil that he had advised Mary to defer her answer for a short time, and that meanwhile he should be glad to have Cecil's "opinion how the same may be so framed, so as neither be pained nor miscontented." He also thought it well to enlighten Cecil again as to Mary's sentiments : she was willing to do anything if "made sure of her title";

---

[1] *Papal Negotiations*, p. 443.
[2] Letter in Philippson, iii. 452-3.

but " to enter into a demand and find a repulse, it would much offend her, being of such courage," etc.[1]

Maitland's communication was skilful, but it was also perfectly fair and above board. Before Elizabeth's letter was received he had, on December 7th, written to Cecil about the affairs of the Guises, and he expected that some mention of it would have been made in Elizabeth's letter. Receiving no answer to either of these two letters, he again wrote Cecil on the 26th, to the effect that he was delaying Mary's answer until he had his advice, as from long experience he knew how his mistress should be dealt with. Shortly after dispatching this letter he received one from Cecil of which only the concluding part remains, but which plainly contained no reference of any kind to Elizabeth's letter. We also learn from a letter of Maitland's of January 15th that Cecil, in a letter of January 3rd, professed to be " something offended " that Maitland had ventured to write for his advice.[2] Cecil's resolute silence could thus hardly be interpreted in any other way than that Elizabeth was acting without the advice of her Council ; but, in any case, in view of the silence, it would have been folly to have made any great pretence of humility or even conciliation towards Elizabeth.

In her reply Mary therefore stated her views not only plainly, but with all due emphasis. Waiving the consideration of the altered circumstances and the question of the treaty's regularity, she put it to Elizabeth, was it reasonable to expect that she could willingly ratify a treaty, so deeply prejudicial to her own interests and prospects ? " How prejudiciall that treatie is to sic title and interes as be birth and naturall discente of zour

---

[1] Haynes, *State Papers*, p. 373.   [2] *Scottish Papers*, i. 573, 581, 588.

awin linage may fall to us, be veray inspectioun of the
treaty itself, ze may," she said, " easelie persave."   She was
not ignorant of the attempts that had been made to
act towards her, as if she had no connection with the
" blude of Ingland " ;   but she hoped Elizabeth would
be loath that she should receive so manifest an injury,
" as wnterlie to be debarrit from that title, quhilk in
possibilitie may fall unto us."   She was prepared to do
all in regard to the treaty that in reason might be
required of her, or rather to enter into a new one
of a more satisfactory kind : and she concluded with
the hope that she and Elizabeth might meet together, when
she would " mair clerelie persave the sinceritie " of her
" gude meanyng " than she could " express in writing."[1]
Nominally, the letter was that of Mary, but the voice of
it was also that of Lethington ;   and Elizabeth's correspondence device having thus

> "redounded as a flood on those
> From whom it sprang,"

could not be further persevered in.

As St. Colme was passing through London to Scotland,
Elizabeth sent with him a short letter to Mary in reply
to a private letter of hers of January 4th, about her uncle,
in which she also stated that she had no leisure, before
St. Colme's departure, to answer her letter on the treaty ;
but the longer Elizabeth pondered the Maitland-Mary
letter, how to frame a reply must only have puzzled her
the more.

With a view of helping Elizabeth out of her preposterous predicament, and of staving off a definite

[1] Labanoff, i. 123-7.

answer on the main question, Cecil now began to hold
out hopes of an interview. Cecil's opinion, repeatedly
urged, was evidently a plain hint as to Elizabeth's wishes ;
and ultimately Maitland thought fit to reply that his
sovereign was so transported with affection, that " she
respects nothing so she may meet with her cousin "—that
she was, indeed, more earnestly bent on the interview than
her councillors dared to advise, unless there were some
assurance of good results from it. Maitland was influenced
mainly by Mary's wishes. She was eager, impulsive and
rash, and she had no knowledge of Elizabeth's incapacity
for friendship : but Maitland discerned that if, after all,
Elizabeth did not mean business on fair terms, the interview could end only in a hopeless quarrel.

Meanwhile, both by her "good words" and her
kindly actions, Mary was at least puzzling, if not con-
vincing, the doubting and deeply pondering Randolph,
who, his mind much relieved that the Marquis d'Elboeuf
was now about to return to France, was, notwithstanding
all his former desperate suspicions, rather disposed to
conjecture her meaning to be good than suspect the
contrary to what he both saw and heard.[1]

It was now even currently, though doubtless erroneously,
reported that the Cardinal of Lorraine had persuaded
Mary to embrace the religion of England—a comparatively
mild form of Protestantism ; and the report was making
the preachers " ronne allmoste wylde : of the which theie
bothe saye and preache, that yt is lyttle better then when
yt was at the worste ! " " I have not," adds Randolph,
" so amplye conferred with Mr. Knox in these matters,
as shortlye I muste : whoe upon Sunday laste gave the

[1] *Scottish Papers*, i. 596.

crosse and the candle such a wype, that as wyse and
lerned as hymself wysshed him to have hylde his peace!
He recompenced the same with a mervilous vehemente
and persinge prayer in thende of his sermonde, for the
contynuance of amytie and hartie love with England." [1]
But, of course, the peaceful and united Britain for which
Knox prayed was one without " cross or candle," and one
in which he hoped that the young girl, his sovereign,
who was prepared, apparently, to adopt the religion of
England, might have neither lot nor part.

In regard to the interview, however, Randolph, writing
on February 28th, thought that unless Elizabeth refused
it, it would pass any man's power in Scotland to stay it : [2]
indeed Randolph, now delivered from his early nightmare,
seemed both desirous and hopeful of a friendly understanding between Elizabeth and Mary. But on the same day,
Maitland sent to Cecil one of his striking letters, which
Cecil must have read with somewhat mixed emotions. " He
had," he said, " in a maner consecrated himself to uniting
this isle in friendship." He had " pressed " this purpose
of his in " Queen Mary's days " [in the hope, we
must believe, that the Scottish Mary, and not Elizabeth,
should succeed the English Mary], and already he had
pressed it in many diverse ways in Elizabeth's time ; " and
ever," he said, " as one occasion doth fayle me, I begyn
to shuffle the cards off new, always keping the same
grownde." [3]

Maitland's late shuffling of the cards was not quite
satisfactory either to Elizabeth or Cecil ; but they had to
play the game with a view not merely to a temporary

---

[1] *Scottish Papers*, i. 603.   [2] *Ibid.*, 607.

[3] *Ibid.*, 609-10.

triumph, but to the final result ; and Maitland and Mary had a very strong hand.

Thus, whatever Elizabeth's suspicions as to Mary might be, she deemed it best to drop the private correspondence expedient, which clearly promised defeat, and to take up or pretend to take up that of the interview. This she seems to have announced in good-humoured and even jocular terms to Mary, in a letter which was handed to her in the presence of Randolph on March 28th. Unhappily we know nothing as to even its general tenor. She did not discuss its contents with Randolph, but he wrote to Cecil that she laughed heartily all the time of reading it, after which she said she was much beholden to Elizabeth for sending her so long a letter, and hoped that when they saw each other, she would better know her heart than she judged from her writings : which, if a reply to Elizabeth's expression of dissatisfaction with the Maitland-Mary letter, was very neatly and nicely put.

From a letter of Throckmorton's of March 31st, we learn that the Council of Scotland were rather perplexed about the interview. Unless the differences between Mary and Elizabeth were previously settled, they were wholly averse to it ; and there were also other difficulties, which they had stated by St. Colme to the Duke of Guise, one of them being that she might, after all, be constrained to agree to some unreasonable conditions. The Duke, however, favoured it, though suggesting the advisability of holding it near the Borders ; [1] and Mary having learned that the Cardinal thought it convenient,[2] it was resolved to proceed with the arrangements.

Dr. Hay Fleming affirms that the Cardinal of Lorraine

[1] *For. Ser.*, iv. No. 967.   [2] *Scottish Papers*, i. 630.

hesitated to give his consent ;[1] but on April 21st the
Bishop of Amiens wrote to Mary : "It was easy for your
uncle to come to a decision, and all are of one mind in
praising the interview between your two Majesties, seeing
therein that which is properly due to you not only there
but throughout Christendom. I think that the Queen of
England has so much good judgment, and is so well advised,
that therein she will not forget anything."[2]

A bad accident to the Queen, whose horse fell with
her between Falkland and Lochleven, delayed her return to
Edinburgh ; but on May 19th the Privy Council of Scotland
gave their advice in favour of the interview, on condition
that proper guarantees were obtained for the safety of her
person ;[3] and on the 25th Maitland set out for England.
The cardinal points of his instructions were that Mary
was not to be pressed with any matter that might be
prejudicial to the realm, and that he was to seek to discover
what modification in the treaty Elizabeth would be disposed
to agree to, it being understood that if she required its
ratification, rigorously as it stood, the meeting could not
take place.[4]

Maitland professed to Mary to be very well satisfied with
his reception by Elizabeth, and advised her to do what
she could to stimulate Elizabeth's affection by writing to
her as "gentle and loving letters" as she could devise.[5]
This Mary was quite prepared to do, but the religious
trouble in France had already begun to cast a sinister
shadow over the negotiations. The recrudescence of the
political influence of the Guises in France, made possible

[1] *Mary Queen of Scots*, p. 71.   [2] *Papal Negotiations*, p. 447.
[3] *Reg. P. C.*, i. 206.   [4] Keith, ii. 142-4.
          [5] Letter in Philippson, iii. 455-8.

by the apostasy of the King of Navarre, tended greatly to strengthen the position of Mary in Scotland. It might also lead to a new alliance between the two countries, and it encouraged Catholic hopes both in Scotland and England. A new element of uncertainty was thus introduced, and Throckmorton, who had formerly advised that Elizabeth should, if possible, come to an amicable understanding with Mary, was as early as April 17th expressing his doubts as to the prudence of Elizabeth, in the unsettled condition of French affairs, making a long journey from London to have an interview with the Queen of Scots.[1]

The Privy Council of England were now, on account of the changed situation in France, also opposed to the interview. They were apparently, in this, mainly influenced by dread of the possible dangers to Protestantism; but Elizabeth, neither so deeply interested in Protestantism as her Council nor so straightforward in her method of dealing with her political difficulties, was not moved by their strong representations. If she had no intention of proceeding with the interview, she told that to no one ; or if, which is more probable, she merely intended to make use of the interview to beguile Mary, she gave no sign of this, except possibly to Cecil, and resolved, as before, in the case of the letter device, to follow her own programme.

To Throckmorton, Mary lamented her uncles' " unadvised enterprise," of the success of which she appeared to be in doubt, and which would in any case tend, as she said, to make Elizabeth colder towards " her and hers." She discovered in it, probably, the first indication that her interests and theirs might not always coincide, and

[1] *For. Ser.*, iv. No. 1015.

that there could hardly be the same unity as of old in
their aims.

On June 10th Maitland wrote that if the troubles in
France were compounded, or ended, by the close of June,
the meeting would take place.[1] With this letter Mary
received one from Elizabeth which pleased her so much
that she placed it "into her bosom next to her skin" ;
and she proposed to send her a "ringe with a diamond
fashioned lyke a harte," and to express the signification
of the symbol by "wryting in a fewe verses."[2] It
is, however, worth noting that Lord James, now Earl of
Mar, liked the resolution—unless matters mended in France
—to defer the interview "marvillous well." It would
be better, so Randolph reported him to have said, for
Elizabeth to defer the meeting than not to send help to
the Huguenots against, of course, Mary's uncles of Guise :
"as he saythe, *Amicus Socrates, amicus Plato, magis amica
veritas.*"[3]

About the end of June, news having reached Elizabeth
that peace would be made with the Prince of Condé, it
was agreed, on July 6th, that the meeting should take
place at York, or, in default thereof, at some convenient
place between it and the river Trent, at some date between
August 20th and September 20th. With this joyful news
Maitland returned to Mary, who immediately began to
make preparations for her journey, sending out letters on
July 15th to all her nobility to meet her with speed at
Edinburgh.[4] With Maitland, Elizabeth sent to Mary her

---

[1] Philippson, iii. 456.

[2] *Scottish Papers*, i. 632 ; Mary's intention of sending a ring is referred
to as early as February.

[3] *Ibid.*, 633.   [4] *Ibid.*, 640.

portrait. She enquired of Randolph, "How lyke thys was unto her lyvelye face?" who, he says, trusted her Grace would shortly "be judge therof her self, and fynde myche more perfection than coulde be sette forthe with the art of man." This, said Mary, was the thing she had always most desired, and she hoped that when they had spoken, their hearts would be so eased that "the greatest greef that ever after shalbe betweene us, wylbe when wee shall tayke leave thone of thother." [1]

It is hardly likely that these ecstasies of Mary, exaggerated and artificial as in some sense they were, were absolutely hypocritical; on the contrary, they seem to show that she desired, if possible, both to win Elizabeth's friendship and to give her her own. This also appears to have been the policy which her uncles of Guise hoped she would pursue. "The Queen of England," wrote to Mary the Bishop of Amiens, who enjoyed their confidence, " among other great virtues, has ever made herself respected in Christendom for being a princess of her word, and makes it evident that she desires your good favour and friendship. Madame, I feel assured of this, that your presence will increase her desire to remain your good, firm and stable friend."

Dr. Hay Fleming has remarked that while Maitland affirmed to Cecil and Randolph that Mary was in earnest in seeking Elizabeth's friendship, he told to the Spanish ambassador "a somewhat different tale." [2] But this was as late as March, 1563, and even so, it was hardly a different tale. True, he said that the Queen of Scots, by the time he spoke, "understood that these unfulfilled hopes had for their object to keep her in suspense and doubt about the marriage, and even to force her into a match with the

---

[1] *Scottish Papers*, i. 639.   [2] *Mary Queen of Scots*, p. 73.

Earl of Arran, or a still meaner suitor."[1] But neither
Maitland nor Mary could understand this until after
Elizabeth had deferred the interview ; the anxiety of both
Maitland and Mary for it was evidently quite sincere,
and they hoped for the best.

Later the designs of Elizabeth began more clearly to
manifest themselves ; and even then Mary, as Maitland
said, did her " best to continue somehow on the present
footing of friendship " with Elizabeth, in the hope that
if Elizabeth " found herself embarrassed by France, she
might be glad of the intervention of the Scots Queen,
and the agreement might be effected between them at the
same time " ; but until Elizabeth had clearly shown her
hopeless falsity, Mary was, seemingly, disposed to believe
in the possibility of winning her friendship.

In the way of Maitland's desired consummation there
were of course immense difficulties—difficulties by reason
of the strange idiosyncrasy of Elizabeth, difficulties on
the part of the English Council and the English Parliament,
difficulties on account of differences in religion, difficulties
arising from the question of marriage ; but had not Mary's
uncles of Guise—who hoped that Elizabeth's anxiety to
be on good terms with their niece would debar her from
interfering with their projects in France—cut somewhat
before the point, the interview must have taken place.
What might have come of it, it is idle to speculate ; but
though Elizabeth could hardly have hoped so much by
it for herself, as for herself Mary hoped to achieve, its
postponement marks another turning point in Mary's career.

The rivalry of the two queens was neither to be
moderated, nor destroyed, nor confirmed by personal

[1] *Spanish State Papers*, 1558-67, p. 307.

intercourse with each other ; and whoever was to blame for the postponement of their meeting, it was from Elizabeth that the decision as to postponement always came. At the very time that Randolph was penning his account of Mary's anticipatory flutterings, Elizabeth was setting about the preparation of the postponement message. But this change of intention can hardly be attributed to caprice.

Writing on July 17th, the Duchess of Parma relates the arrival some days previously of news from Throckmorton of " the breaking out of hostilities between the King of France and the rebels " ; [1] and in sending Sidney on July 15th to announce to Mary the postponement of the interview, Elizabeth affirmed that the renewal of hostilities in France was due to an act of treachery on the part of the Duke of Guise.[2]

According to Sidney, who had an interview with Mary on the 23rd, Mary manifested her grief at the postponement " not only in woordys but in countenans and watery eyes " ; and, but for the fact that she had some previous " inkling " of his message from Mar and Maitland, she would have shown her sorrow much more, the bad news having deferred his interview for a day and driven her into such a passion of disappointment that she took to her bed. Nevertheless she proposed to accept Elizabeth's considerations as reasonable, and anticipated with great pleasure the prospect of an interview in the following year. In order to satisfy Mary that she was in earnest, Elizabeth suggested that it should take place at York or at Elizabeth's castles of Pomfret or Nottingham, at any time between May 30th and the last day of August following,

---

[1] *Spanish State Papers*, 1558-67, p. 254.   [2] Keith, ii. 149.

the time and place which Mary preferred, to be intimated to her before the last of "August next," Elizabeth accepting "before the last of October." According to Maitland, Mary would have accepted Elizabeth's proposal out of hand, but on his advice it was determined first to consult the Council.[1]

The Council, while on August 15th declaring that nothing had altered their opinion as to the possible advantages of the meeting, were even more chary than before in expressing an opinion as to whether it was safe to "commit hir body in England," and therefore referred the place of meeting and the security to herself.[2] Mary thereupon resolved to comply with Elizabeth's suggestion, and at Perth ratified, on August 20th, the old conditions for the interview, fixing it to take place on June 20th in the city of York.[3] But she had then no anticipation that in a few months Elizabeth would, in France, be waging war against her uncles.

[1] *Scottish Papers*, i. 641-42.   [2] *Reg. P. C.*, i. 217.
[3] Labanoff, 150-6.

CHAPTER V

HAMILTONS AND GORDONS

MARY'S position as a Catholic sovereign carrying on
her government, if she was really carrying it
on, by means of officers of state avowedly Protestant,
and ruling a people the Protestant portion of which,
mainly by their determination and ardour, had an apparent
ascendancy, was not only quite anomalous : it was, on
account of the rigidity of Scottish Protestatism, under
the rampant direction of Knox, both humiliating and
perilous. But Mary may at first have realised but imperfectly the peculiarities of her position ; and at any rate,
except for temporary exhibitions of irritation and distress,
there was little sign that her political or ecclesiastical
difficulties greatly troubled her youthful good spirits.

Mary's anticipations of the future were, we must suppose,
coloured in the main with the roseate hue peculiar to
her period of life ; her horizon, if not unclouded, was
not as yet troubled or threatening. She had, it is true,
no certain assurance of the fulfilment of her more splendid
ambitions ; but, light of heart and strong of purpose, she
did not permit her hopes to be smothered by anxieties.
The time had not, as yet, come for any decided parting
of the ways as regards anything of importance—her
marriage, her relations with Elizabeth and England, the

final trust to be placed in her brother, the religious con-
stitution of her State, or possibly even her own religious
profession.   All the early arrangements as to the character
of her rule in Scotland were tentative, and, it might be,
transitory ; her eyes were directed towards a variety of
possibilities and some kind of transformation scene which
would reveal to her a new world.

Meanwhile, Mary, with youthful lightheartedness, was
resolved to have as good a time as her present circumstances
would permit.   Strikingly though her new surroundings
contrasted with the brightness and splendour of France,
there was in their rudeness and roughness a certain novel
piquancy ; and hardy and resolute, notwithstanding her
luxurious upbringing, she resolved to make the best of
them.   In France she had learned to appreciate outdoor
sports and amusements, and for these, at least, she had in
Scotland ample opportunity.   While within easy reach of
some of her palaces there were extensive lowland forests,
she was accustomed also to attend the gatherings, organised
by the Highland nobles, in the wild mountainous regions
for the hunting of the deer ; and for almost daily occupation she had the fascinating pastime of hawking.   One
of her favourite outdoor games was shooting at the
butts ; and she was also accustomed to play at pall-mall,
and even at golf, though, we must suppose, hardly in the
accomplished fashion of the modern lady golfer.

The custom of running at the ring does not seem
to have been practised much by the Scottish nobility ; but on
Sunday, November 30th, 1561, a special display of this
exciting amusement took place, under the auspices of
the Marquis d'Elboeuf, on the Sands of Leith, among
others who took part in it being her half-brothers, Lord

Robert and Lord John. They ran, says Randolph, " six against six, disguised and apparelled, the one half like women, the other like strangers, in strange masking garments. The Marquis that day did very well ; but the women, whose part the Lord Robert did sustain, won the ring. The Queen herself beheld it, and as many others as listed." [1]

Sunday amusements of this character were of course quite in accordance with French custom ; nor had the new Puritanico-Jewish method of Sunday observance as yet—notwithstanding certain recent statutes of the Edinburgh magistrates [2]—become established amongst Scottish Protestants. Whether there were many spectators, we are not told, but the gay d'Elboeuf and the grave and Protestant Randolph, who was a spectator, found, at their first interview with each other, a pleasant topic for conversation on the feats of that day ; and it may be that Knox, who, it would appear, was silent on the subject in his sermons, had he passed that way would not have turned away his eyes from beholding the bright and spirit-stirring spectacle. On the Friday and Saturday following, Mary had solemn masses performed in memory of her husband, and again, on the Sunday following, there was a repetition of the mirth and pastime on the Sands of Leith. [3] " At the first anniversary of her husband's death," remarks Dr. Hay Fleming " the Scottish court seems to have been particularly joyous " ; [4] but the sarcasm is founded on a lack of acquaintance with French customs. Even yet, the day annually dedicated in Paris to mourning for the dead is succeeded by feasting and mirth.

[1] Keith, ii. 120.   [2] *Burgh Records of Edinburgh*, 1551-71, p. 85.
[3] *Scottish Papers*, i. 579.   [4] *Mary Queen of Scots*, p. 58.

From the picture by Francis Pourbus, in the possession of the Royal Society.

GEORGE BUCHANAN.

During the long winter evenings there was for Mary, besides her needlework, the recreation of dice and the cards for which she, for a time, developed a passion. She had doubtless also, at some period of the day, a few quiet hours which she devoted to reading and study, or the practice of music ; after dinner she was accustomed to read Latin under the direction of George Buchanan. She also brought with her from France the game of billiards ; and in a game in 1565 with her and Lord Darnley as partners against the famous beauty, Mary Beaton, and Randolph, the latter were the winners.[1]

In Mary's time there was no place of public amusement in Edinburgh, nor is there any indication of her patronage of rope-dancers, or players, or similar public performers ; her principal indoor social recreations were the masques and dancings by which banquets were usually followed, and in which she usually herself took part. As a change from the gaiety and publicity of the court, she was accustomed, occasionally, to retire to the quietude of St. Andrews, where she made a show of renouncing her sovereign cares and occupations, and living as a plain burgess wife. But she was in nowise addicted to moroseness and gloom. " Her common talk," writes Knox, " was, in secreat, sche saw nothing in Scotland but gravitie, which repuyned alltogether to hir nature, for sche was brocht up in joyusitie; so termed sche her dansing, and other thinges thaireto belonging." [2] What these were, Knox wisely preferred to hint rather than specify ; but the actual fact was that Mary had been continuing to conduct herself with a prudence and propriety which were the despair of Knox, who was conscientiously " resolved to ruin or to rule "

[1] *Scottish Papers* ii. 142.   *Works*, ii. 294

her :   his very vague, though violent, references to
" Scouparis, dansaris and dalliaris of dames," are evidence
sufficient that his prejudices were stronger than his facts.

Mary was not greatly tied by conventions ; her manners
were frank and friendly, and she greatly delighted in the
accomplished art of dancing, for which she had a peculiar
genius ; but her main protection in her novel and difficult
position was her latent sovereign reserve.

Major Martin Hume [1] ventures to promulgate the
theory that the main source of Mary's fascination was her
power of sensuous allurement.   Such a theory would doubtless elucidate to the meanest understanding the Châtelard
incident, and the Rizzio, Darnley, and Bothwell episodes ;
but it seems to me to be inconsistent with what is generally
recorded of the impression she produced on those who
came into close contact with her.   Even Knox hints at
nothing of the kind ; and in a remarkable passage—which
has been curiously overlooked by her champions—he, as late
as 1566, while affirming, probably on no adequate evidence,
that " her dame heard more than we will wryte,"
ventures to say nothing more definite of Mary, confirmed
" idolater " though she was, than that " what sche was and
is, herselff best knows, and God (we doubt not) will
declair." [2]

Randolph also, much as he dreaded her cleverness, makes
no reference to the quality propounded by Major Martin
Hume ; indeed he came to have a very high estimate of
her womanly gifts and graces, though she in no way
succeeded in turning his head.

The most noticeable characteristic of Mary's intercourse
with her nobles and officials was, in fact, her free and open

[1] *Love Affairs*, p. 5.   [2] *Works*, ii. 319.

friendliness, without the least touch of coquetry. She prepossessed them in her favour by her tact and good nature, and secured their goodwill by her own self-respect. Indeed, had she been the exact type of woman Major Hume supposes, it would, from the time of her arrival, have been a very "mad world" in Scotland ; but one of the most surprising circumstances of her earlier sovereignty was, considering her great powers of fascination had she cared to exercise them, the manner in which she kept free from love-entanglements with the eager young Scottish nobles, and avoided encouraging delusive hopes in those who were overweeningly ambitious.

In this connection, considerable confusion has arisen through a general misinterpretation of the story of the "enchantment whereby men are bewitched," a misinterpretation from which even Dr. Hay Fleming, meticulously interested in correctness of detail though he be, has not escaped. Dr. Fleming refers to it thus : "there being about her, as the godly Kingzeancleucht supposed, 'some inchantment whareby men are bewitched.'" [1] But Kingzeancleucht supposed no such thing as this : what he actually said was, " I have bene here now fyve dayis, and at the first I hard everie man say, 'Let us hang the Preast' ; but after that thai had been twyse or thrise in the Abbay, all that fervency was past. I think thair be some inchantment whareby men are bewitched." [2] He thought there might be, not figurative or personal, but actual and impersonal, sorcery in the business. The comments of Knox indicate this clearly enough : " And in verray deed," he writes, " so it came to pass ; for the Queen's flattering words, upoun the ane pairte, ever still crying, 'Conscience,

[1] *Mary Queen of Scots*, p. 48.   [2] Knox, ii. 227.

conscience : it is a sore thing to constreane the conscience ' ; and the subtile persuasionis of hir suppositis (we mean evin of such as were judged most fervent with us) upoun the other parte blynded all men, and putt thame in this opinion, sche will be content to hear the preaching." That was the whole matter of the enchantment, and Lord James and Maitland had a share in it as well as Mary.

The Scottish family which, immediately after her arrival in Scotland, gave Mary most annoyance was the Hamiltons. While in France, Mary, as we have seen, proposed to her mother a marriage between Arran and Mademoiselle de Bouillon, daughter of Diana of Poitiers. We are not told what either her mother, or Arran or the Duke, thought of this way of disposing of the hand of him, who supposed himself next heir after Mary to the Scottish crown ; but the hopes of the Hamiltons were not so lowly as to agree to any such alliance.

Arran had, as we have seen, been rejected in dubious terms by Elizabeth, just before the death of Francis II., and, immediately on the news of the death, the old purpose of the Duke of marrying him to Mary was at once revived. It was now the main hope of the Protestants, though the likelihood of any such event was, says Randolph, " agaynste thopinion of all the doctors." [1] Arran, who seems to have been enamoured of Mary, could hardly have committed an act of greater imprudence than to presume to make offer to her of the hand, which only a few weeks before had been rejected by Elizabeth : and the arrival of Mary in Scotland after Arran's suit had been refused, looked like the final blow to the highest Hamilton ambitions.

The Hamiltons and their friends formed, thus, a nucleus

[1] *Scottish Papers*, i. 523.

From an old engraving.

JAMES HAMILTON, THIRD EARL OF ARRAN.

of discontent, which Knox no doubt would have appealed to, had he resolved that Mary's Mass should be put down by force. Apparently Arran wished to foment the opposition to Mary's Mass for purposes of his own : the Duke resolved not to come to the court unless sent for, and Arran expressed his intention of staying away as long as the Mass remained. While he was ostentatiously posing as a malcontent, a rumour arose on November 16th that he had crossed the frith with a strong company to carry Mary off ; but the report was at least premature, and, according to Randolph, it originated in a rash speech of his in crossing the frith. " Why is yt not as easye to tayke her owte of the Abbaye, as ons yt was intended to have byne done unto her mother ? "[1]

While matters with Arran were in a condition which, on account of his mental instability, were rapidly becoming deplorable, the situation became further complicated by a wild frolic of d'Elboeuf, Bothwell, and Lord John, who forcibly entered a merchant's house in pursuit of a " good, handsome wenche," supposed to be Arran's mistress. The unseemly incident aroused much indignation amongst the extreme Protestants, who desired to make it the occasion of disgracing d'Elboeuf.

Mary could hardly be expected to inflict severe punishment on her uncle, but she severely reproved the roisterers, whereupon Bothwell and Lord John swore that next night they would do the like, in despite of any one that would say them nay.[2] Learning of their boast, the Hamiltons assembled in the market-place, with jack and spear, to be ready for the fray ; but while Bothwell was still in his lodgings assembling his supporters, the common bell was rung, Lord James,

---

[1] *Scottish Papers*, i. 569. [2] *Ibid.*, 583.

Argyll, and Huntly, representing the Queen, appeared on the scene, and proclamation having been made that every one should depart to his home on pain of death, "within half an hower thereafter ther was never a man seen." [1]

Next day, the Duke and Bothwell were summoned to the court, when the Protestants convoyed the one and the Catholics the other; but, to "avoider cumber," Bothwell agreed to leave the town.

Meanwhile Arran was proposing to return to France, where Protestantism was supposed to be now in the ascendant; but on January 17th he went to Linlithgow and made his peace with the Queen. [2] On February 8th, he condescended to be present at the marriage of Lord James (Earl of Mar) to the daughter of the Earl-Marischal; but next day he fell sick, and so remained during the rest of the festivities.

Randolph, who had had a good deal of talk with both father and son, wrote on February 28th that while the father was so inconstant, saving in greed and covetousness, that in three moments he would take five purposes, the son was "so drowned in dreames and so feedethe hymself with fantasies, that either men feare that he wyll fawle into some dayngerus and incurable sycknes, or playe, one daye, some made parte that wyll brynge hymself to myschef." [3]

The next step in Arran's eccentric behaviour was his reconciliation with Bothwell. Efforts had been made both by the Queen and Council to bring this about; but while Bothwell was willing to meet Arran half way, Arran was not in a condition of mind to be reconciled to anybody, and least of all to Bothwell, his hatred against whom "I see,"

---

[1] Knox, ii. 322.   [2] *Scottish Papers*, i. 597.   [3] *Ibid.*, 609.

wrote Randolph, "is immortal."[1] All that he could be
induced to do, was to come under obligations to keep the
peace to him ;[2] but Bothwell, bent on a full reconciliation,
sought for this purpose the good offices of Knox, who
was bound to Bothwell by what Knox terms the "obligations of our Scottish kindness" [kinness], his ancestors
having been feudal dependants of the earl's predecessors.
When Knox succeeded finally in arranging an interview
between them, Arran, without waiting for Bothwell's
apologies, cordially embraced him, saying, "Yf the hearttis
be uprycht few ceremonyes may serve and content me."[3]

The result of Arran's frankness was that, from being
mortal enemies, the two strangely assorted earls appeared to
become, almost in the twinkling of an eye, inseparable
friends, all Edinburgh and most of Scotland being in
wonder at their sudden familiarity, "at preachings, hunting,
and otherwhere."

On Thursday, March 26th, they dined together, after
which Bothwell, with Gavin Hamilton, went to the Duke's
house at Kinneil. Next day, Arran appeared before Knox
in great distress, affirming that Bothwell had suggested to
him a plot for removing the Queen to the Castle of Dumbarton and slaying Lord James, Lethington, and others
that "now misguide her." Knox, who perceived that he
was "stricken with frenzy," sought to soothe him as well as
he could, and advised him that, since he had, as he said,
refused to entertain Bothwell's proposal, it would be better
to do nothing further in the meanwhile ; but Arran, with
insane obstinacy, persisted in his purpose of revealing
Bothwell's treason, and, after writing a letter to the Queen,

---

[1] *Scottish Papers*, i. 585. [2] *Reg. P. C.*, i. 203.
[3] Knox, *Works*, ii. 325.

who was at Falkland, rode to Kinneil. There, after
an unpleasant scene with his father, whom he afterwards
accused of favouring Bothwell's plot, he was, on going
to his bedroom, locked in ; but he made his escape on
Easter Eve from the house, by tying together the sheets
of his bed, and, attired only in his doublet and hose,
arrived at the house of the laird of Grange, near Burntisland,
on the morning of Easter Tuesday, when, besides telling
his story against Bothwell and his father, he began, says
Randolph, to rave and speak of strange purposes, " as of
divels, witches and such lyke." [1]

It was only too evident that Arran was out of his wits ;
but both he and his father had, since Mary's arrival in
Scotland, been behaving in such a manner as to arouse
strong suspicions in regard to their loyalty, while Bothwell's
readiness for any wild enterprise against Lord James was
not difficult to credit. According, also, to Randolph,
when Bothwell arrived to purge himself he was found guilty,
on his own confession, in some points.[2] When brought
before the Council, Arran persisted in his accusation against
Bothwell, but finally withdrew his whole charge against
his father ; and it would appear that there was now in
his mad brain some hope that his revelation of Bothwell's
purpose, would help him towards his marriage to the
Queen.[3]

Though no credit could be given to Arran's wild talk, it
was determined to confine him, mainly, apparently, to hold
the Hamiltons in check. As Randolph puts it, Mary must
have " ofte wysshed in her harte for no worce occasion
than nowe she hathe, to do with hym as she dothe." [4]

As for the poor old Duke, no one was much in dread

---

[1] *Scottish Papers*, i. 614.   [2] *Ibid.*   [3] *Ibid.*, 615.   [4] *Ibid.*, 620.

of him personally ; and all that was demanded of him was
the deliverance to the Queen of Dumbarton Castle.   On
May 14th Arran, Bothwell, and Gavin Hamilton, commendator of Kilwinning, were brought from St. Andrews
to Edinburgh Castle, Arran riding in the Queen's carriage
on account of his frenzy.[1]   Bothwell, a few months afterwards, made his escape and lived to take part in more
stirring events ; but Arran's public career was at an end,
and, though he survived Mary by over twenty years, he
never permanently recovered his wits.   The Duke, who,
when brought before the Queen at St. Andrews, had
lamented his own and his son's hard case, with " teares
tritlinge from his cheekes," as if he had been a beaten
child,[2] had now not only lost his game, but lost it in a
manner pitiable almost beyond words ; and in a few years
his disappointment was to be rendered still more bitter
by Mary's marriage to the son of Lennox.

As for Mary, we have the testimony of Randolph that,
from the time of her arrival in Scotland, she had been
conducting herself towards the Hamiltons with the utmost
forbearance, knowing " how many they are and how
allied " ;[3] and it must have been an inexpressible relief
to her to be delivered from further overtures of marriage
from Arran, all the more that it was supposed that he
was the suitor Elizabeth intended to press upon her in
connection with the treaty negotiations.

Next to the Hamiltons, the Scottish family which was
the cause of most perplexity to Mary was the Gordons.
While the Hamiltons were embarrassing on account of their
Protestant pretences, the Gordons were so by reason of

---

[1] *Diurnal of Occurents*, p. 72.   [2] *Scottish Papers*, i. 619.

[3] *Ibid.*, 617.

their endeavours to force her hand in regard to Catholicism; and both had ulterior ends to serve which were incompatible with Mary's purposes. Whatever, also, her final aim, she was determined to effect it in her own way and allow her hand to be forced by no one.

In December, 1561, the Cardinal of Lorraine told the Cardinal Commendone that his niece had written to the Pope a letter in which she made "him professions of the greatest readiness rather to die than swerve from obedience to his Holiness, and the Apostolic see";[1] but she was clearly becoming more and more desirous to allay the anxieties of the Protestants as to her ultimate intentions, while, also, she doubtless wished to do nothing that might awaken suspicion in Elizabeth, as to the sincerity of her professions of friendship. In these circumstances, the resolution of the Pope to send to her de Gouda on a Special Mission must have been particularly embarrassing to her. The mission was accidentally delayed, so that de Gouda did not arrive in Scotland until the arrangements for Mary's interview with Elizabeth were nearing completion; and though he landed at Leith on June 18th, he did not obtain an audience until July 25th, after she learned that Elizabeth had postponed the interview.

During all this while, de Gouda had been in close hiding: the rumour that a Papal nuncio was in Scotland had aroused a great storm of indignation amongst the Protestants, and Randolph was exercised as to whether he could remain in Scotland, should Mary receive him. The interview, to which Maitland was privy, took place while her brother Mar and others were at the sermon; but the conference lasted so long that Mar almost caught

[1] *Papal Negotiations*, p. 87.

them together, and Randolph came to know that it had
taken place.   Maitland, in excusing it, told him that since
the envoy desired to speak with her, she could hardly
do less than see him ; but he assured him he would " return
in vain," and that the present political situation would
be in no way disturbed.[1]

In making such a declaration, he was fully justified by
the general tenor of Mary's conversation with de Gouda.
While assuring him, as she had assured the Pope, that
she " would rather die at once than abandon her faith,"
she let him know that the times were altogether in-
opportune for any movement on behalf of the restoration
of Catholicism.   When he exhorted her to follow the
example of Mary of England, she plainly told him that
the position, and that of the kingdom and nobility, of the
English Queen were very different from hers, while to
the request that she should send a deputation of bishops to
the Council of Trent, she replied that she would consult
with the nobles as to how it was to be done, but " under
present circumstances with little hope of success."   Even as
to the future, she was notably reticent, virtually declining
to give him any of her confidence : when he spoke of a
college for training ecclesiastics, " she replied," he says,
" in one word, that this might come in due time, but was
impracticable just then, and so dismissed us."[2]

Even had Mary not been desirous to await the further
development of events, one great difficulty in committing herself to a Catholic rising was that she could
put no faith in Huntly, of whom Randolph wrote on
February 6th, 1560-61, that if his craft "were not so
well known that no man wyll truste hym ether in worde

---

[1] *Papal Negotiations*, 143.   [2] *Ibid.*, pp. 112-61.

or deade, he were hable for his good mynde to God
and his countrie to do myche myschef." [1] How keenly
he and the Gordons felt the rejection by Mary of their
offer to take her under their protection, we may infer
from the story of his wife's consultation with her
"familiars"—*i.e.* her witches—as to whether Mary would
reach Scotland in safety. We must believe that these
oracles gave her an answer as satisfactory to her as,
when he heard the story, it was to Randolph—" that the
Queene shall never set her foote in Scottyshe ground." [2]
But when Mary did, nevertheless, arrive, Huntly hastened
by post-horses to Edinburgh, only to find himself superseded, as her chief confidant, by her brother. At the
beginning, his presence in Edinburgh was of some service
to her in securing the maintenance of her Mass ; but
the excess of his Catholic zeal was, meanwhile, almost as
embarrassing to her as the efforts of those who desired
to deprive her of the exercise of her religion.

Notwithstanding that Châtelherault—this was after the
Arran incident—and Huntly expressed themselves in favour
of Mary's interview with Elizabeth, it was supposed that
they would seek to excuse themselves from accompanying
her into England, the one on account of a diseased arm
and the other on account of a sore leg ; but the postponement of the interview by Elizabeth delivered them from
their dilemma.

Having been disappointed of her journey to England,
Mary now determined to undertake a progress in the
north, going as far as Inverness. In Aberdeen there
had been an expectation that she would visit that city
earlier ; but the journey had been delayed, it may be,

[1] *Scottish Papers*, i. 513.   [2] *Ibid.*, 543.

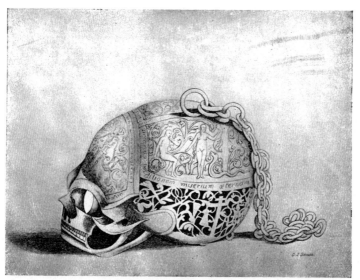

A MÉMENTO MORI WATCH.
Presented by Mary Queen of Scots to Mary Seton.

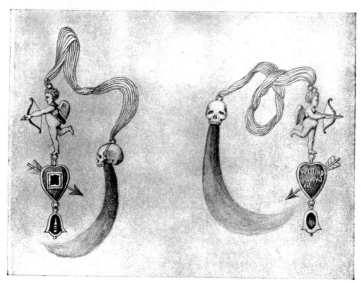

ENAMELLED JEWEL.
Presented by Mary Queen of Scots to George Gordon, fourth Earl of Huntly.

on account of her unsatisfactory relations with Huntly, who, as early as January, had fallen into discredit ; and the visit now undertaken, was probably intended to be of a different kind from that which she had previously contemplated. Most likely before she set out, her purpose was to take measures to curb the influence of Huntly in the north. For this there were various reasons : (1) It would tend to allay the restiveness of the extreme Protestants, who at their assembly in June had framed a special petition to her against the Mass and toleration of the Catholics ; (2) the visit of de Gouda suggested the necessity of taking every precaution against a premature Catholic rising, for Mary, while she knew that de Gouda was doing what he could to stir the Catholics into action, was doubtless unaware that from the elusive Huntly he had failed to obtain so firm an answer as he expected ;[1] (3) it was advisable, in view of her future intentions, to do everything she could to gratify her brother, and she now purposed to put him in the possession of the earldom of Moray, whether Huntly said nay or not ; (4) it was politic to produce on Elizabeth the impression that she was not supremely devoted to the interests of Catholicism ; and (5) there was the quarrel with Huntly's son, Sir John Gordon, the exact character of which has hitherto been misunderstood.

On June 27th, Sir John Gordon had been sent to the Tolbooth for a savage attack on Lord Ogilvie of Airlie, whom he had severely wounded in the arm ; but, a few days afterwards, he made his escape. This Sir John, the third, and the second surviving, son of Huntly, had already a remarkable record. The ground of his quarrel

[1] *Papal Negotiations*, p. 154.

with Lord Ogilvie was an action by Ogilvie in regard to certain lands, which Ogilvie of Findlater had bequeathed to Gordon, instead of to his son James Ogilvie of Cardell. According to Randolph, the son had been disinherited for two astounding reasons : (1) soliciting his father's wife, who was his stepmother, to " dishonesty " with him and other men, and (2) conspiring to lock up his father in a dark room and keep him awake until he became mad. Furthermore, it was the strange stepmother who persuaded Findlater to disinherit his unfilial son in favour of Sir John Gordon, who, after Findlater's death, either married the widow or made her his mistress.[1] In an order of the Privy Council she is referred to as " the pretended spouse " of Sir John Gordon[2] ; and at any rate, having, according to Randolph, cast " hys fantasie unto another," he, because she would not give the lands to him, "locked her up in a close chamber."

It is possible that the so-called marriage was invalid, and that Huntly was now scheming for a marriage between his son and the Queen. Gordon of Gordonstown, in his *Earldom of Sutherland,* even affirms that Mary was in love with him, and this writer may have been so informed by his mother, Lady Jean Gordon, whom Bothwell divorced in order to marry Mary ; but Sir John must have been unduly confident on this point. In any case, it was charged against Sir John that from the very first he intended, if he could, to capture Mary on her arrival in Aberdeen ; and Mary herself told Randolph that among the shameful and detestable practices Huntly intended to use against her, was to have married her "wher he wolde."[3]

---

[1] *Scottish Papers*, i. 656.   [2] *Reg. P. C.*, i. 218.
[3] *Scottish Papers*, i. 665.

But it is also clear that among other intentions of Mary, before she set out for the north, was to deprive Sir John of his lands of Findlater ; for she had in her train James Ogilvie of Cardell, who was the Master of her Household, and has left in French a journal in which he noted where the Queen dined and slept each day.[1] The significance of the presence of Ogilvie with the Queen has hitherto been overlooked, Chalmers, who mentions the circumstance, failing to recognise that Gordon and Ogilvie were at deadly feud.

Mary began her journey to the north on August 11th, and on the 13th reached Stirling, where, on the 14 and 15th, meetings of the Privy Council were held to consider the question of the interview. Before leaving Stirling she had a conference with Mar, Maitland, and Randolph in regard to a proposal of Elizabeth to send help to the Prince of Condé, while the irrepressible Knox also made his appearance to present to her, in support of the proposal, a supplication in the name of the Church.

On the 18th she left Stirling for Perth. On account of the Letters Patent for Mary's interview with Elizabeth being dated at Perth, August 24th, and a letter of Mary, to the magistrates of Edinburgh being dated at Coupar Angus, on August 21st, while a meeting of the Privy Council was held at Edzell on the 25th, Dr. Hay Fleming [2] makes her proceed by Coupar Angus to Perth, while, in fact, Coupar Angus lies between Perth and Edzell, which, besides, would be more than a day's journey from Perth. The cause of the discrepancy is a mistake in the Perth date, probably due to the copyist who wrote the MS.

[1] It was at one time in the possession of George Chalmers, and a translation of it is included in his MSS. collection in the University of Edinburgh.

[2] *Mary Queen of Scots*, p. 74.

in the Cottonian Library. According to the journal o
Ogilvie, Mary left Perth on the 21st.

Proceeding by Glammis, where she was on the 26th,
Mary reached Old Aberdeen on the 27th. Here, according
to Knox, Huntly and his lady, "with no small tryne, re-
maned in court, was supposed to have the greatest credyte,
departed with the Quene to Buchquhane, met hir again at
Rothymay, looking that sche should have passed with him
to Strathbogye"; but since Sir John Gordon broke his
promise to enter into ward in Aberdeen, she avoided
Strathbogie and "passed through Strathyla to Innerness."[1]

Sir John having, on August 31st, appeared before a court
of justiciary in the Tolbooth of Aberdeen, he was, by the
Queen's direction, ordered, on September 1st, to enter
himself in ward in the Castle of Stirling.[2] The Queen left
Aberdeen on the same day in the expectation that Sir John
would obey; but learning that he had no intention of doing
so, she declined, says Randolph, in a letter of September
18th, to come to Huntly's house, "though looked and
provided for."[3] Argyll and Randolph, at Huntly's request
and by leave of the Queen, stayed at Huntly's house for
two nights, where they found his "cheere" to be "mervilous
great, his mynde then suche, as yt appered to us, as ought
to be in anye subjecte to his sovereigne."[4] But Randolph
learned later that his "mynde" was mere pretence; and
had the Queen gone to Strathbogie, it was his intention
either to have got her into his hands or to have cut off
Moray and Lethington.

On Mary reaching Darnaway, an order, on September
10th, was issued against Sir John, for not only neglecting

[1] *Works*, ii. 353.   [2] *Reg. P. C.*, i. 218-19.
[3] *Scottish Papers*, i. 651.   [4] *Ibid.*, 652.

From an old print.

OLD ABERDEEN.

to enter himself in ward, but for assembling his followers in order " to brek the hale cuntre sa fer as is in his power." [1] Here also it was announced that the Queen had created Mar, Earl of Moray, and had given him a grant of the earldom in place of that of Mar claimed by the Erskines.

On reaching Inverness—which she did, not on the 9th, as Randolph states, but on the 11th—she purposed to lodge in the castle, but was refused entrance by the keeper, Alexander Gordon, deputy of Huntly's son, Lord Gordon. The castle was a royal building of which Huntly had charge as Sheriff of Inverness ; and for the keeper to refuse the Queen entrance to it, until he had authority from Huntly, was the very insolence of treason. On learning that the country people were assembling to the Queen's assistance, the Gordons sent word to him to surrender it, which he did ; but, for his previous contumacy, he was hanged over the battlements.

After remaining in quiet at Inverness for five days, the Queen, convoyed by great numbers of horse and foot, proceeded to Spyine, a seat of Patrick Hepburn, Catholic Bishop of Moray. The Bishop may or may not have been a confederate of Huntly, whom he had formerly joined in inviting the Queen to Scotland ; but, enemy though he must have been to the Queen's brother, he had no option but to hide his discontent at his triumph. Huntly was himself keeping at home ; but Sir John Gordon was insolently hovering on the skirts of the Queen with a large band of followers, and it was supposed that he would make his attack at the passage of the Spey.

Meanwhile, her free and open-air life, with its spice of adventure, exactly accorded with Mary's temperament,

[1] *Reg. P. C.*, i. 219.

and the change it had wrought in her bearing quite surprised Randolph. " In all these garbullies," he wrote to Cecil, " I assure your honour I never sawe her merrier, never disamayde, nor never thought that stomache to be in her that I fynde ! She repented nothynge but, when the lardes and other at Ennernes came in the mornynges from the wache, that she was not a man to knowe what lyf yt was to lye all nyghte in the feeldes, or to walke upon the cawsaye with a jacke and knapschall, a Glascowe buckeler and a broode swerde." [1]

The Queen's scouts brought word that the Gordons had a thousand men concealed in the woods near the Spey ; but two miles before she reached it, intelligence arrived that they had disappeared. As she passed Findlater, "standing hard on the sea," she summoned it to surrender ; but this being refused, and its capture being impossible without cannon, she passed on, and arrived at Old Aberdeen, "cleane owte of danger," on September 22nd.

Next day she made her deferred entry into the New Town of Aberdeen, where, according to Randolph, she was received with many tokens of welcome, " as well in spectacles, plays, enterludes and other as theie culde beste devise." [2] It was her original purpose to have remained some time in Aberdeen, in order to put the country in quietness; and she now resolved, after consulting how to reform the country, to begin at the " head," and unless Huntly delivered up his son, to use all force against him " for the subverting of his house for ever." For this purpose she levied a hundred and twenty harquebussiers, and sent to the south for such experienced soldiers as Lord Lindsay, Kirkcaldy of Grange, and Cockburn of Ormiston, while

[1] *Scottish Papers*, i. 651.   [2] *Ibid.*, 653.

cannon were also procured to take by storm Findlater
and other houses held against her.

Huntly, meanwhile, sent his son, Lord Gordon, to the
south to consult Gordon's father-in-law, Châtelherault ;
and meanwhile he resolved to temporise. He was ready
to appear with an armed force for Mary's assistance against
his son ; but unless accompanied by an armed force, he
preferred retirement. In dread of capture, he neither slept
in his own house nor more than one night in one place.
This becoming known to Mary's generals, and that it
was his custom to occupy his house during the day,
Kirkcaldy, with the Tutor of Pitcur and twelve attendants,
started from Aberdeen so as to reach Strathbogie at
twelve o'clock, when the Earl would be in the house for
his dinner.

It was calculated that the small company would not alarm
the Earl, Kirkcaldy's intention being to seize the entrance
to the house, until the arrival of a larger force under
Lord John and others ; but the more advanced portion
of this force had spurred on rather quickly, and appearing
on the horizon, about a mile distant, as Kirkcaldy was
in parley with the porter, attracted the attention of the
watchman on the tower, who immediately raised the
alarm. The Tutor of Pitcur had ridden round to
the back ; but Huntly, without boot or sword, got over
a low wall where his horse was in waiting, and on his
fresh and swift mount soon outdistanced all pursuit.

On the return of his pursuers from their fruitless chase,
his lady set open to them the gates and doors of the
castle, but could make them but sorry cheer. They
found that everything had been removed from it save
a few beds of the worst sort ; but the chapel remained

"garnished," and on being asked why she had not de-furnished it also, the Countess replied that she was sure the Queen would not be offended with that. She had already shown the chapel—"fayer and trymlye hanged, all ornaments and masse robes reddie lyenge upon the autour, with crosse and candels stondinge upon yt"[1]—to a former envoy of the Queen; her expectation being that the Queen would use it on her visit to Strathbogie.

Since Huntly had thus shown his heels to the royal deputies, no other course was open than to regard him and his son as confederates; and at a meeting of the Council on October 15th it was decided that unless on the following day he appeared to answer to the things laid to his charge, he should be put to the horn.[2] This decisive step had become absolutely necessary, for, two nights before, Sir John Gordon, with some 150 men, had surrounded a captain and some soldiers lying in a village near Findlater and taken fifty-six harquebuses from his men.

Shortly before this, Huntly had sent a boy, professedly with two keys, one of the house of Findlater and the other of that of Auchendown, and the intimation that they were left void; but the keys were rejected, the Queen's answer being that "she had provided other means to open those doors."[3]

Strathbogie, being demanded, was now refused; but though the key of it had not been sent, it also was "voyde," Huntly having retired to his Highland fastness in the wilds of Badenoch. Had he continued his elusive policy, he might have baffled his enemies for a long time. Meanwhile the Countess, on the 20th, came within two

---

[1] *Scottish Papers*, i. 655.   [2] *Reg. P. C.*, i. 219.
[3] *Scottish Papers*, i. 658.

miles of Aberdeen, desiring speech of the Queen, who declined to receive her. Thereupon she seems to have persuaded her husband to take action, for, immediately on her return to Strathbogie, he began to assemble his followers, with whom he marched to Aberdeen "with purpose," according to Randolph, "to apprehend the Queen and to do with the rest at his will."

Though contemporary authorities differ as to the number of Huntly's men, some putting it as low as 700 and others as high as 1,200, there is a general agreement that his only hope of victory was in the treachery of the Queen's followers. There is also general agreement that many of his followers deserted him during the night. According to Knox, when Huntly saw that there was no hope from treachery he resolved to retire ; but from fatigue, for he was corpulent and in indifferent health, he did not rise until ten o'clock, and he was then too unwell and too puzzled to adopt a decisive resolution. His position, on the Hill of Fare, which rises to a height of over 1,500 feet, was well adapted for enabling him to strike a crushing blow on his opponents, should the treachery he hoped for occur; but, as it turned out, the extent of marshy ground at the foot of the hill caused him to be virtually caught in a trap.

Huntly's men, writes Randolph, "had encamped on the top of a hill, where horse could hardly come to them, and were driven by shot of harquebus into a low mossy ground, where the horse dealt with them a good space, at length forcing them into a corner, where by reason of the hill and marsh ground, they could not escape. There were they set upon, and at the shock, the vanguard (either for faintness of heart, or other thing

suspected) gave back, many casting away their spears ready
to run.   The Earl of Moray and his company being
behind them, seeing the danger, came so fiercely on, that
he caused them to turn again, and so stoutly set on the
enemy that incontinent they gave place, and 120 and
more were taken, and eleven score or thereabout slain.
Huntly's whole company was not above 500, some say
he fought before he was taken—others the contrary." [1]

Immediately on being set on horseback before his
captor, Huntly dropped down dead—a strangely dramatic
ending to a career remarkable for nothing but its constant
inconsistencies, created by the impossibility of reconciling
sometimes his patriotic prejudices, but oftener his worldly
interests, with his religious or superstitious convictions.
Two of his sons, the bold Sir John, and Adam, a youth
of seventeen, were captured uninjured, but Lord Gordon
was still absent in the south.

The body of the Earl, after being disembowelled in
Aberdeen, was sent south to Edinburgh in a ship, which
also carried the more precious articles of furniture from
Strathbogie Castle, the Queen designing to appropriate them
to her own use.[2]   The body was kept until the meeting
of Parliament in the following year, when, in accordance
with the brutal usage of the time, it was brought to the
bar in order that an act of forfeiture and attainder might
be passed against him, declaring his "dignity, name,
honour and memory" to be extinct ;   and his posterity
"unable to enjoy any office, honour, or rank within the
realm." [3]   Sir John—after a confession which exists only

[1] *Scottish Papers*, i. 665.
[2] For list, see *Inventaires de la Royne Descosse* (Bannatyne Club).
[3] Crawford, *Officers of State*, pp. 87-8.

in contemporary gossip—was, on November 2nd, executed
in presence of the Queen, who attended in order to silence
doubts as to her consent to Moray's proceedings, but was
necessarily quite overcome by the trying ordeal.   The
younger brother Adam was pardoned, and lived to become
the hero of the old ballad "Edom o' Gordon," and to
fight for the Queen after her escape from Lochleven.
Lord Gordon, who, on February 8th, was sentenced to
be executed, drawn and quartered at "our soverain's plesor,"
she also spared ; and being delivered from prison after
her marriage to Darnley, he was, in conjunction with Bothwell,
to be fatefully connected with her later misfortunes.

Mary left Aberdeen on November 5th, travelling by
Dunottar, Craig, Bonytown, Kincardine, Arbroath, Dundee,
Perth, Tullibardine, Drummond, Stirling and Linlithgow
to Edinburgh, where she arrived on the 21st.[1]   Shortly
afterwards she had a somewhat mild attack of influenza,
at this time very prevalent in Edinburgh.   It was then
regarded as a new disease, and therefore pleasantly entitled
the New Acquaintance.   Moray and Maitland suffered
from it at the same time as Mary.

By Catholics abroad, the proceedings against Huntly
were mostly regarded as symptomatic of Mary's helplessness.
De Gouda, who had left Scotland on September 3rd, attributed Huntly's overthrow simply to the "heretical bastard-
brother of the Queen " ;[2] but de Quadra, the Spanish
ambassador in London, learned that Huntly had determined
to "sieze the Queen of Scots and turn out Lord James
and other heritics that govern,"[3] which was undoubtedly
Huntly's final aim.   Mary's account of her dealings with

[1] Chalmers's MS. Collections in the University of Edinburgh.
[2] *Papal Negotiations*, p. 156.   [3] *Spanish State Papers*, 1558-67, p. 270.

Huntly, sent to her uncle, the Cardinal of Lorraine, un-happily perished in 1865 in a fire at a London book-binder's, whither it had been sent by the British Museum authorities ; but from a letter of the Cardinal to the Emperor, it is clear that she blamed no one but Huntly and his son for their calamity.

"When the practice was discovered," wrote the Cardinal, " she took such good order to raise men at once, that she had enough to offer battle, in which, thanks be to God, the victory remained with her, and she has had such punishment inflicted on the vanquished, that she now finds herself at peace as she was before." [1]   Father Pollen assumes that Mary, in asking the Cardinal, in a letter of January 30th, 1562-3, to make her excuses to the Pope if she had failed in any part of her duty towards religion, meant this to be understood as " a confession of fault " in connection with the Huntly incident ; [2] but since she had thanked God for Huntly's defeat, it is difficult to see how she could charge herself with any fault in the matter.

Mary's letters to the Pope and the Cardinal, in which she now expressed a determination to establish Catholicism in Scotland at the peril of her life, [3] indicate the beginning of a new phase in her policy. It was not merely that she found it needful to disavow all sympathy with Elizabeth's action on behalf of the French Protestants, or that she was deeply hurt, as she must have been, at Elizabeth's conduct towards her uncles, but that she now discerned that Elizabeth was mainly intent on humbugging her.

The general drift of the evidence—including the statements and attitude of the Guises—is toward the conclusion that for some time Mary was really sanguine

[1] *Papal Negotiations*, pp. 163-4. [2] *Ibid.*, p. lviii. [3] Labanoff, i. 175-180.

of coming to a satisfactory understanding with Elizabeth. There was of course the primary difficulty in regard to religion, but it is by no means certain that either Elizabeth or Mary made much account of this. In her interview with the Papal nuncio, Mary had dwelt mainly on the difficulties of her position, and was very indefinite as to what she could accomplish on behalf of Catholicism ; but she now saw that she might require to put her main trust in the Pope and Catholicism, in order to secure the recognition of her English rights.

Curiously enough, hardly had Mary dealt what seemed almost a death-blow to Catholicism in the north of Scotland, than she learned that Elizabeth had committed herself to a crusade against Catholicism in France, as represented by Mary's uncles. On the day after Huntly's defeat and death, Randolph entered her supper-chamber and handed her Elizabeth's letter announcing the fact. He could make nothing of her countenance as she read it ; but the resumption of her "mirthe," after reading it, must have been due to deep mortification and the desire to conceal it. Nor could the expression of the hope that next year she would journey as far south as she had done north, have been intended as other than an attempt to lead Randolph astray. But when she had time to collect her thoughts, she called him into her chamber and frankly told him that she thought Elizabeth was meddling in a matter that was no concern of Elizabeth's, though she was not disposed to make her action a ground of quarrel with her.[1] A day or two afterwards, on learning that Elizabeth, who had been ill, had recovered from an attack of small-pox, she expressed her

[1] *Scottish Papers,* i. 663.

pleasure at the news that " her beautiful face will lose none of its perfections." [1]

But if Mary was not yet disenchanted of all hope of any advantage from Elizabeth's goodwill, it had now become imperative, by reason of Elizabeth's action against the Guises, that she should receive from her some more decided token of friendship than empty promises. By her cordial relations with Elizabeth, she was now, as Maitland represented to Cecil, in danger of losing both the friendship of her uncles and her French dowry, while to " countervail these dangers " she had at present only Elizabeth's love, which was " but inclosed in her owne harte *et non transgreditur personam.*" [2] The force of this reasoning was also brought home to Mary in a vivid manner by the rumoured deliberations of the Council, when Elizabeth, during her late illness, lay apparently at the point of death. Had she died, there would, most likely, have been hopeless confusion as to who should succeed her ; and it may be that the knowledge of her Council's dilemma gave to Elizabeth as much satisfaction as to Mary it gave uneasiness.

Maitland learned—he put it as mildly as possible— that the Council had intended to prefer another to his mistress ; Villemort affirmed that he was told by a clerk of the Council that only one of the Council favoured her claims ; and de Quadra reported to Philip of Spain that out of fifteen or sixteen of the Council there were as many opinions, and that while the Catholics were divided between the Queen of Scots and Lady Margaret Lennox, the favourite of the two was Lady Lennox, who was considered " devout and sensible," which, it would seem, the Catholics had begun to doubt whether Mary was.[3]

[1] *Scottish Papers,* i. 666.   [2] *Ibid.,* 667.   [3] *Spanish State Papers,* 1558-97, p. 263.

Still, whatever her real sentiments, Mary had to keep up, for a time, the old pretences. "Of thys nation," wrote Randolph on December 3rd, "onlye thys maye be sayde, that the quene her selfe, how well somever she favour her uncles, that yet she lovethe better her own subjectes ; she knowethe the necessitie of my sovereigne's frendshipe to be greater than a preste bablinge at an autour ; she is not so affectioned to her masse that she wyll leave a kyngdome for yt." [1]

That Elizabeth was acting deceitfully and had never really had any other intention than to mislead Mary, is hardly open to question ; but Mary's deceitfulness cannot so certainly be determined, for the reason that she was ever compelled to counter the deceit of Elizabeth ; and she was also accessible to influences—friendship, gratitude, trust in the goodwill of others—by which Elizabeth was almost incapable of being affected.

Knox, it is true, did not agree with Randolph's rather roseate view of Mary's intentions. Of "these matters," we are told by Randolph, they often communed together, but they differed a good deal in judgment : Knox, wrote Randolph, "hath no hope (to use hys own termes) that she wyll ever come to God or do good in the common welthe ; he is so full of mystruste in all her doynges, wordes, and sayenges, as thoughe he were ether of Godes previe consell, that knewe howe he had determined of her from the begynnynge, or that he knewe the secretes of her harte so well, that neither she dyd or culde have for ever on good thought of God or of his trew religion." [2]

But what chiefly exercised Knox was, that whether

---

[1] *Illustrations of the Reign of Mary*, p. 109.
[2] *Scottish Papers*, i. 672-3.

Mary accepted the Protestantism of Elizabeth or not, she would never sit at his prophetic feet, or rather, would not sit under them. Moray must have known this, and Maitland, Morton, and others were already in semi-revolt against the arrogant pretensions of the Protestant ecclesiastics, and would have welcomed the national acceptance of the modified and unobtrusive Protestantism that prevailed in England. But mere dread of Elizabethan Protestantism, was with Knox a sufficient reason for exerting himself to the utmost as marplot in the negotiations between the two sovereigns.

At this time, also, Knox was sorely exercised by Mary's manifest sympathy with the Guises.   On the Sunday before Randolph wrote of his communings with him, Knox had been inveighing " sore agaynste the Quenes dansynge and lyttle exercise of her self in vertue or godliness." [1]   Mary, therefore, called him before her, and, as Randolph said, wished him to speak his conscience, as he would answer before God, as she would also in her doings.   Knox asserts that the occasion of her dancing " excessively till after midnight " was news received by her that persecution had begun in France.[2]   But here his memory played him false ; the rejoicing of Mary took place, as we learn from Randolph, not in the spring but in December, the cause being seemingly the fall of Rouen.

Since Knox's memory was at fault as to the occasion of the dancing, not much faith can be placed in his recollection of their conversation ; but it would appear that he denied having railed generally against dancing, or against the Queen's little exercise of herself in virtue or godliness : what he objected to was that she made more account of

---

[1] *Scottish Papers*, i. 673.   [2] *Works*, ii. 330.

dancers and fiddlers than of Knox, and that she danced, as the Philistines did, for the pleasure she took "in the displesour of Goddes people." Curiously enough this explanation appeared to satisfy Mary: on learning that he had been less employed in maligning her generally than in giving vent to his ill-humour at the Guisian victory, she was inclined to make allowance for him. His words, she said, were sharp enough as he had now spoken them, but they were not such as had been reported to her. She was quite aware that he and her uncles were not of the same religion ; but if he heard anything of herself that "misliked" him, she hoped he would come and tell her of it, and she would listen to him.

This attempt to disarm him rather took Knox aback : what he desired was the privilege of rebuking his sovereign's delinquencies, not in private but in public. With naïve presumption he therefore proposed that Mary should either "frequent the publict sermon," so as to listen in public to what he had to say against her, or, at least, afford him an opportunity of fully expounding to her the "form and substance " of the reformed doctrine : otherwise, rather weakly and rudely added he, he declined to be taken away from his book "to wait upon her chalmer-doore." Mary, thereupon, pleasantly reminded him that he would not be always at his book ; and, though he affirms that she there and then turned her back upon him, we must believe that he had no answer ready to her very pertinent remark. At the same time, Knox was correct in supposing that his private colloquys with her would be of no advantage to him, for the fact was that she was now meditating as to the possibility of a new course of action, not merely towards him but towards Elizabeth.

CHAPTER VI

MATRIMONIAL INTRIGUES

IN February, 1563, it was resolved to send Maitland on a Special Mission to England, nominally with a view to offer the mediation of Mary in order to bring about peace with France.[1] But besides his instructions in regard to this, he was provided also with other instructions to be used if the cause—entirely another cause than peace with France—"sa requiris, and at his discretioun."

These last instructions were to the effect that should any discussion arise in the English Parliament as to the succession to the crown, he was to desire Elizabeth to see that nothing was done prejudicial to Mary's title ; further, he was, if necessary, to appear before Parliament and declare its validity, and should this be denied, he was solemnly to protest that she was "injurit and offencit," and would seek for such remedies as were provided "for thame that ar enormlie and accessivelie hurt."[2] Though the discussion in Parliament was unfavourable to Mary's claims, no definite decision was arrived at, and apparently Maitland deemed uncertainty better than a distinctly hostile decision ; but the unsatisfactory attitude of the Parliament and Elizabeth now determined him towards a method of action, about which he had, of course, no intention of taking

[1] Instructions in Keith, ii. 188-91 ; and Labanoff, i. 162-4.
[2] Keith, ii. 191-2 ; Labanoff, i. 167-9.

After a painting by Sir Antonio More.

DON CARLOS,
Son of Philip II. of Spain.

Elizabeth into his confidence. But before we follow him in his remarkable secret mission, it is necessary to take notice of an unpleasant experience of Mary, which was rolled as a sweet morsel under the tongue of the gossips both at home and abroad.

Amongst those who accompanied Mary to Scotland in the suite of Damville, son of the Constable of France, was the poet Châtelard. He was of good family, being descended by the mother's side from the Chevalier Bayard ; but it was to his poetical and musical accomplishments, he was indebted both for his own good opinion of himself and the consideration shown him by his patrons. Like other poets at the French court, he was, poetically, a fervent adorer of the young Queen of Scots ; and after the inflated fashion of the time he celebrated her in verses, which she acknowledged by some kind of poetic compliments.

Châtelard had returned to France with his patron ; but on Mary's southward journey from Aberdeen he presented himself at her supper-table near Montrose and handed her a letter from his master, which the watchful Randolph noticed that she read with great contentment, though he was afterwards informed by Maitland that it did not in any way concern Elizabeth.[1]

On his way through London, Châtelard is stated to have told a friend that he was going to visit his lady love ;[2] but this does not help us much to understand the final *dénouement*. In any case, he was most cordially received by Mary, who gave him the use of a sorrel gelding which had been presented to her by Lord Robert ; was stated— though it may be falsely—to have supplied him with

---

[1] *Scottish Papers*, i. 669
[2] *Spanish State Papers*, 1558-67, p. 314.

pocket money to enable him to dress as a French *galant* of the time loved to be dressed ; and manifested a friendly enjoyment of his society and conversation.

After the occurrence of the scandal, Randolph wrote that Mary had shown " over-great familiarity " to " so unworthy a creature and abject a varlet "—a familiarity " too much to have been used to his master himself by any Princess alive " ; but Randolph was seemingly unaware of the consequence accorded to poets at the French court. Mary was, moreover, a special enthusiast about poetry. She probably petted Châtelard, somewhat after the fashion that musicians are accustomed to be petted by ladies now, and treated him, most likely, with a friendly familiarity that would have been out of place, had the social distance that separated them not been, in her eyes, a barrier to any misunderstanding of its meaning. Had she been in the habit of violating the proprieties, the insinuations against her in the case of Châtelard might have a certain plausibility ; but the Châtelard incident stands alone, if it even can be said properly to stand. Indeed it stands chiefly in the highly coloured narrative of Knox, which is in his most offensive vein.

Being prejudiced up to the eyes against Mary, as a persistent practiser of " idolatry " and open contemner of his ecclesiastical pretensions, he treated her with the same contumely as the religious disputants of those times were accustomed to treat each other. Prepared to lend a greedy ear to any story against her, he apparently, in this instance, allowed unauthenticated gossip quickly to crystallise into what he deemed solid fact, which he then dressed up in the rhetorical fashion of which he was a master. Even Froude puts aside, in this instance, the prejudiced rhetoric of Knox, and does not think that Mary had anything "worse to accuse herself of than thoughtlessness."[1]

The mere fact that an enamoured and vain poet chooses to suppose that a sovereign lady, who has treated him with condescending kindness, is in love with him, is evidence of nothing except the extent of his own enamourment and vanity ; and the conduct of " the little Frenchman," as Maitland terms him, betrays such a mixture of idiocy and baseness as puts him beyond serious consideration, as a witness in regard to Mary's conduct.

But by whatever motive Châtelard was inspired, he, on the night on which Maitland set out for England, found an apparently providential opportunity of putting his design into execution. While Mary was engaged until past midnight in earnest political conference with her brother and Maitland, this love-sick poet, or Huguenot dastard, slipped quietly into her chamber and hid himself below her bed. In this ridiculous position he was discovered by two grooms, who had the good sense quietly to remove him and refrain from mentioning the incident to the Queen until the morning, when, on learning of his adventure, she ordered him to leave the court.

This lenient treatment encouraged Châtelard to follow her on her journey towards St. Andrews, and on the evening of February 14th he presented himself before her at Burntisland, when only one or two of her gentlewomen were with her. Randolph's first version of the incident was that while two of the Queen's gentlewomen were present, Châtelard set on her in so impudent a fashion that Mary was forced to cry for help, and that on her brother Moray appearing, the Queen commanded

[1] *History*, cab. ed., vii. 48.

him to put his dagger in him, but that Moray, as he was about to obey a natural impulse, reflected that it would be better to reserve him for justice.[1]

Knox, who had got hold of this version of the incident, not only found it impossible to let it go, but embellished it after his picturesquely effective fashion. Moray "fell," says Knox, "upon his knees befoir the Quene and said, ' Madam, I beseak your Grace, cause not me to tack the blood of this man upoun me. Your Grace hes entreated him so familiarlie befoir, that ye have offended all your Nobilitie ; and yf he shalbe secreatlie slane at your awin commandiment what shall the world judge of it ? I shall bring him to the presence of Justice, and let him suffer be law according to his deserving.' ' Oh,' said the Quene, ' ye will never let him speak ? ' ' I shall do,' said he, ' Madam, what in me lyeth to saiff your honour.' " [2]

The suggestion, which Dr. Hay Fleming [3] is not disinclined to accept, that Knox got the story from Moray is (1) unnecessary, for Randolph evidently got it from another source, (2) is in itself hardly credible, for if Moray desired to save his sister's honour, he would not proceed to expose her honour to the hostile Knox, and (3) is impossible, for the story was a mere invention of the gossips.

At a later date, Randolph learned that Châtelard's appearance at Burntisland was his second escapade—his aim being to explain away the awkward circumstances of his former adventure.[4] Though his intention was an aggravation of his original offence, it could not occasion such a dramatic dagger scene as that portrayed by Knox; but it

---

[1] *Scottish Papers*, i. 684.
[2] *Works*, ii. 368.
[3] *Mary Queen of Scots*, p. 314.
[4] *Scottish Papers*, i. 685.

demanded the application of stern measures. He was therefore sent a prisoner to St. Andrews, where, after a trial —the records of which have, however, perished, owing to an unfortunate blank in the court book of justiciary from May 1562 to May 1563—he was executed in the market-place, on market day, February 22nd.

Brantôme, who, of course, was not present, states that before his execution he read for his eternal consolation Ronsard's Hymn to Death, that he sought to fortify himself otherwise neither by aid of a spiritual book, nor minister nor confessor, and that, on concluding his consolatory hymn, he turned in the direction of the Queen's lodging and cried aloud, "Adieu the most beautiful and cruel princess of the world." In a manner Brantôme is corroborated by Knox, who says : "In the end he concluded, looking unto the heavens, with these words, ' O cruelle Dame,' that is, ' cruell maistress.' What that complaint imported, luvaris may devine ";[1] but Knox differs from Brantôme in affirming that Châtelard died penitent ; and in this he is corroborated by Randolph. Knox says that he made a "Godly confession," by which he could only mean a Protestant profession, and we learn also from Brantôme that Châtelard was a Huguenot.[2]

This fact, in itself, gives a colour of likelihood to Mary's statement to Maitland, as reported by Maitland to the Spanish ambassador, that Châtelard had confessed that he had been sent by persons of distinguished position to compromise, if possible, her honour. The name of the lady who had inspired Châtelard was, according to Maitland, Madame de Curosot ; but Mary had affirmed to him that other names also were involved which could not be intrusted

---

[1] *Works*, ii. 369. [2] *Œuvres*, ed. Buchon, ii. 148.

to letters.[1] This also was the name mentioned by Chantonnay to Philip, and Teulet explains it as the cypher name of Châtillon, the lady referred to being the first wife of Admiral Coligny.[2]

Father Pollen, oblivious of the fact that Curosot was the name mentioned not merely by Chantonnay, but by Maitland, accepts the authority of the Papal nuncio for Madame de Cursol;[3] but though this also was the name mentioned by Madame de Guise to the Venetian ambassador,[4] the original source of the information was Maitland; and Madame de Guise, not being able to interpret the cypher name, probably misunderstood the reference.

The unpleasant excitement of the Châtelard incident had hardly subsided before Mary, on March 15th, was shocked by the news that her favourite uncle, the Duke of Guise, had died on February 24th from a pistol shot by the Huguenot boy assassin, Poltrot; and a few weeks later came intelligence that the Grand Prior had succumbed to an attack of cold.

Before learning of this latter bereavement, Mary, deeply moved by her sense of loss in the death of the Duke of Guise, had "renewed" to Randolph all her griefs and adventures since her husband's death, and, as an excuse for her extreme manifestation of sorrow, she remarked that she was practically almost destitute of friends.[5] In her solitary sorrow a sympathetic letter from Elizabeth seems to have really touched her naturally keen susceptibility to kindness: according to Randolph she read it not without tears, and she expressed to him her conviction that it was most needful

---

[1] *Spanish State Papers*, 1558-67, p. 314.   [2] Teulet, *Relations*, v. 3.
[3] *Papal Negotiations*, p. 164.
[4] *Venetian State Papers*, 1558-80, p. 356.   [5] *Scottish Papers*, ii. 2.

From a contemporary engraving.

FRANCIS, DUKE OF GUISE.

for both of them that they should be friends, " and I perceave," she said, " yt to be Godes will yt sholde be so : for
I see nowe that the worlde is not that, that we do mayke
of it, nor yet are theie most happie that contynue longeste
in yt." [1]

Does not this suggest that had Elizabeth been able to
have reciprocated sincerely Mary's offers of friendship, the
reconciliation of their differences was not beyond attainment ?
Should Elizabeth determine not to marry, Mary, if her
succession rights were admitted, might have Elizabeth at a
certain disadvantage ; but she would have almost no reason
for disturbing Elizabeth. But what Elizabeth desired was
to have everything her own way—to avoid any recognition
of Mary as her successor, and at the same time either to
prevent Mary's marriage, or to cause her to marry some
one who would not endanger Elizabeth's sovereignty.

The death of the Duke of Guise, while it removed a
possible occasion of estrangement between Mary and Elizabeth, weakened for the time being Mary's power to induce
Elizabeth to come to terms with her. Maitland told de
Quadra that his mistress had hoped, by delivering Elizabeth
from her embarrassment with France, to effect an agreement
with her. Of the difficulties to be surmounted she was
well aware ; but with the powerful backing of the Duke
of Guise, she hoped in some way to bring Elizabeth to the
adoption of a reasonable compromise. But since she was
now deprived of this important leverage, Maitland resolved
on an alliance with Spain, through Mary's marriage to
Don Carlos.

If we are to believe Maitland's representations to Mary,
the negotiations were really opened not by him but by

[1] *Scottish Papers*, ii. 2.

the Spanish ambassador, de Quadra ;[1] but Maitland knew
of Mary's inclinations towards such a match, and he was
also, as he told de Quadra, proceeding "on the principle
that it was not fitting that the woman should seek a
husband."[2] From de Quadra's letter of March 18th we
gather that it was Maitland himself who suggested the
reopening of the negotiations, though de Quadra admitted
that he had done all he could to entice him on. Maitland
declared that he was certain (1) that Mary would never
marry a Protestant, and (2) that she would "not take
a husband, Catholic or Protestant, from the hands of the
Queen of England, even if by this act alone she could
be declared her successor," because she knew that the
husband offered would be one of Elizabeth's subjects, and
that after she had married beneath her she would have
the same difficulties in regard to the succession as before.

These remarkable statements went to the root of
Mary's political difficulties, and of those of Maitland and
Moray as well. Neither Maitland nor Moray were now,
be it remembered, their own masters : they had either
to humour and manage their sovereign, or face a desperate
political crisis. It is, apparently, from failing to recognise
the tremendous complexities of the situation that Professor
Hume Brown commits himself confidently to the opinion
that Maitland and Moray gave their support to the Spanish
marriage, "assuredly not from a desire that it should ever
take effect, but from the hope that the fear of such a
contingency would force the hand of Queen Elizabeth."[3]

The only direct evidence on which the Professor seeks to

---

[1] Letter of May 9th in Philippson, iii. 459.
[2] *Spanish State Papers*, 1558-67, p. 310.
[3] *History of Scotland*, ii. 96.

base this strong opinion is a letter of April 30th—probably
by Kirkcaldy of Grange—to Randolph, in which occurs
the sentence : " the Quene mother " [Catherine de Medici]
"hathe written to our Quene that Lid. said to her that all that
was spoken of the marriage with Spain, was done to caus
England grant to our designs." [1] The conclusiveness of
this evidence is not apparent ; but since the step taken
by Maitland was a very remarkable one, it may be pointed
out (1) that the story of Kirkcaldy, or whoever the
person was, may have been mere hearsay, (2) that, since
Maitland wished to use Catherine, he might desire also
to bamboozle her, (3) that there is evidence that Catherine,
if told such a tale, did not believe it, for, according to
the Abbate Mina, an intimate friend of the Cardinal of
Lorraine, she never was so scared in her life as by the
resumption of the Spanish negotiations,[2] and (4) that so
far from using the Spanish negotiations as a means to
influence Elizabeth to " grant to our designs," Maitland
carefully concealed them from her.

It might have been argued, with greater plausibility,
that Maitland and Moray were seeking merely to humour
Mary ; that, knowing how bent she was on the match,
they resolved, by prosecuting negotiations which they
believed would be unsuccessful, to disabuse her mind
of the idea that they were bent on preventing their success ;
and that they hoped, once Mary came to recognise the
hopelessness of the negotiations, she would be so far clear
for an understanding with Elizabeth.

It is at least by no means unlikely that Moray, who
had a curious aptitude for bending to the storm and waiting

---

[1] Knox, *Works*, vi. 540; *Scottish Papers*, ii. 61.
[2] *Papal Negotiations*, p. 465.

his time, was influenced by some such motives ; but it must be borne in mind that Maitland and Moray had to solve the double problem of managing Mary and thwarting Elizabeth. If their diplomacy seems now to assume very much the appearance of mere groping and stumbling in the dark, the darkness was created not by them but by the peculiarity of the ecclesiastical problem, and the idiosyncrasies of the two female sovereigns to whom, by a curious freak of fate, the charge of the destinies of Britain were at this time committed.

Moreover the ultimate aim of Maitland, Moray, and the great bulk of the Scottish people, no less than of Mary, was to secure recognition of the Scottish succession; and if it be said that they acted unwisely in pressing for a settlement of this, that really the main thing after all was Protestantism, the answer is that even the bulk of the nominal Scottish Protestants had not the supreme interest in Protestantism that Knox and the clerical leaders had, and that, moreover, it is vain to argue against an overpowering national sentiment.

It would, further, appear that Maitland and Moray had a Protestant scheme of their own : they deemed it possible that under the new arrangement Scotland might be governed, independently, as a Protestant kingdom. Maitland intended, apparently, to stipulate for the preservation in Scotland of something resembling the *statu quo* in religious matters. To Mary he wrote that de Quadra, to remove the scruple about religion, had shown him that his master was not " ane sworne *soldato del papa*," but a wise politic prince who governed the different nations under his rule according to their own humour.[1]

1 Philippson, iii. 462.

This, at any rate, represented Maitland's own attitude towards the religious disputes of the time ; and, though his attitude was plainly not Moray's, nor probably Mary's, the scheme he had in view for Scotland was apparently a Protestant regency under Moray. The Queen of Scots, he might reasonably suppose, would desire to reside rather in Spain than in Scotland ; and since this would imply a sort of Scottish regency under Moray, there were probably to Moray attractions in the scheme, from a worldly, as well as from a Protestant, point of view.

But whatever Maitland's real aims, and however far he and Moray were at one, it is plain that Maitland was doing his utmost to further the Spanish match. When he learned that the Cardinal of Lorraine, without consulting Mary, had taken upon himself to negotiate with the Emperor for the marriage of Mary to the Archduke, he " sent off in furious haste to the Cardinal, begging him not to negotiate the marriage, as the Scottish people would not consent to it and it would cause confusion." [1]

The objections to this match—apart from Mary's high ambition to be the greatest Queen-consort in Europe— were (1) that it was impossible for Mary to marry a Catholic prince who was not prepared to maintain her position in Scotland by force, if necessary, of foreign arms, and (2) that it was incumbent on her to form such an alliance as would enable her, if necessary, to assert by force of arms her right to the English throne, should Elizabeth die childless.

To the Cardinal, on the other hand, the interests of his niece were now a matter of subordinate importance : his main concern was that they should not interfere with

[1] *Spanish State Papers*, 1558-67, p. 422.

his own interests and the interests of France—though he was also anxious for the triumph of Catholicism in Scotland. Unhappily for his niece, while still cherishing this latter sublime purpose, he now objected to its being effected by her marriage to Don Carlos, which he was as anxious now to prevent as he had formerly been to promote. It was, however, impossible for Mary either to accept the Cardinal's view of the matter, or to be blind to the character of his manœuvre ; and to be wounded in the house of her friends, as the Cardinal was seeking to wound her, must have been inexpressively distressing.

With the more definite Austrian and Spanish proposals there were intermingled hints as to possibilities of a French marriage ; but in this last case rumour was entirely at fault. So far as Catherine de Medici gave countenance to such a possibility, she did so merely to entice Mary from the Spanish marriage, while Maitland, on the other hand, strove to make such a contingency assume to de Quadra the semblance of more than possibility, simply with a view to further the Spanish negotiations.

As for Catherine, her main aim was, of course, to entangle Mary in the Austrian match. Except for the fatal enmity between her and Mary, and her dread of the revival of a preponderating Guisian influence, she had every reason to prefer a marriage that would restore French influence in Scotland ; but, unable to brook the thought of Mary resuming her old position in France, she earnestly backed up the endeavours of the Cardinal to win Mary's assent to the Austrian marriage.[1] Catherine's advocacy would have tended rather to prejudice Mary against the proposal,

[1] Letter of Raulet, March 21st, 1563   Add. MSS. (B. M.), 19,401 f, 441, first quoted in Philippson, ii. 197.

even had it been otherwise acceptable ; but the Cardinal, by his unwarrantable precipitancy, had, in a measure, committed Mary to the negotiations ; and, besides, she probably thought it advisable to veil for a time the negotiations for the Spanish marriage.

On May 15th Randolph wrote to Cecil that it had "come to this point that if she finds it good, the Duke will, out of hand, send hither his ambassador and proceed to the consummation hereof with all convenient speed." She even proposed that du Croc should report to Elizabeth "both the occasion of his coming hither, and the state of things ; "[1] and on June 15th Middlemore was able to send word from Paris to Elizabeth that du Croc had been empowered both to thank the Emperor and his son for the offer, and to "note well the personage of the Duke, to learn his nature and conditions, and his living and revenues."[2]

The most of this was, however, mere fencing on Mary's part, her chief aim, according to Maitland, being "to drop the business politely."[3] How deeply Mary was hurt at the manœuvring of the Cardinal and Catherine, she even obscurely manifested to Randolph, who, not dreaming how repugnant to her were the Austrian proposals, wrote on April 10th to Cecil, "I maye also further assure your honour that whatsomever theoccation is, thys Quene hathe somewhat in her harte that wyll burste owte in tyme, which wyll manifeste that some unkyndenes hathe passed betwene them that will not be easlye forgotten."[4]

By June 26th, at least, the Cardinal knew of Mary's extreme aversion to the match, and was much perplexed

---

[1] *Scottish Papers*, ii. 8-9.   [2] *For. Ser.*, v. No. 912.
[3] *Spanish State Papers*, 1558-67, p. 422.   [4] *Scottish Papers*, ii. 5.

what to do ; [1] but he was not debarred by his knowledge of her objections from, in her name, prosecuting the suit, for he hoped, by doing so, at least to prevent the Spanish match.

But with the aid of diplomacy so marvellously adroit as that of Maitland, it seemed for a time that the Cardinal and Catherine would be baffled ; and from August to November reports reached Elizabeth from Paris of the " marvellous fear " of the French lest a marriage-treaty with Spain had been, or might yet be, concluded. Maitland's quite unwarrantable suggestion to de Quadra as to the possibility of a French marriage so perturbed Philip that, on June 15th, he wrote to de Quadra that he had decided to " entertain negotiations," though he candidly stated that he would have preferred to support the Austrian marriage.[2] On his return to London Maitland had some difficulty in knowing how to represent to de Quadra the prospects in regard to the French marriage, but he endeavoured to feed the Spanish alarm as best he could, by " frankly " telling de Quadra " that a person of rank in France had told him that if his Queen could only wait a couple of years she could no doubt marry the King." [3]

As we shall see, Elizabeth, scared by what she had learned of the Austrian negotiations, was endeavouring to lure Mary from her apparent purpose by mingled threats and promises ; but Maitland, though he made his own use of Elizabeth's professions to spur Philip to more definite steps than he had hitherto taken, had really no intention of recommending Elizabeth's proposals to Mary. His half-pretences had, however, a strange effect on

[1] *Documentos Inéditôs*, xxvi. 447.
[2] *Spanish State Papers*, 1558-67, pp. 332-3.   [3] *Ibid.*, 339-40.

de Quadra, who actually sent "an English gentleman, on behalf of other noblemen and gentlemen, to Scotland to offer the Queen the service and assistance of the Catholics in case she will marry the Archduke."[1] So completely, indeed, was de Quadra deceived by the ruse of Maitland that he was even afraid Maitland might do his messenger "some harm."

When de Quadra sent the messenger, he had not as yet, be it remembered, received Philip's reply of June 15th, and Maitland also had left for Scotland in uncertainty as to Philip's attitude to the proposal. On receiving Philip's reply, de Quadra, dreading to commit to writing any statement on the subject, sent to Mary "a trustworthy person" to say what he had "to convey to her." This was Louis de Paz, who, in order to conceal his journey to Scotland, went by Ireland. Necessarily his message was one of the most welcome Mary ever received, but on his return to London to report to de Quadra, he unhappily found him so ill with the plague that he died within six hours.[2] Before de Quadra's death Philip had written to him, on August 15th, giving his consent to the formal commencement of negotiations,[3] and had de Quadra lived it is by no means unlikely that the marriage-treaty might have been fully concluded ; but without the impulse of de Quadra'a advocacy, Philip's resolution finally failed him.

Learning of de Quadra's illness, Mary resolved to send her French secretary, Raulet, to London. But before Raulet set out, de Quadra had been three or four days dead, and by the advice of Diego Perez he therefore went over to

---

[1] *Spanish State Papers*, 1558-67, 341.   [2] *Ibid.*, p. 346.
[3] *Documentos Inéditos*, xxvi. 460.

Brussels, where he put himself into communication with Cardinal de Granville.[1] He also entered into communication with the Duchess of Parma and with Chantonnay, Philip's minister at Paris. But for the persistency of Catherine de Medici and the Cardinal of Lorraine, his efforts might have been successful. Catherine removed Philip's fears of the Charles IX. marriage, and she necessarily confirmed his fears of a possible Franco-Anglican alliance. As for the Cardinal, he had recourse to the Pope, who, in ignorance of the Cardinal's project, had hitherto supported the Spanish suit.[2] The Pope did not commit himself to any direct opinion, but instructed Visconti to inform Philip of the conversation he had had with the Cardinal on the subject.[3]

Meantime Diego Perez had strongly recommended to Philip to conclude the Marian alliance ; and on October 12th Philip wrote to the Duke of Alba stating his difficulties. On the 21st the Duke sent a long and detailed reply.[4] Being strongly of opinion that Catherine intended that Charles IX. should marry Mary, he recommended that Philip should do his utmost to support the Austrian marriage. Against the proposal of a Spanish marriage, he pointed out the danger of an Anglo-French alliance and the incapacity of Don Carlos for a position of such tremendous responsibility.

Greedily ambitious though he was, Philip lacked the nerve necessary to enable him to run a great risk. Alba's representations, being reinforced (1) by a dangerous illness

---

[1] Cardinal de Granville to Philip, September 14th, in Weiss's *Papiers de Granvelle*, vii. 209-11.

[2] *Mémoires de Castelnau*, ed. Labourier, i. 326.

[3] *Papal Negotiations*, p. 179; see also Philippson, ii. 214-217, and Gachard, *Don Carlos et Philippe II.*, i. 207-22.   [4] Weiss, vii. 223-44.

After an engraving by Cock.

PHILIP II., KING OF SPAIN.

that happened at this time to befall Don Carlos, and
(2) by the indirect recommendation of the Pope through
Visconti, decided him to give his support to the Austrian
marriage, though, for the time being, the resolution
was to be kept secret.[1] Kept secret it, however, could
not be from Mary, who evidently soon came to know
that a deadly blow had been dealt to her hopes.. Early
in December, Randolph found that she had become unwell ;
and on the 21st he reported that " some think the Queen's
sickness is caused by her utterly despairing of the marriage
of any of those she looked for."[2]

Mary's chequered and eventful history now reaches a
new turning point. The splendid vistas of ambition which
the prospect of the Spanish marriage had revealed were
now all but dissipated, and they were dissipated mainly by
the Pope and his henchman, her uncle of Lorraine. While
retaining her old Catholic preferences in religion, she
therefore became more and more inclined to play her own
political game; and indeed she had no other choice. But
she was now fighting a losing battle. Her severance from
French and Spanish help was to be fatal to her. She had
now, almost alone, to beard two great and irreconcilable
foes : the extreme Protestantism of Knox and the selfish
rivalry of Elizabeth were the two portentous dragons
guarding the entrance to her political paradise. Henceforth, therefore, Mary's case was well-nigh desperate ; and
moreover, as always, the luck, that there was, was dead
against her.

Throughout 1563 the rumour of the Austrian negotiations—for owing to the secrecy of Philip little was heard

[1] *Historische Zeitschrift*, vol. xi. (1864) p. 296.
[2] *Scottish Papers*, ii. 30.

of the Spanish negotiations—had, however, been a source
of sore anxiety both to Knox and Elizabeth. All throughout this year everything seemed to be going against the
great Protestant priest, who, had his power been equal
to his ambition, would already have either bent his sovereign
to his wishes, or procured her dethronement and captivity,
as in the end they were procured. But the proceedings
of the Parliament in May seemed to postpone indefinitely
his hopes of triumph. The " styncken pride " manifested
in the gorgeous apparel of the ladies at its opening, was
evidence of how much the Queen's "joyusitie," and her
love of brightness and splendour had infected noble dames
who were nominally disciples of the puritanic Knox ; and
moreover the Queen herself was, clearly, very popular ;
and her tact and oratorical art enabled her to produce a
great effect in her opening speech. " The first day," writes
Knox, " sche maid a paynted orisoun ; and thair mycht have
bene hard among hir flatteraris, ' Vox Dianae ! ' The
voce of a goddess (for it could not be *Dei*) and not of
a woman ! God save that sweet face ! Was thair ever
oratour spack so properlie and so sweitlie ! " [1]

As for the actual proceedings of the Parliament, they
were notable mainly for the barbarous and degrading
ceremony of the forfeiture of Huntly in the person of
his dead body, and for the modification of the Acts against
adultery and of those for the manses and glebes in such
a fashion that, according to Knox, " no law and such Actes
were boyth alyk." [2] But the distinguishing feature of the
Parliament—that which made it inexpressibly disappointing
to Knox—was not what it did, but what it failed to do :
it entirely avoided the burning question as to the establish-

---

[1] *Works*, ii. 381.   [2] *Ibid.*, 383.

ment of what Knox termed "Religion." As yet Scotland
was not definitely committed to the make-believe of a
national religion ; and whether, after all, it would be
Protestantism or Catholicism was by no means certain.
The failure of Moray and Maitland to press for the
establishment of Protestantism, coupled with the supposed
negotiations for an Austrian marriage and the manifest
popularity of the Queen, filled Knox with almost overwhelming despair. So deeply did he distrust the purposes
not only of Maitland but of Moray and other Protestant
leaders, that he says, "familiarlie after that tyme thei spack
nott together more than a year and half." [1]

Supposing that their reluctance to do his bidding was
owing to difficulties connected with the marriage negotiations, Knox, in a sermon preached before the rising of the
Parliament, thought fit to indulge in an impassioned
vituperation against the leniency towards the Queen's
religion : " Ask yea of hir," he said, " that which by Goddis
word ye may justlie requyre, and yf she will not agree
with you in God, ye are not bound to agree with hir in
the Devill." And he concluded thus : " Duckis, brethren
to Emperouris, and Kingis, stryve all for the best game :
but this, my Lordis will I say, (note the day, and beare
witness efter), whensoever the Nobilitie of Scotland professing the Lord Jesus, consentis that ane infidell (and all
Papists are infidelles) shal be head to your soverane, ye
do so far as in ye lyeth to banishe Christe Jesus from this
Realme ; ye bring Goddis vengeance upoun the countrey,
a plague upoun yourself, and perchaunse ye shall do small
conforte to your soverane."

Knox himself ingenuously confesses that this manner

[1] *Works*, ii. 382.

of speaking was judged, both by Papists and Protestants, to be "intolerable"; and it is therefore small wonder that when, at Mary's command, he appeared in her presence, he found her in a "vehement fume." To Mary's query, "What have ye to do with my marriage? or what ar ye within this Commounwealth,"[1] the reply of Knox was "a subject borne within the same."[2] The retort has been admired by some as an assertion of what are supposed to be democratic rights. So far as it bore this appearance, it must have sounded very strange in the ears of a queen accustomed to the absolutism of France; but it implied the assumption, on the part of Knox, of a somewhat false humility, for it was not in the capacity of a mere subject, or as a mere layman, that he was taking upon him to forbid Mary's banns, but as the leader of Protestantism in Scotland, and the ordained prophet of the Most High.

So much for the Protestant danger that was lying in wait for Mary. From the side of Elizabeth the peril was in reality only the more serious in that, for the nonce, it assumed the guise mainly of excessive, if somewhat fantastic, friendliness. It was when Maitland was in London, in the spring of 1563, that Elizabeth first broached the eccentric suggestion that Mary might do worse than accept from Elizabeth, Elizabeth's own too notorious lover, Robert Dudley. Elizabeth's strange infatuation for Dudley, and—it was even supposed—Elizabeth's connection with the strange death of Dudley's wife, Amy Robsart, had been for some time the talk and wonder of Europe; and Elizabeth's friendly offer to Mary was as nearly as possible analogous to the proposal of one king that another king

[1] *Works*, ii. 385-6.   [2] *Ibid.*, 388.

After the picture in the collection of the Marquis of Salisbury.

AMBROSE DUDLEY, EARL OF WARWICK.

should marry his cast-off mistress. But the curious pretence of Elizabeth was that in bestowing on Mary the lover she held so dear, she was giving her the completest possible pledge of friendship; and, with all its fantasticality, the pretence had a certain plausibility.

To Maitland, Elizabeth had regretted that the Earl of Warwick, Dudley's brother, " had not the grace and good looks of Lord Robert, in which case they each could have had one "; but this being seemingly impossible, she was apparently not only willing but anxious to sacrifice her own strong affection, for the benefit of the two kingdoms and the promotion of her sister sovereign's happiness. It may be that her original purpose was to grope Maitland as to Mary's intentions ; and if in this she did not succeed, she was successful in entirely nonplussing him, though he hid his inward confusion, as cleverly as possible, by jocularly suggesting that Elizabeth should first marry Dudley herself, and his mistress, if she survived Elizabeth, could have the reversion of him and the English crown after Elizabeth's death.[1]

Elizabeth was then unaware that any definite foreign marriage negotiations were in progress, though she might well suspect that Maitland was entrusted with some errand of the kind. When, a few months afterwards, she learned of du Croc's mission, as Mary for strategical reasons desired that she should, she availed herself of Maitland's presence in London, on his return from France, to warn him that if Mary married either the Prince of Spain or the Archduke, " she could not avoid being her enemy," while if Mary married to " her satisfaction she would not fail to be a good friend and sister to her and make her heir." This,

[1] *Spanish State Papers*, 1558-67, p. 313.

then, was the position which Elizabeth professed to take up ; but the difficulty was that while her threats were really vain, should Mary marry Don Carlos, no trust could be put in her promises, even should Mary seek to comply with her conditions.

Elizabeth's first definite move after sending Maitland her peremptory message, was, on August 20th, to instruct Randolph to warn Mary against the Cardinal of Lorraine's effort to secure for her " a husband in the Emperor's family." If, further, Randolph were " pressed to say what would best content us in her marriage," he was to suggest, as his opinion, " some person of noble byrth within our realme," and to hint at the possibility of " yea perchance suche as she wold hardly thinke we could agre unto." [1] The person so mysteriously referred to could not—after Elizabeth's earlier hints to Maitland—be regarded as other than Elizabeth's paragon, Robert Dudley. But if Mary appeared disinclined to rise to such tempting bait, Randolph was to " descend further," and say that he thought " some other noble person of any other countree, being not of such a greatness, as suspicion may be gathered that he maye intende trooble to this realm, might be allowed." [2]

This move was weak and illogical. If Mary were assured of the succession, would she not be less likely to trouble Elizabeth's realm ? And, on the other hand, could Elizabeth give a definite guarantee in regard to the deter- mination of the succession ? Granted also, that Mary's marriage to a powerful foreign suitor could hardly be assuring to Elizabeth, it was not to be expected that Mary could sacrifice her own interests simply for the preservation of Elizabeth's peace of mind. Randolph, when he delivered

---

[1] *Scottish Papers*, ii. 19-20.   [2] *Ibid.*, 20; *Ibid.*, 23.

Elizabeth's remarkable message, was therefore indirectly
made to feel that it had failed wholly of its purpose and
that he was cutting a rather ludicrous figure. The cordiality
of his reception could hardly have been exceeded, but Mary
so plied him with questions as, it would seem, fairly to
bewilder him ; after which she still further nonplussed him
by asking him to put down his " sovereign's mind shortly
in writing." [1]

All that Randolph could gather from the interview and
from other sources was that he feared, " she was more
Spanish than Imperial," which was, if it indicated the
likelihood of the Spanish match, a very black look-out for
Elizabeth. Nor could the communications of Maitland
and Moray to Cecil be at all reassuring as to the success
of Randolph's mission. Maitland had previously regretted
to Cecil that his representations to Elizabeth had not been
" at all tymes so weyed as I think the wecht off the cause
did requyre " ; [2] and after he had heard Randolph's message,
Moray, in reply to some " friendly advyce " from Cecil,
reservedly remarked that it was not to Mary's honour
to " impede and stop " the suit of princes, nor could he
advise her Highness to do so.[3]

That Mary, also, was not greatly impressed by either
Elizabeth's dark threats on her still darker promises, was
manifested by a memorandum given by her to Randolph
in which she desired that Elizabeth would definitely state
(1) " quhome she can allow and whom she cannot lyke with
the particular respectis and considerations moving hir
thereunto," and (2) " by what way she intendis to procede
to the declaration of our richt to be hir next cousine." [4]

---

[1] *Scottish Papers*, i. 22. [2] *Ibid.*, 21.
[3] *Scottish Papers*, ii. 23. [4] Philippson, iii. 472.

The independent and almost jaunty air assumed by
the Queen and by Maitland and Moray, coupled with
Knox's revelation, on October 6th, to Cecil of the " plainness
of his troubled heart," [1] was evidence that Elizabeth was
then quite out of her reckoning.   In December, Randolph
returned to Scotland with protests against an Austrian,
French, or Spanish marriage, and a promise that Elizabeth,
if once satisfied as to Mary's " choice in her marriage,"
would " proceed to the inquisition of her right by all good
means in her furtherance." [2]

But it now appeared that Mary was not so much
at ease regarding her foreign prospects as formerly—
not that there was the slightest chance of Randolph
succeeding any better than before in inducing her to enter
Elizabeth's parlour.   For some time her trust in Elizabeth
had been dead and " damned " ; but she was now less
openly scornful of Elizabeth's offers, and more disposed
to fall in with her game of procrastination.   Maitland,
whom Randolph found at Haddington taking possession
of the abbacy—given to him by Mary for services, which
would have a little startled Randolph had he been fully informed what they were—told him that Mary had been unwell.
Her illness he attributed to her having " danced over long
to celebrate the feast of her nativity " ; [3] but on arriving
in Edinburgh he found that the illness was of a somewhat
confirmed character, that her " grief was marvellous secret,"
and that she wept when there was " little apparent occasion."
Moray and Maitland he also found to be conciliatory,
though Maitland wished that Elizabeth " had dyscended
into more particularities." [4]   On the other hand, Mary

---

[1] *Scottish Papers*, ii. 24.   [2] Keith, ii. 216.
[3] *Scottish Papers*, ii. 28.   [4] *Ibid.*, 29.

appeared to have no desire to discuss her matrimonial matters with Randolph, and at different interviews put him off with general talk.

What definite information Mary then possessed as to Philip's attitude towards her marriage to Don Carlos is hard to tell ; but evidently her ardent hopes had suffered some kind of blight. In January, 1564, she however resolved to send Raulet to Flanders in order, if possible, to resume negotiations through Cardinal de Granville. Of Raulet's mission, there and in France, particulars are very scanty, for the reason that all his important instructions and information were communicated to the parties concerned orally : but, while evidently in charge of a variety of indirect intrigues, his main errand was to bring pressure to bear on Philip, and to frustrate in every possible way the counter-moves of Catherine and the Cardinal of Lorraine. After Raulet's final return to Scotland, Kirkcaldy of Grange wrote on May 5th to Randolph that by what he could learn he had not been " welcome to the Queen-mother " [Catherine], that Mary was now beginning altogether to dislike her, and was also complaining of her uncles and had said thus, " Seying that they have no respect to hir weill, scho will do the best scho can for hir self." [1] In February Mary also thought fit to send Stephen Wilson to Rome to give the Pope assurance of her fidelity ; but the Pope, in his letter to her carried by Wilson, made no reference to matrimonial matters, and confined himself to exhortations as to the best means to be used for " the preservation and maintenance of the Catholic religion." [2]

---

[1] *Scottish Papers*, ii. 60. For various letters connected with Raulet's mission, see Labanoff, i. 196-215, and also Weiss, vol. vii.

[2] Weiss, vii. 396-7.

Either, as Philippson [1] surmises, in the spring of this year—while Raulet was in the Netherlands—or in the late summer, Castelnau was sent by Catherine de Medici, first to make offer to Elizabeth of the hand of Charles IX., and then to proceed to Scotland to propose to Mary her acceptance of the younger brother, the Duke of Anjou. Both offers were grotesquely absurd, and neither could have been meant seriously. To Castelnau Mary replied— and, we must believe, in perfect sincerity—" that all the kingdoms and countries of the world did not touch her heart so much as France "; but that she could not go even to France as a secondary personage, and that, " grandeur for grandeur," she " preferred the Prince of Spain." Neither in the spring nor by autumn had she altogether lost hope of the Spanish marriage ; but her main wish in referring so confidently to the Spanish match was probably to revive Catherine's fears about it, which, Mary may have hoped, if they reached a very high pitch, might lead to the offer of the hand of Charles IX.

But having to deal not only with Catherine but with the Cardinal, who was bending all his efforts to concuss her into the Austrian match, Mary was between them deprived of the only two suitors, marriage to one of whom would have met satisfactorily the necessities of her political situation. On June 1st the Papal nuncio at Vienna was writing that Catherine had been working on Elizabeth's fears in regard to Mary's marriage to the Prince of Spain, mainly to drive Elizabeth to that " peace which is just concluded," and that it was now expected that the Cardinal of Lorraine would come to Vienna " to arrange the Queen of Scotland's marriage to the Archduke." [2] But though the Papal nuncio

[1] *Marie Stuart*, ii. 239.   [2] *Papal Negotiations*, p. 180.

F om a drawing by François Clouet in the Bibliothèque Nationale, Paris.

Phot by A. Giraudon, Paris.

CHARLES IX. IN 1570.

knew much, he did not know everything ; naturally he supposed that what the Cardinal decided in such a matter would be law, as of old, to the Cardinal's niece ; and it may be that the Cardinal, as little as he, dreamt that Mary would show the resolution she was now displaying to have her own way. It was the strength of Mary's will that was more or less perplexing and baffling the different high personages who, for reasons of their own, were so interested in her future. She had made up her mind that in this matter she would be made a tool of by no one—as a matter of course not by Knox nor by Elizabeth, but also neither by Moray nor by Maitland, and—what was more remarkable —neither even by her uncle nor the Pope.

Largely dowered with the womanly inability properly to calculate possibilities where her strong desires were concerned, Mary had not yet utterly resigned hope of success in the Spanish negotiations. We gather from a letter of Philip to Cardinal de Granville, of August 6th, 1564, that de Granville had advised Mary to defer the matter until the arrival of de Silva, de Quadra's successor, in London ; but though nominated ambassador in January, he did not arrive in London until June 18th ; and, for some reason or other, Mary did not adopt the course with de Silva that de Granville advised. De Silva having, however, on July 18th, written to Philip that he had given a somewhat dubious, though negative, answer to a query of Elizabeth as to the likelihood of the marriage of Don Carlos to Mary, Philip, on August 6th, wrote that since the Cardinal of Lorraine had offered Mary's hand to the Emperor for the Archduke Charles, the proposal to marry her to his son Don Carlos must be considered at an end.[1]

[1] *Spanish State Papers*, 1558-67, p. 371.

On the same date Philip also informed de Granville that
after a full examination of the question he had come to the
conclusion that in view of the character and temperament
of his son, of the unlikelihood of the marriage accomplishing the triumph of Catholicism in Britain, and of the
fact that the Cardinal of Lorraine had proceeded so far
as he had done in the Austrian negotiations and had
partly committed him to support them, he had reluctantly
come to the conclusion, unpleasant though he knew it
would be to the Queen of Scots, to cede his rights to
the Archduke ; but should the French seek to substitute
Charles IX., he was prepared to reopen the question
of Mary's marriage to his son.[1] To de Silva he also wrote
in similar terms, but at the same time advising him,
should Mary seek to reopen negotiations through him,
to support as warmly as possible the claims of the
Archduke.[2]

There is no evidence of any attempt on Mary's part
to enter into communication with de Silva—doubtless because she was informed by de Granville how matters stood ;
but since, in view of Philip's qualifications, de Granville
could hardly represent the matter as absolutely closed, it is
not surprising that in September she endeavoured through
Beaton, her ambassador in Paris, to induce Don Francis
de Alava to take it up.[3] Necessarily the endeavour was
unsuccessful ; for as matter of fact she was the mere
shuttlecock of French and Spanish rivalry ; and Philip
regarded her marriage to the Archduke in the light of
a compromise.

Though, through de Silva's communication, Elizabeth

---

[1] Weiss, vii. 211-16.   [2] *Documentos Inéditõs*, xxvi. 521.
[3] Teulet, v. 4.

was probably relieved from her anxieties as to the Spanish
match, she was, by it, necessarily confirmed in regard to
the probability of the Austrian suit ; and it was therefore
as incumbent on her as ever, to distract Mary by vague
promises, menaces, and suggestions. At first—with
characteristic indirectness—she avoided naming Dudley in
so many words ; but Mary, who could not be blind to
the farcical nature of Elizabeth's hints, was at first in no
way anxious to bring Elizabeth to the point, and viewed
mainly with quiet amusement the comedy with which
Elizabeth was entertaining her.

Even after she had recovered her health, Mary was in
no hurry to resume her conference with Randolph, her
time being passed mainly in the mirth, pastime, and
banqueting peculiar to the season of the year ; but at last
Randolph—who had virtually been remonstrating with
Cecil about being entrusted with such a fool's errand [1]—
was permitted to say his say. After various interviews and
much contradictory and perverse talk on the part of Mary
—at one time liking well to hear of the marriage, at another
affirming that "the weddous life is best" ; sometimes
asserting that she may marry where she will, and again
that she is sought of by nobody—he was given to understand that the negotiations could make no further progress,
until Elizabeth definitely named the suitor she proposed
for her.

Unless, therefore, Elizabeth was prepared to efface
herself, and allow Mary to follow her own devices, she
had no option except to play her trump card. Not that
it could possibly serve any good purpose to do so, for
neither her ludicrous coaxings nor her veiled threats in

[1] *Scottish Papers*, ii. 43.

any way affected Mary as they were intended to do. Elizabeth—the slave partly of her own strange idiosyncrasies, partly of her difficult circumstances—was doomed to play, towards Mary, a part that to the onlooker was bound to seem unworthy, when it was not merely laughable. In her own view she had now no option but to authorise Randolph to proceed with the farce; and on March 5th, 1564, he therefore " named in speciall the Lord Roberte, saying no less of hym than your Majestie's letter imported." To Elizabeth, Randolph reported that " yt pleased her grace to here me with meetly good patience"; but from the details of his letter to Cecil we gather that her patience had been a little tried. Unlike Elizabeth, Mary usually came directly to the point. " ' Now, Mr. Randolph,' said she; ' dothe your mistress in good erneste wyshe me to marrie my Lord Robert?' I assured her it was so. ' Is that,' said she, ' conforme to her promes to use me as her syster, or daughter, to marrie hir subject?' "

These queries were but lamely answered by Randolph, and again Mary pressed him with the question: " What yf the Quene my syster sholde marrie herself and have children, what have I then gotten? whoe wyll judge thys to be wyselye done of me, or who wyll allowe it? or yf she wolde gyve me, were yt never so myche, what assurance have I?" And her final, and very proper, conclusion was, "Though I have lyttle cause to mystruste your mestres, or to thynke otherwyse than well of her: yet in matters of suche dyffecultie, good and large advisemente must be taken, as I, for my part, in thys intende to do." [1]

The weak point in Elizabeth's diplomacy was that Mary had ceased to credit the possibility, on any conditions,

[1] *Scottish Papers*, i. 56-7.

of a satisfactory settlement being arrived at, at Elizabeth's instance, in regard to the succession : Mary's weak point was the present vagueness of her marriage prospects ; but she had not, in this respect, by any means reached the limit of her resources. On Mary's foreign prospects Elizabeth's diplomacy had at present no effect. So far as they were concerned Elizabeth was wholly astray—she was in reality fighting with shadows.

True, Moray assured Randolph that the Emperor was "a continual earnest suitor to the Cardinal for his son," with whom he was offering 2,000,000 francs yearly during his life and 5,000,000 after his death ;[1] but Moray knew that his sister had no intention of accepting the suit ; and as for Don Carlos, had he been obtainable, no threats or promises of Elizabeth's would have prevented Mary's acceptance of him. Mary was thus entirely at her ease in regard to Elizabeth's diplomacy ; and since in itself it was very good fun, it was not surprising that at supper, after her talk with Randolph, she was "merrie inoughe," and that Randolph, in subsequent conversation with her and Moray, Argyll, and Maitland, found them all in a bantering mood.

And while Elizabeth was, so to say, massing her forces against a merely imaginary foe, she was virtually providing Mary with an opportunity of getting within her defences from an entirely new direction. Should the Spanish negotiations not succeed, as now seemed but too likely, she could fall back on what was in reality her only remaining resource, a marriage with Lord Darnley ; and that she was able to do so, she owed entirely to a false move on Elizabeth's part.

[1] *Scottish Papers*, i. 55.

On April 14th Randolph wrote to Cecil that a friend
" of good knowledge and judgment" had expressed to him
the opinion about Mary that "whear somever she hover,
and howe maynie tymes somever she duble to feche the
wynde, I beleve she wyll at lengethe let fawle her ancre
betwene Dover and Barwicke." And he added, not at
all to Randolph's liking, "thoughe perchance not in the
porte, haven, or roode, that you wyshe she sholde!"[1]

If there was any subject of Elizabeth that could be
deemed a fitting match, genealogically, for Mary, it was
her half-cousin, Lord Darnley ; and the reticence both of
Mary and Elizabeth as to this possibility was a significant
sign of how little trust there was between them. But
while this was so, Elizabeth had already, while bent on
another purpose, begun to play into Mary's hands.

Margaret Douglas, Darnley's mother, had herself rival
claims to the English throne with Elizabeth and Mary
Stuart ; and, being an inveterate and unwearied intriguer,
she had more and more set her hopes on the English
throne, for her boy, if not for herself. But with the death
of Francis, Mary Stuart's prospects of the support of the
English Catholics were immensely improved, and Lady
Margaret, recognising this, proposed that the widow and
she should cease their rivalry and join their forces by a
marriage alliance. But at this period Mary was ruled by
the opinions of her relatives of Guise ; and even if she
had not been, the Darnley marriage had not attractions that
could compare with a marriage to Charles IX. or Don
Carlos. Meantime she had Darnley in reserve should these
prospects fail, for she knew that Lady Margaret could have
no dearer hopes than such a marriage.

[1] *Scottish Papers*, i. 59.

Lady Lennox renewed her advances on Mary's arrival in Scotland, and on this account she was in November, 1561, summoned by Elizabeth to London. It being also discovered that she had been engaged in dealings with the English Catholics, her husband, in the spring of 1562, was sent to the Tower, and Lady Margaret and her son were confined in the house of Sir Richard Sackville at Sheen. Towards the close of the year they were, however, set at liberty ; and when Elizabeth began to have suspicions of the renewal of the foreign marriage negotiations, she began to make an ostentatious pretence of receiving them into special favour. To Maitland she broached the subject of the restoration of Lennox to his Scottish estates, and on June 16th, 1563, she addressed to Mary a formal letter on the subject. Lennox and his wife were now also constant attendants at court and were made much of, while Elizabeth professed to find special pleasure in Darnley's performances on the lute. This ostentatious patronage of the Lennox family continued for more than a year ; and when de Silva, in June, 1564, went to pay his respects to Elizabeth on his arrival in London, it was Darnley who was sent on her behalf to lead him into her presence-chamber.[1]

Whether the ruse, if it puzzled, in any way, perplexed Mary is doubtful ; it could at least have no influence in lessening her efforts to secure the hand of Don Carlos ; should she succeed in this, she could afford to laugh at Elizabeth's efforts to dispose of the succession. At first, however, she appears to have made no reply to Elizabeth's suggestion ; but as she turned the matter over, she, in the discouraging condition of the Don Carlos suit, discerned that to fall in with the suggestion, while it could

[1] *Spanish State Papers*, i. 364.

not do her harm, might in the end serve a very good purpose.

As yet there were no definite indications that Mary's hopes were turned towards Darnley. In December, 1563, the much pondering and perplexed Randolph was of opinion that she would not take him, if Elizabeth were to offer him ;[1] and although in February Moray and Maitland mentioned Darnley's name, Randolph was persuaded that they "mean nothing, nor find in him any great thing" ; indeed Maitland gravely told him that he found no man in the world so fit to match with his sovereign "as he whom we desier" [Dudley].[2] If this was not the opinion either of Maitland or even of Moray, it was probably the opinion of Knox, who in October, 1563, actually wrote a letter to the scandalous Dudley, with the view of inducing him to use his favour and credit with Elizabeth to advance "the purity of religion."[3]

But Randolph, believing that for the Dudley match he had the best wishes not only of Knox and Moray but even of Maitland, must have been a little bewildered to find that a proposal—emanating from Elizabeth at his suggestion— that the long-deferred interview should now at last take place, was received with indifference, and that the Council, on June 4th, determined for "diverse reasons" that it should not take effect.[4] Further, with Randolph, who early in June returned to London, Maitland sent a letter to Cecil, in which he told him that "gentle lettres, good wordes, and pleasant messages be good meanes to begyn friendship amongst princes, but I tak them to be to slender bandes to hold it long fast."[5] These signs of distrust,

[1] *Scottish Papers*, ii. 32.   [2] *Ibid.*, 45-6.   [3] *Ibid.*, 25.
[4] *Ibid.*, 63-4.   [5] *Ibid.*, 65.

coupled with the news, which arrived about the same time, that Lennox had at last obtained leave from Mary to return to Scotland and sue for his own right, were to Elizabeth a little disquieting. Elizabeth's patronage of the Lennoxes had clearly failed of the effect she intended. Whatever the new move on Mary's part might signify, it was a serious disturbance to Elizabeth's diplomacy; and by her next step, Elizabeth only floundered more deeply into the morass towards which she had blindly wandered.

With the curious maladroitness which, notwithstanding her subtlety, was accustomed to conquer her in sudden emergencies, she wrote to Moray and Maitland suggesting the advisability of Mary revoking the leave that had been given to Lennox, her plea being that some of her [Elizabeth's] friends in Scotland misliked his home-coming. To this Moray replied that he was quite unaware of any mislike in Scotland to the recall of Lennox; but he suggested that if Elizabeth, for reasons of her own, desired that he should be stayed, it would be better that she herself should put her veto on his journey.

With more incisiveness, as well as cleverness, Maitland reminded Cecil that the recall of Lennox had been suggested by Elizabeth; that though Moray—this was a quite admirable touch—as a Stewart might wish to see Lennox restored, he himself, and, he believed, the Queen, had simply desired to oblige Elizabeth; that as to whether Lennox came or not, he took "to be no greate mater up or downe," and that the Queen his mistress saw no danger in the matter to "move her to put her reputation in doubt before the world by breach of promise."[1] This implied reproof was all the more unpleasant to Elizabeth in that it indicated

[1] *Scottish Papers*, ii. 67-9.

that she was being quietly laughed at. We also learn
from Sir James Melville's *Memoirs* [1] that Mary had written
Elizabeth a letter on the subject, which, being necessarily
unanswerable, Elizabeth professed to deem " so dispyttful
that she believed all frendship and famyliaritie had been
given up."

By this time, however, the recall of Lennox had become
to Mary a matter of more pressing importance than it was
in May ; and it was deemed incumbent to begin with
Elizabeth a new system of tactics, which was inaugurated
by the mission to her, in September, of Sir James Melville.
When it was decided to send Melville, Mary must have
known from de Granville Philip's decision as to Don Carlos.
Philip's letter had placed the Spanish match so far outside
the bounds of at least probability as to lend, in Mary's
eyes, a special interest to the visit of Lennox.

Major Martin Hume, apparently unaware of Philip's
letter to de Granville of August 6th,[2] supposes that even three
months later Mary was " still in the belief that Don Carlos
was to come to Flanders to marry her " ; [3] but if at any
time in 1564 Mary cherished any such conviction she
must have been exceedingly sanguine, for Raulet's mission
had been quite unproductive, all that Granville could advise
her to do being to defer further attempts at negotiation
until the arrival of de Silva in London.

We must therefore suppose that Mary's boasts to Castelnau, if uttered in the spring, were mainly bluff ; and they
could be nothing else if uttered after de Granville told her
of Philip's decision in favour of the Archduke. True, as
we have seen, she was in September seeking to get at

[1] p. 117.   [2] Weiss, vii. 211-16.
[3] *Love Affairs of Mary Queen of Scots*, p. 204.

Philip through Don Francis de Alava in Paris. But Beaton met with absolutely no encouragement in his efforts to interest de Alava in her case ; nor was he more successful when he sent his brother to London to sound Louis de Paz on the subject.[1] All that Louis de Paz could tell him was that he had no information to communicate, and that he neither knew when he might have it, nor what its character might be. If also a letter from the Duchess d'Archot, which Mary in a letter of January 3rd, 1565,[2] refers to as "dated October 4th," had reference to a final decision on Philip's part, absolutely vetoing all further negotiations, it gave her no surprise, her comment being merely that it was satisfactory to know that there was no longer such a possibility, since she could not now be blamed for proceeding too hastily.

Mary made a last appeal to Philip even when her arrangements for the Darnley marriage were approaching completion ; but from the beginning of 1564 she never had any definite grounds for the opinion that she would be able "to carry through the Spanish plan." We cannot therefore suppose, with Major Martin Hume, that Mary now wished to have Lennox and his son in her keeping and at her mercy, so that they "might not be turned into instruments of attack against her by Elizabeth, when, by a *coup de main*, Scotland became Spanish and Catholic."[3] Such a device would have been more in keeping with Elizabeth's methods than those of Mary ; but besides, it would have been unnecessary, for (1) Elizabeth, by setting up Darnley, could appeal only to Catholic sentiment, and (2) we cannot suppose that the Catholics—once Mary was

---

[1] *Spanish State Papers*, i. 399.   [2] Labanoff, i. 249.
[3] *Love Affairs*, p. 208.

married to Don Carlos—would allow Elizabeth to make them her catspaw.

The ostensible objects of Sir James Melville's mission, his instructions for which are dated September 18th,[1] were (1) to express Mary's regret that anything she had written on the recall of Lennox should have given pain to Elizabeth, (2) to make arrangements for a conference, which had already been proposed, at Berwick on the subject of the Dudley marriage, (3) to obtain as authentic information as he could in regard to the attitude of Parliament towards Mary's claim to the succession, and (4) to induce Elizabeth, if possible, to declare publicly her preference for Mary as her successor. For Mary's purpose no better messenger could have been selected than the experienced and suave Sir James, with whom also Elizabeth would be less on her guard than with her old acquaintance Maitland, whose resolute goodwill had become a source almost of terror both to Cecil and Elizabeth.

The real aim of Melville's mission was (1) to preserve the make-believe of friendliness between Mary and Elizabeth, so that Darnley might have leave to visit Scotland, though this was to be brought about indirectly through Lady Lennox, and (2) to do everything possible to probe Elizabeth's intentions. Elizabeth used all her wiles to charm and befool him, but the result was hardly what she fondly expected. On the contrary, she so displayed to him her characteristic feminine weaknesses and vanities that his record of his interview with this quite unique sovereign lady is by far the most vivid and entertaining presentment of her personality that we possess. Here we are concerned with it mainly as it bears on Elizabeth's relations with Mary. While it

---

[1] Labanoff, i. 231-4

amusingly exhibits Elizabeth's keen jealousy of the charms and accomplishments of her "good cousin," it also shows how anxious she was to produce a favourable impression on Melville of her own idiosyncrasy and intentions. Her professed desire being to treat Mary as a sister, she wished Melville to realise how unkind and unsisterly it was, on Mary's part, to show distrust in her by coquetting with foreign alliances.

The suggestion that Mary should marry Dudley was to be interpreted as a special token of Elizabeth's favour, and a sufficient pledge of her intentions in regard to the succession. In her instructions to Randolph and Bedford for the conference at Berwick, she even affirmed that she would like nothing better than that the Queen of Scotland, after her marriage to Elizabeth's old lover, should live with her in England in "household." [1] To impress Melville with the earnestness of her desire for the success of Dudley's suit, she caused Dudley to be created Baron Denbigh and Earl of Leicester in Melville's presence ; but she quite spoiled the impression she intended to produce, by the impromptu of "putting her hand to Dudley's neck to tickle him smilingly." Elizabeth, truth to tell, was, in some respects, an utterly preposterous person. That she should dream of the possibility of befooling Melville by such amusing pranks, only shows that on certain occasions she was capable of bidding temporary farewell to her common sense.

When Mary—who had in all minor matters an admirable tact, acquired by quite a different early training from that of Elizabeth—had from Melville his relation of her sister sovereign's cantrips, her amusement could have been

[1] *Scottish Papers*, ii. 80-1.

equalled only by her distrust. With her customary directness she asked Melville, as he tells us, " whether I thocht that Quen menit trewly towardis her as weill inwartly in hir hart as sche apperit to do outwardly by hir speach ? " And she could have been in no way surprised by Melville's answer, " that ther was nather plain dealing nor vpricht meanyng, but gret dissimulation, emulation and fear, that her princely qualities suld overschone, chace hir out, and displace hir from the Kingdom." [1]

If also anything had been wanting to confirm Melville's conviction as to Elizabeth's insincerity, this was supplied by the instrument she was utilising for her ridiculous expedient. To the newly made earl himself, the plight in which he was being placed by Elizabeth was so uncomfortable, that he could not refrain from making Melville the confidant of his perplexities and grief. As Melville was being carried by his barge down the Thames, Leicester asked Melville how Mary regarded the proposed match ; and when Melville answered, as he was instructed by Mary to do, very coldly, not only was Leicester's *amour propre* stung to the quick : he discerned that his dilemma was both absurd and perilous. He therefore protested to Melville that he had never cherished so proud a pretence as to marry the Scottish Queen, that the project emanated from his enemy Cecil, and that he knew that, should he himself show any desire for the marriage, he would lose the favour of both Queens. Apparently he wished the farce ended as soon as possible.

Thus—apart from the dispatch of Darnley to Scotland, which Melville indirectly did much to bring about— Melville's mission to England had been successful entirely

[1] *Memoirs*, p. 129.

After the picture in the collection of the Marquis of Salisbury.

ROBERT DUDLEY, EARL OF LEICESTER.

in the manner that Mary had desired. It supplied her with the full and authentic information necessary to deal with Elizabeth's strange proposal. She was now certain that Elizabeth did not mean her to marry Leicester, that the proposal was made only to puzzle her, and to fan hostility in Scotland to a foreign marriage, and that in regard to the succession there was nothing to be hoped for from Elizabeth.

When therefore it was arranged that commissioners from the two queens should meet at Berwick, on November 18th, to proceed gravely with the discussion of Elizabeth's proposal, each party was convinced that the other had no serious intention of coming to an agreement, though neither party apparently knew how far they were themselves suspected. By "each party," the principals, rather than the agents, are however to be understood. On the English side there was perhaps only Elizabeth—with whom Cecil could hardly have been in full sympathy—and on the Scottish side there were Mary and Maitland. How far Moray coincided with the views of Mary and Maitland we do not know ; but as a Protestant he may have been inclined to favour the Leicester match, which Mary of course did not favour, and which Maitland knew was a sheer impossibility.

As for the English commissioners, Randolph and Bedford, they were evidently under the delusion that Elizabeth's offer of Leicester was *bona fide*, though so far as concerned any arrangement in regard to the succession, their instructions[1] were little better than a farce. The position taken up by Elizabeth was that Mary should place her whole trust in Elizabeth's goodwill, of which

[1] *Scottish Papers*, ii. 80-1.

she professed to have given the strongest possible pledge, by offering her the hand of her notorious lover, now created, in Mary's honour, Earl of Leicester.

Elizabeth's idea was that her grotesque offer placed Mary in a dilemma, and might embarrass the foreign negotiations ; but, having some fear that it might be accepted, she now showed a strong desire to emphasise her disinclination to take any step towards settling the succession. So far from seeking to allure the Scottish commissioners by specious promises as to the succession, she rather deemed it advisable to scare them from any definite decision in favour of Leicester, by making it apparent that she would not bind herself to exert herself in any way on Mary's behalf : she instructed her commissioners (1) to reduce the Scottish commissioners to the meanest straits and conditions, and (2) to see if her offer " is like to take place."

Small wonder therefore was it that Mary and Maitland should find the dealing of the English commissioners " marvellous strange," and conclude that nothing was meant by it but drift of time ; but since they were loath to break off negotiations, they would report, they said, what had passed, and deal further with Randolph in Edinburgh.[1]

This they did ; but while the sanguine Randolph reported that Mary had " no great misliking of the late conference," thinking that " things were now more earnestly meant than before,"[2] a somewhat different story was told by Moray and Maitland in their letters to Cecil. The truth was that Randolph knew as little of Elizabeth's as of Mary's intentions, and was quite unsuspicious of

[1] Scottish Papers, ii. 94.   [2] Ibid., 95.

the farcical part he was being made to play. Discerning therefore that he was a mere cypher, Moray and Maitland, without—so they affirmed—the knowledge of Mary, resolved to make, through Cecil, a last appeal to Elizabeth's good sense. To render their appeal effectual, they saw it was needful to represent their case as urgent—more urgent than it really was ; and, in a letter of December 3rd, they professed that " these practices "—practices for a foreign marriage—were coming on so quickly that the matter must be determined one way or another without delay.

They themselves, they said, did not wish to have recourse to foreign friendship could they avoid it, and were prepared to do what they could to induce their mistress to " embrace such marriage, friendship and alliance as in reason ought to content " Elizabeth ; but it was above all things necessary that Elizabeth should deal " frankly " with them : if she did so, they would do their utmost to overthrow " all foreign practices," but if she persisted in the course she was following, she need not find it strange " yf we thereafter change our deliberations as caus shalbe ministred, and seke to salve our selffis the best way we can." [1]

As to what course of action on Elizabeth's part would satisfy them, there was probably some difference of opinion between Moray and Maitland ; but, for various reasons, Moray's policy is more of a mystery than Maitland's. As a precise Protestant, Moray was seemingly bent either on correcting or overthrowing his sister, and he could hardly be blind to the probability that, in the latter case, he would be her successor. Maitland's attitude towards

---

[1] Scottish Papers, 96-7.

religion, on the other hand, closely resembled that of Elizabeth, and he was troubled mainly with the political difficulties of Mary's Catholicism : he had nothing to gain but everything to lose should Mary be overthrown ; his main aim was to make her rule as great a success as possible, and to obtain with Elizabeth an arrangement which, if— in the unlikely case of Elizabeth having children—it did not lead to the Scottish inheritance of the English crown, would remove a dangerous cause of discord between the two countries.

Moray was, however, probably as much impressed as Maitland with the dangers of the situation : if he was privately persuaded that the best possible arrangement both for Scotland and himself was that the crown should be placed on his own head, the difficulties in the way of this desired consummation might seem meanwhile insuperable. It may even be that he desired that Mary should accept Leicester. But if this is credible of Moray it is not credible of Maitland, who, besides enjoying, as he must have done, much more of Mary's confidence than her morose brother, was untroubled either by such possible ambitions as those of Moray or by his conscientious Protestant scruples.

From Cecil's reply to Moray's and Maitland's letter we learn that, at the Berwick conference, Maitland proposed that Elizabeth should, " saving in some places prohibited," allow Mary to marry where she would ; and in considera- tion of the prohibition of the influential suitors—Don Carlos, the Archduke, and Charles IX. were those whom Elizabeth specially objected to—should grant her some years' revenue out of England, and by Parliament establish her succession to the crown next to that of Elizabeth and her children. Regarding this proposal Cecil sarcastically remarked that he saw that Maitland could tell how to make a bargain ;[1] but Maitland denied having spoken of any revenue from England ; and this being omitted, the bargain could hardly be termed other than reasonable : indeed it was the only bargain that promised to meet the necessities of the case. And if Maitland knew how to make his bargain, Cecil revealed that Elizabeth had really no desire to make a bargain of any kind. His letters were a mere repetition of the old impossible conditions in a more burlesque form than ever. Elizabeth would in no way widen Mary's choice of a suitor. The main recommendation of Leicester, according to Cecil, was that he " was dearly and singularly esteemed " [this was substituted for the awkward word " beloved," which was not fully obliterated] " of the Queen's Majesty " ; and at the special instance of Elizabeth he had to intimate that, in regard to the succession, she would proceed only " in terms and conditions mete for friendship, but not in waye of contractyng."[2]

To such transparent trifling Moray and Maitland could only—after explanations as detailed and polite as those of Cecil—reply, that if Elizabeth was determined to do nothing in regard to the succession, " then (to speak roundly) may you conclude also absolutlie that we will never have the credit to induce our mystres to marye ane Inglisman." Indeed, had Mary accepted the notorious Leicester on Elizabeth's terms, she would have made herself the laughing-stock of Europe ; and, as Moray and Maitland said, while they could not press Elizabeth to do what she was not inclined to do, so they saw no reason why the present " amity should be dissolved," though their mistress married where her heart was best inclined.[3]

[1] *Scottish Papers*, ii. 103.   [2] *Ibid.*, ii. 104.   [3] *Ibid.*, 109.

Subsequently, Maitland, on his own account, continued to ply Cecil with arguments and appeals : and in the last one, of February 1st, 1564-5, he, in order, if he could, to kindle an answering enthusiasm in Cecil, professed to lay bare to him his heart. As no man's heart, he said, was void of ambition, he already imagined within himself what glory it would be for Cecil and himself, not only in life but after death, " in the mouthes of posterity, to be named as medlars and chefe doars in so godly and honorable a work as is the union off these two nations, which so long have continewed ennemyes, to the greate decay off both " ; and he strove to fascinate the very English Cecil with the imagination of how, in this case, their report with posterity, in ages to come, would be more honourable than even those that did " most vailyeantly serve King Edward the First in his conquest, or Kyng Robert the Bruce in the recovery of his countrey." [1]

But even had Cecil been capable of being moved by the higher patriotism that inspired this splendid letter, he was hopelessly hampered by the whimsical selfishness of Elizabeth ; while of course Mary was in no way devoted to either country. Thus the two Queens, between them, deprived Cecil and Maitland of the glory which Maitland fondly hoped might last for them, when, otherwise, the memory of both would be brought to oblivion. Though not for long ages will oblivion overtake the memory of either, the glory of neither is exactly what Maitland hoped it might be ; but if Maitland's reputation with posterity is somewhat tainted, the nature of his difficulties and perils has to be considered. Moreover, the taint may possibly be shown to have been partly imaginary ; and in any case he

[1] *Scottish Papers*, ii. 118.

ST. ANDREWS.

From an old print.

cannot be robbed of the glory of having done his utmost to avert the calamities that were now awaiting his country and his queen.

As for Mary, it is difficult to see how she could have acted otherwise than she was doing. The wholly gulled Randolph—gulled by his own mistress—still diligent in what he did not know was a mere fool's errand, had come in the beginning of February to St. Andrews, bent as before on furthering Elizabeth's insincere proposal. There he found the Queen in a merchant's house, living in that quietness and simplicity for which she often took a fancy. She was apparently in high spirits ; and, telling the anxious-minded diplomatist that she merely wished him, meanwhile, to be " merrie, and to see howe like a bourgeois wife " she could live with her " little troupe," gaily upbraided him for seeking to interrupt her pastimes with " his greate and grave matters."

One day, however, when riding out with him after dinner, she thought fit to talk to him of France, of the honour she had received " to be wyfe unto a greate Kinge," of the many friends she still had there, of the close connection still subsisting between France and Scotland, and of how her relatives had pressed her, and were still pressing her, to agree to their desires in her marriage.

How then, she asked, could any one advise her to forsake friendship offered and present " commodotie " for mere uncertainty ? Would even Elizabeth approve her wisdom in doing so ? And when the well-meaning, but blundering, Randolph sought to use the opportunity to press for an answer to the Leicester suit, she, with a grave face, professed her readiness to place herself in his " mistress will," if Elizabeth would only remove the succession stumbling-block. She altogether preferred that, inhabiting the same isle, they should live together as sisters, rather than that they should become estranged to the hurt of both ; but she warned him that unless they came to a definite friendly agreement, it would pass the power of both of them to live as friends, whatever they might say or do.[1]

So far as argument went, Mary had as much the better of Randolph as Maitland had of Cecil ; and her warning was to be amply justified. To give special point to it she caused her ambassador in Paris to adopt various methods to impress the English ambassador with the notion that she was then engaged in France in negotiations of great importance.[2]

They were, however, only so far effective that they convinced Elizabeth of the need of inventing a new diversion, which, if it could not turn Mary from her supposed intention of accepting a foreign suitor, would at least embarrass and complicate the situation. She now permitted Darnley to pay a visit to Scotland ; but she had as little desire that Mary should marry Darnley as she had that Mary should marry Leicester. Had she wished her to marry Darnley she had only to say so, and Mary would not have boggled at Elizabeth's lack of definiteness about the succession : for in the end she accepted Darnley not only without any arrangement about the succession, but without Elizabeth's leave. Married to Darnley, she was prepared to take her chance as to the succession ; and had Elizabeth remained friendly, this was perhaps the one arrangement that could have met the necessities of the case. No other marriage could have been more accordant with Maitland's wishes, for no other rendered the succession so secure ; and while,

[1] *Scottish Papers*, ii. 120-3.   [2] Labanoff, i. 259.

with Elizabeth supporting Mary in her choice, Moray could not have ventured, as he did, to oppose the marriage, it would probably have been acceptable to all but the more extreme Protestants ; for in Elizabeth they would have had a pledge of Protestant support.

But for her antipathy to the Knoxian Protestantism, Mary, in such a case, would have been deprived of any strong political reason for persisting in her efforts to maintain Catholicism. It was really the political necessity created by the underhand hostility of Elizabeth, that was to drive Mary towards the wild project for the restoration of Catholicism that was to work her ruin.

Darnley's arrival in Scotland at this particular juncture exactly harmonised with the process of circumstances and events which, with an inevitableness almost appalling in its precision, was dooming Mary to disaster. The first part of the process had now been completed. France had done for her all that it was to do. There her character had been formed, her ecclesiastical leanings determined, her peculiar aspirations and ambitions awakened, her tastes, opinions and habits matured. During her earlier years her relatives of Guise had been entirely devoted to her interests, and for their own sakes—more than hers, though they were sincerely attached to her—they had raised her to the great position of Queen-Consort of France. But to her and her French relatives the whirligig of time had brought rivalry, instead of the old unity, of interests.

By doing his utmost—for selfish reasons of his own—to prevent the Don Carlos marriage, which he had formerly suggested and promoted, the Cardinal had put a term to Mary's confidence in him ; he had formed her after a model of his own, but had been compelled to place her beyond his immediate influence. She was no longer prepared implicitly to accept his political guidance ; she scorned the political advantages he was professing to secure for her ; and he had now practically ceased to be a factor in the determination of her future. Unhappily, in robbing her of Don Carlos—personally undesirable though he was— the Cardinal had, her training and circumstances being such as they were, deprived her of what was almost her one chance of political salvation. He had placed her in a political bog from which extrication was hardly possible. There was just a chance of extrication by the Darnley marriage : there was apparently no other chance ; but this chance, if badly used, might simply sink her, as it did, deeper in difficulties than ever.

CHAPTER VII

THE DARNLEY MARRIAGE

ON Mary refusing to prohibit or delay the return of Lennox to Scotland, Elizabeth had hardly other option than to allow him to visit it ; and, having determined to permit his visit, she had to adopt the attitude of seeking to further his interests there. It was on the " recommendation of her good sister, the quene of England," that Mary suggested to the Council his restoration to his estates, which was proclaimed at the Cross of Edinburgh on October 9th, 1564, and confirmed by Parliament in the following December. Ostensibly also to show her goodwill to Elizabeth, Mary paid elaborate attention to his comfort —furnished his lodgings with hangings and costly beds of her own, entertained him at those splendid banquets in which she specially delighted, and arranged a series of pastimes and festivities in his honour.

On October 27th she also formally reconciled Lennox to his ancient rival, the weakly foolish old Duke of Châtelherault, whose fortunes had now fallen on very evil days, his fond daydreams as to the future royal greatness of his house having been altogether belied, and belied in a manner that was peculiarly disheartening. On the part neither of Lennox nor the Duke could there be any sincerity in the reconciliation. Indeed the two rivals could not have spoken together in private without a violent quarrel, and never could be other than mortal foes. Randolph relates that they never met but in the " Princes' sight," and that the Duke assured him that nothing was meant by the arrival of Lennox than the undoing of his house, his only hope now being in God and Elizabeth.[1] Necessarily the restoration of Lennox to his estates was a great blow to the power of the Duke in the west of Scotland, but it soon began to appear that he had a much greater errand in view.

To allay the apprehensions of the Protestants, Lennox made it a point to be specially exemplary in his attendance at " the sermonde " ; to aid his popularity among the nobles he made great " cheer " at his lodgings, where, besides dining many of the lords, he banqueted the " four Maries and some other delicate dames " in attendance on the Queen ; he also entertained the Queen herself at supper, on which occasion she favoured him with a display of her accomplishments as a dancer, and, afterwards playing with him at dice, lost to him a jewel of crystal set in gold ;[2] he spent his money more lavishly than he even could afford ; and he presented also choice and costly presents—sent by his clever and eager wife Meg from London, through Sir James Melville—to the Queen and the principal lords. The general rumour in Scotland towards the end of October was that both the Countess and Darnley were on their way to Scotland ; and Randolph found that there was a " marvellous good liking of the young lord," and that many desired to have him in Scotland.

According to the same authority, Lennox was also " well friended of Lethington," who, it was supposed,

[1] *Scottish Papers*, ii. 91.   [2] *Ibid.*, 88.

After the picture in the Royal Collection.

MATTHEW STEWART, EARL OF LENNOX,
Regent of Scotland.

would "bear much with the Stewarts," by reason of his love to Mary Fleming.[1] The Darnley match was already "through all men's mouths," as a "thing concluded in the Queen's heart"; and it was asserted that Lethington was wholly "bent that way." Randolph, indeed, thought that he had good reasons to suppose the contrary, both in regard to Lethington and the Queen; but he was able to "assure" Cecil of nothing, "mens doings so alter, and their minds so uncertain that he is wisest who assures leist."

The reports of Randolph, so far from disconcerting Elizabeth, apparently only confirmed her in her resolve to fly the Darnley kite. If a definite foreign marriage was contemplated by Mary, the presence of Darnley in Scotland might not turn her from her purpose, but it would at least add to the prevailing political confusion. Thus, shortly after his long conference with Mary at St. Andrews, Randolph learned to his utter bewilderment that Leicester, as well as Cecil, had made "earnest means" for Darnley's license to come to Scotland, and that their inexplicable request had been granted. He was, however, sent solely at the instance of Lady Lennox, who again represented the visit as a mere family affair—he was to see the country and the Scottish estates and to return to England with his father.

Thus Elizabeth gave neither encouragement nor warning about the Darnley suit. She was professedly as anxious as ever for the success of that of Leicester; but if she was, then it was merely absurd to put Darnley in Mary's way. She could have, therefore, no other intention than mischief. With the foreign match, the Leicester match, and the Darnley match to divide and bewilder

---

[1] *Scottish Papers*, ii. 86.

Scottish opinion, Mary, Elizabeth may well have hoped, would be very much puzzled how to decide ; or, should she decide, the difficulty of realising her hopes might be insuperable. What led Elizabeth so utterly astray was that the supposed foreign negotiations were—much of course to Mary's regret—a mere myth.

By what was thus clearly a false step in Elizabeth's diplomacy, it came about that on February 18th, 1564-5, Mary, at Wemmys Castle, on the beautiful shores of Fife, met her " fate," in the person of the long, lady-faced lad who, when Melville was in London, appeared to be so high in the good graces of Elizabeth. Ostensibly the two cousins —who were to influence so darkly each other's fate—met merely as relatives ; but probably Lennox had, on his son's behalf, made some kind of marriage overture to Mary, for she told Melville that at first she took his proposals in evil part, though she was favourably impressed by him as " the lustiest and best proportioned lang man she had sean." [1]

A tall and athletic youth of some nineteen years of age, remarkably well set up by the diligent practice of manly exercises, Darnley had also been carefully trained in music, dancing, and the more graceful accomplishments ; and his late attendance on Queen Elizabeth must have helped to give ease and readiness to his address. His appearance and manner were at first rather prepossessing, and, until his head had become turned by the success of his visit, his courtesy gained him general approval. But his essential defects of character could not long be hid ; and his new circumstances acted with the artificial power of a hothouse in developing them. On a first acquaintance he was, to

[1] *Memoirs*, p. 134.

From the picture in the collection of the late Earl of Seaforth.

HENRY STEWART, LORD DARNLEY.

use Randolph's words, " well liked for his personage " ; but
so soon as he became familiar he generally aroused hostility
mingled with contempt. His bodily size and strength
belied the character of his personality. Though expressing
a certain physical vigour, his self-assured, yet babyish
countenance, crowned by its close-cropped yellow hair—
for, like Mary and her brother Moray,[1] he had the princely
complexion of the royal Stewarts of those days—was both
intellectually and morally weak ; and while doltish, proud,
obstinate and passionate, he yet, physically strong though
he was, possessed, as Mary, to her utter contempt, was to
discover, a " heart of wax."

It was not, probably, till she married him that Mary
plumbed the depths of Darnley's inanity ; but, with her
clever wits sharpened by her experience in such a school of
human nature as the French court, can it be credited that
she fell blindly in love with this raw and conceited boy ?
Or is any such theory needed to account for her eager determination to marry him at all hazards ! Since what the pious
would term the " leadings of Providence " had apparently
decided that, if her political aims were to be accomplished,
her choice of suitors was now restricted to the " fayre
yollye yong man," she was naturally disposed to take the
most favourable view of him she could ; and she may
very well have thought—as women are apt to think—that
she would be able to fashion him into something much
better than he was.

Also, when all was said, Darnley was quite as presentable
a husband as either the sickly and fractious Francis II.—
whom, for the sake of the fair kingdom of France, she would

---

[1] Moray was not the black-avised person that Mr. Hewlett, in the *Queen's
Quair*, makes him out to be.

again have been prepared quite joyfully to welcome as a
nominal husband, had a second choice of him been possible—
or the half-mad Don Carlos, of whose lurid peculiarities
she must have learned something from her sister-in-law,
but whom she nevertheless deemed, with his great pos-
sessions, the best possible husband the wide world could
afford her. Since the friends of Don Carlos would
have none of her, she was fain to be content with the
strong but stupid stripling, whom her old friend the
Cardinal and her deadly rival Elizabeth had practically,
though quite against their real intentions, foisted upon her.
In himself, he was no fitting match for her, and she
would not have looked over her shoulder to him, had
he not been, apparently, both the one means of deliverance
from her desperate political difficulties, and the best means
of attaining, for herself or her descendants, the English
throne.

After staying a night at Wemmys Castle, Darnley
paid a visit to his father, then residing with his great
friend, Atholl ; but on Mary's return from Fife he proceeded
to Edinburgh, his purpose evidently being to lay siege
to the heart of the illustrious and world-famed beauty.
On Sunday, February 26th, Randolph and he were entertained by the circumspect and secretly pondering Moray to
dinner. Never perhaps did three persons meet at a meal,
on such apparently cordial terms with each other, who
in their secret intentions were so entirely at logger-heads.
But as yet their antagonism was merely in the chrysalis
stage. The brusquely polite Moray was no doubt taking
his own soundings of the shallow but self-confident boy
he was entertaining ; the boy was probably inwardly
resenting the great state of the bastard, and his quiet

assumptions of superiority ; and the deluded Randolph was content to write to Cecil that Darnley's behaviour was "very well liked." After dinner Darnley accompanied Moray to the kirk to hear Knox preach ; but neither of the thoughts of Knox when he saw him there, nor of the words which Knox uttered on this notable occasion, nor of the remarks of the ill-assorted pair, Darnley and Moray, as they left the sacred building, have we any record. In the evening the Queen and her ladies, as well as Darnley, were Moray's guests ; and, after Darnley had seen the Queen and various ladies dance, Darnley, at Moray's suggestion, led out the Queen and they danced a galliard together.

What were Moray's intentions in this friendly patronage of Darnley ? Was he simply obeying his sister's suggestion, was he seeking to humour her so as to prevent her taking any hasty resolution, or did he think that Darnley's marriage might be feasible, if the opposition of Elizabeth could be overcome, or was he simply leading her on towards a fatal false step ? It is hard to tell what he meant ; but we must believe that he was now cognisant that a great crisis was approaching, which would test to the utmost his courage and his wit.

As for Mary, we are told by Randolph that from her tour round the coasts of Fife she had, notwithstanding the cold and storms, returned "lustier than when she went forth."[1] Life was acquiring a new interest to her, not because of the mere prospect of her marriage to a silly boy, but because her long wait for something to turn up was reaching its close, and negotiations, uncertainty, and suspense would soon be at an end. If Elizabeth had determined not to untie for her the Gordian knot,

[1] *Scottish Papers*, ii. 128.

she had determined to cut it. She knew that the peril
of doing so must needs be great, but she possessed in an
extreme degree the womanly faith that would, if it could,
remove mountains ; and peril had greater attractions for
her than dull monotony.

Randolph, who, as representative of Elizabeth in
Scotland, had been fraternising with Darnley—lending him
horses and doing him, as he said, all the honour and
service he could—had, deluded simpleton that he was, got
to entertain the conviction that Mary had not the least
thought of marrying Darnley, since, so he supposed, it
was Elizabeth's good pleasure that she should marry
Leicester : her frequent and friendly talks with Darnley
he was attributing to "her own courteous nature."[1]
Elizabeth's still hopelessly dubious reply about the succession appeared to give Mary discontent ; but the story
of Randolph, that it had caused her to "weap her full" is
not to be credited. The fact was that Elizabeth was
now playing exactly the game that Mary desired : she
was demonstrating that the Leicester suit was a mere
impossibility. The Darnley suit, on the contrary, would
strengthen Mary's claims on the succession, whatever
Elizabeth might do ; and thus it specially appealed to a
Scottish sentiment that was deeper than the religious contentions of the hour.

That it was Darnley's attack of measles at Stirling
in April that sealed Mary's fate cannot be entertained,
for she had hardly other choice than to let her fate be·
sealed. As to the extent of her attendance on him in
his sick chamber, this, most likely, was grossly exaggerated.
His sickness was bound, of course, to cause her the gravest

[1] *Scottish Papers*, ii. 136.

concern ; and knowing how violently opposed the extreme Protestants were to the marriage, she could hardly be certain that he might not fall a victim to some kind of unfair play. If devoted love between her and Darnley was impossible, she had, at least, a strong friendly, as well as selfish, interest in his welfare ; and, never a stickler for the conventions, she was prepared to brave them in order to know for herself how he was faring. But the source of the more definite statements regarding her visits to Darnley is quite unreliable : they emanated from the boasts of Lennox's man, founded on what Randolph terms the " fond tales and foolish reports " of chattering domestics. Rumour was now having a quite golden opportunity, and was making the most of it.

As for Lady Lennox, she was in such a condition of maternal anticipation as to be prepared to believe any-thing ; and that she should—apparently on the testimony of Lennox's man—assure de Silva that Mary had spent a whole night in her beloved son's chamber, is probably proof of nothing more than that Mary had, to avoid curious observation, gone to visit him after nightfall. Randolph, who was at Stirling at the time, neither saw nor learned anything notable, though he tells us that sometimes a re-version of meat came from the Queen's table to the patient, and that the Queen's familiarity bred no small suspicion that there was more intended than merely giving him honour for Elizabeth's sake.[1] Of course, if all that was reported was true, Mary had practically committed her-self to the match ; but Elizabeth, who taxed her with attending on Darnley, notwithstanding the infectiousness of the disease, saw nothing wrong in this, if Mary intended

[1] *Scottish Papers*, ii. 142.

to marry him—as how could she, since Mary was behaving
with much more propriety towards Darnley than Elizabeth
was behaving towards Leicester? Her one objection to
Mary's conduct was that it seemed to be an unmistakable
sign that Mary had taken her bait; she desired that she
should take it, but only that she might be tortured, not
caught, and her aim was now to remove the hook. She now
charged her—as if it had been a crime—with such a desire
to marry Darnley that "if others had not been scrupulous
and fearful to assist the same, she had been affyed [affianced]
to him."[1]

According to an anonymous *Mémoire*,[2] Mary was
secretly married to Darnley by a priest introduced into the
castle by Riccio; but this is apparently a mere inference
founded on a statement of de Foix, the French ambassador
in London, that Randolph, in a letter brought by Maitland,
stated that Mary was already married to Darnley without
waiting for the ceremonies of the Church;[3] while Randolph
certainly wrote nothing of the kind. About the same
time, Lady Margaret told de Silva that the negotiations
were proceeding favourably; and, two days later, she stated
that the marriage was a settled thing.[4] No doubt she had
good reason to be very sanguine; but, probably, she also
wished to prevent the possibility of further negotiations
with Spain. Darnley and Mary may, at this time, have
pledged themselves to one another : what renders even this
unlikely, was the commission Mary gave to Maitland to
state to de Silva that her wishes in regard to Don Carlos
were unchanged, should Philip even yet desire to reopen
negotiations.[5]

---

[1] *Scottish Papers*, 146.   [2] Labanoff, vii. 66.   [3] Teulet, ii. 193.
[4] *Spanish State Papers*, ii. 1558-67, pp. 420, 427.   [5] *Ibid.*, p. 421.

Major Martin Hume has advanced the opinion that Mary's better plan at this time would have been to have played the same game in Scotland that Elizabeth was doing in England : to have kept all parties in expectancy, by refraining from committing herself to any definite arrangement ; [1] but it is difficult to see how Mary could have deferred her inevitable choice, for the simple reason that Darnley could not be detained for an indefinite time in Scotland. His father's leave, which had been renewed for another three months, would probably not be renewed again : it was thus only by making the most of the time at her disposal that Mary could outwit Elizabeth. Apart from this, Mary's position in Scotland was not on all fours with that of Elizabeth in England. Her throne in Scotland was virtually the crater of a volcano. Probably her one chance of safety depended on her ability to make such a marriage as would satisfy Scottish sentiment in regard to the succession—this apart from her own strong wish on the subject. Had she been content to be flouted and befooled by Elizabeth, and had Scotland, also, been so content, then she might have delayed to grasp what was now within her reach : but since neither she nor Scotland were so content, she had hardly any choice but to marry Darnley, and it was really a question of now or never. The adventure was quite as dubious and dark as her return to Scotland ; but it was its inevitable consequence, and she undertook it in a spirit of much greater hopefulness.

Events were now rapidly reaching a crisis, and the leading political personages, who had kept the peace, in such unnatural circumstances, so long, were getting in readiness for a near termination of the truce. As for the

[1] *Love Affairs*, p. 225.

Protestants, Randolph, on April 18th, wrote that "the Godly cry out that they are undone—no hope now of the sure establishment of Christ's true religion ;"[1] and although, for various reasons, there was likely to be a division in their camp, yet the irrepressible Knox was a host in himself—or, as he might have put it, as much to be feared "as 10,000 armed men." For some time he had been refraining from political comment, it may be in the hope that, after all, Mary might accept the disreputable Leicester, whom he had been exhorting, as we have seen, to purify the Church of England. In June, 1564, he had been brought before the Council for praying that the Lord would purge the Queen from idolatry and "deliver hir from the boundage and thraldom of Sathan in the quhilk sche has been brought up and yet remains for the lack of true doctrine ;"[2] but whether the exhortation of the Council led him to modify his petition, or caused him to drop praying for the Queen altogether, we have no record.

In March the marriage of Knox to Margaret Stewart, a girl of seventeen, and daughter of Lord Ochiltree, had caused the tongues of all Scotland to wag, and many of his own friends to wonder ; while the Queen, when she learned his intentions, stormed and raged, even threatening to expel him from Scotland, for presuming to marry one of her own "blood and name."[3] Even if born not in

---

[1] *Scottish Papers*, i. 144.   [2] Knox, *Works*, ii. 428.

[3] *Scottish Papers*, ii. 54 ; Nicol Burne (in his *Disputation concerning the Controversit Headdis of Religion*, 1581) represents Knox as riding to his courtship "with ane great court on ane trim gelding, nocht lyke ane prophet or ane auld decrepit priest, as he was, boi lyk as he had bene ane of the blud royal, with his bendis of taffetie feschnit with golden ringis and precious stanes," etc.

1505 but in 1513, he was now—wasted as he was by his tremendous task—well stricken in years, and within another eight he was to die from sheer physical exhaustion. We must suppose that this young girl, in the early bloom of womanhood, had taken a pious fancy to him ; but in marrying her he was, most likely, actuated—as Mary in the case of Darnley—more by ambition than by love. He had much of the wordly wisdom of the Catholic ecclesiastics, and quite understood the advantages—from what he would deem the religious point of view—of placing himself in a good social position, a position that would bring him into closer social contact with the nobility, and help him to regain the hold on them that he had partly lost. After June of this year, and probably until the spring of 1565, he was unreconciled to Moray ; neither by " word or write " was there any communication between them ; if they accidentally met, they apparently did nothing more than salute each other, though Moray doubtless continued his attendance on the " sermonde." But Moray's toleration of his sister, the Queen, which had wounded so deeply the ecclesiastical heart of Knox, was becoming more equivocal, and the long estrangement between the great twin leaders of Scottish Protestantism was nearing its term—though their concord was not to be accomplished without the severance of the close political partnership between Moray and Maitland. This latter partnership had possibly been already somewhat tried by the Don Carlos negotiations. It was now to be abruptly broken ; and though, outwardly, for a short time it was renewed, they must henceforth be regarded as enemies.

Two days after Darnley and Randolph's Sunday dinner with Moray, Moray again dined Randolph ; but Darnley was not one of the company invited to meet him, his place being taken by the Comptroller, the laird of Pitarrow. Moray's aim was evidently partly to "grope" Randolph's mind. Pitarrow began this portion of his work for him in protesting against Elizabeth sending them a Papist; and Moray still pretended to believe in, and desire, the Leicester match, though he complained that he "had to do all for nothinge, and to gette nothing for all"; but his most characteristic stroke was his secret imploring whisper to Randolph : " Whatsomever ye do with us, contende and stryve as myche as you cane to bringe us from our papystrie." [1]

This committed Moray to nothing ; it merely showed how zealous he was for " true religion "; but what his actual aim was, was another matter. Did he, as all Scotland was beginning to surmise, think that Elizabeth had sent Darnley that Mary might make a match with him ; and did he desire that Elizabeth should take precautions that with Darnley a Protestant " settlement "—to use a modern term—should be effected? Or had he so sounded Darnley as to discover that he was quite an unfit consort for his sister—that her marriage to him would spell disaster to Moray himself, to Mary, and to religion ; and did he therefore desire that Elizabeth should " forbid the banns " ? Mary was now showing almost contempt for the general regulations against the Mass and desiring that " all men live as they list " ; [2] but Elizabeth, also, was now specially countenancing practices that in Scotland were deemed Popish ; [3] and how Moray could hope that Scotland was to be delivered from the dangers of Papistry through

---

[1] *Scottish Papers*, ii. 133.   [2] Randolph, March 20th, in Keith, ii. 268.
[3] *Scottish Papers*, ii. 139.

Elizabeth, is not self-evident. But be this as it may, Moray, by the beginning of April, left the Scottish court with his Queen's disfavour, because he had been so plain of late with her "idolatrye"; and on his return to Stirling at the end of the month he had "worse countenance than he looked for." Indeed it was now perfectly understood that he and the Queen were not at one on the subject of Darnley.[1]

But Moray, it was evident, was not now backed up by Maitland. Maitland, all along, must have pretty well known his man—how far he could compel him to go, and when, in certain circumstances, the split between them would take place. He knew, of course, that he was more a religionist than a unionist, and, withal, probably more intent on his own predominance than the success of his sister's rule. Maitland, we must believe, was more devoted to Mary's political than her religious interests. She had, necessarily, a strong hold on him through his love for Mary Fleming, who, like all the other Marys—whatever she or they might think of Darnley—was devoted heart and soul to the Queen; but his main motives were political. If in heart opposed to the Darnley match, he knew also that, should the Queen determine to marry Darnley, it would be vain to oppose her wishes; but probably he may have deemed the match, even with the drawback of Darnley's personality, the best solution of the succession difficulty. Instead of being perplexed and distressed, as Moray now was, at the course things were taking, he seems to have been in remarkably good spirits.

Thus, on February 28th, 1564-5, we find him chaffing the now very troubled Cecil about his too great immersion

[1] *Scottish Papers*, ii. 144, 147.

in public affairs, and advising him to have, like him, at least one " meary hour of the four and twenty." Cecil, he said, might reply that those " that [like Maitland] be in love, are ever set upon a meary pyn," but he, nevertheless, thought merryness was " the most singular remedy for all diseases." [1] The fact was that Maitland thought— and quite correctly—that Elizabeth and Cecil had rather outwitted themselves, and he also hoped—though here he was partly wrong—that their mistakes might be turned to Scotland's advantage. Elizabeth had no idea, when she sent Darnley to Scotland, how helpless Mary was without him. Maitland knew that Elizabeth had sent him, because of her mortal terror of the phantom of a powerful foreign suitor ; and he was now not without hope of driving Elizabeth into a corner.

With this aim, Maitland therefore set out for London about the beginning of April ; but nothing was immediately known in Scotland as to his mission. Though Randolph, at Maitland's request, conveyed him as far as Berwick, Maitland breathed not a word to him as to his real purpose ; and Randolph still supposed that he was, as Moray was supposed to be, intent on the Leicester suit. His aim was however something quite different from this. It was (1) to obtain Spanish approval of the Darnley proposal, and (2) to bring pressure to bear upon Elizabeth, if not to make a settlement in regard to the succession— which Maitland was in fact prepared to leave for after consideration—at least to raise no objection to the marriage. Should she consent to let the marriage take place without protest, then the objectors to it in Scotland would be powerless to interfere ; and should she make conditions

in regard to Protestantism, then Mary might be compelled
to agree to them.

On the other hand, the approval of Spain was a
guarantee against a Scottish rebellion aided by Elizabeth.
Either in serious earnest, or to avoid wounding Spanish
susceptibilities, Maitland informed de Silva that Mary
was as anxious as ever to marry the Prince of Spain,
should Philip now see his way to reopen negotiations ;[1]
and finding that, while there was no hope of this, de Silva
warmly favoured the Darnley match, he proceeded to press
the matter with Elizabeth.

But Elizabeth, who was probably a puzzle to herself,
puzzled Maitland, as she had puzzled every one else. Besides sending Darnley to Scotland, this superb specimen
of feminine duplicity had been zealously attempting to
lure Mary's possible foreign suitors towards herself, and,
with her almost grotesque advances now to Don Carlos,
now to Charles IX., now to the Archduke Charles, was
carrying on as unconcealed flirtations as ever with Leicester,
whom she was pressing Mary to take off her hands.
While, in April, playing tennis with Norfolk, in presence
of the Queen, Leicester, being very " hot and sweating,"
took the handkerchief out of the Queen's hand to wipe
himself, and when Norfolk swore to lay the racket on
his face for his impudence, the Queen showed herself
" offended sore with the Duke."[2] Shortly afterwards, while
Leicester was suffering from a fall from his horse, she
also went to visit him, in much the same way as Mary
had been visiting Darnley.

Thus Elizabeth's foreign overtures were not meant more
seriously than any other of her devices ; but Maitland's

---

[1] *Spanish State Papers*, 1558-67, p. 422.   [2] *Scottish Papers*, ii. 140.

mission having completely delivered her from the foreign-suitor dread, her main concern now was to prevent the Darnley marriage. Still, the rapidity with which matters had come to a crisis had plainly taken her by surprise; and Maitland's presence in London caused her much anxiety, and even perturbation. Lady Lennox was ordered to keep her apartments; and, after hurrying Throckmorton away to Scotland with instructions, dated April 24th, she recalled him, and, on Maitland's suggestion, Maitland and Cecil held a consultation with him, after which it was arranged that the matter should go before the Council.[1]

The Council, on May 1st, declared the Darnley marriage to be "unmeet, unprofitable and perilous to the sincere amity between the Queens and their realms," but offered "a free election of any other of the nobility either in this wholl realme or ile, or in any other place, being sortable for hir state, and agreeable to both the realms."[2] This pretended generous offer really meant nothing, for the Council virtually reserved the right to veto any other proposed arrangement. Still, they were not such knaves or fools as to so much as mention the notorious name of Leicester. Not so, however, the unscrupulous Elizabeth, though, in her new instructions to Throckmorton, she reserved mention of it until the latter part of the document, which latter part was penned wholly by Cecil,[3] so as to preserve its privacy.

The first part of the instructions, representing the views of the Council, was to the effect that since Maitland was "tied" to his message for Darnley, it was Elizabeth's wish that some other persons should be sent with sufficient

---

[1] *Spanish State Papers*, 1558-67, p. 428.
[2] *Scottish Papers*, ii. 151.   [3] *Ibid.*, 151-2.

authority to conclude " for some more meter marriage."
If it were answered that the offer was " very general,"
he was to reply that a short conference would soon make it
" in effect spetiall." And then followed the individual
proposals of Elizabeth : if he found the Queen inclined
to forbear the marriage with Darnley, he was to declare that
Elizabeth could promise nothing about the succession, unless
Mary married Elizabeth's own notorious lover. And the
sum of the matter was (1) that with Darnley she could
not grant her her goodwill, (2) that with Leicester she
might have it, and (3) that she would assent to her
marrying with any other than Darnley with " more or less
mesure " of goodwill, but only with Leicester would she
" inquire, judge or publish her title." She was still
enigmatic as to what she would actually do in regard to the
title, but not so enigmatic as she had been, for the simple
reason that there was very little chance indeed that Mary
would marry Leicester. Compared with that of Mary,
Elizabeth's policy had at least the disadvantage that its
duplicity could not be hid.

Mary's policy, throughout the whole series of the
trying negotiations, had been scrupulously correct. In
Elizabeth's attitude towards the succession she had a
sufficient excuse for seeking an influential alliance ; and,
after all, she had as much right to marry any of the
foreign suitors as had Elizabeth, who, had she thought
of marrying any of them, would have done so without
leave asked of Mary. And as for the Darnley proposal,
Mary seems to have been cherishing the hope that
Elizabeth would not seriously object to it. Of this there
is even pretty clear proof.

Mary was now in such high spirits that, on Easter

Monday, she and others of her ladies dressed themselves
as "bourgeois wives" and went through the town of
Stirling collecting money from each man they met for a
banquet. Apparently the banquet was for her attendants,
and the Queen herself was present thereat, to the great
wonder, says Randolph, of man, woman and child,[1] though
there was really nothing much to wonder at. Be this
as it may, after the flying post arrived, on Saturday,
with the news that Maitland was "not so welcome as he
looked for," she and her ladies, according to Randolph,
appeared to become downcast and sad, and there were no
further signs of frolic. Not only so, but Mary's impul-
siveness, held in check so long, could be held in check no
longer.

Instead of waiting the arrival of Maitland and of the
formal message of Elizabeth through Throckmorton, she
resolved to take time by the forelock and gain the support
of as many of the nobility as possible for the marriage,
before the message of Elizabeth arrived in Scotland.
Knowing also that the person in Scotland she had most
to dread was her half-brother Moray, of whom she was
said to have affirmed that he would "set the crown on
his own head,"[2] she, on his arrival in Stirling, suddenly
placed before him a paper, which she desired him to sign,
pledging him to do his utmost to promote the marriage ;
and on his desiring time to consider, and affirming the
necessity of some guarantee in regard to "Christ's trew
religion," she had a violent quarrel with him.

On May 5th, Mary also dispatched John Beaton,
brother of the Archbishop, to intercept Maitland on his
way north, and with a letter in her own hand to him

---

[1] *Scottish Papers*, ii. 148.   [2] *Ibid.*, ii. 153.

asking him to go back immediately to London and intimate to Elizabeth that since Mary had been "so long trayned with fayre speeche and in thende begyled of her expectacion, she did mynd with thadvice of the estates of her own realme, to use her own choyse in marriage, and to take suche a one as in her opynyon should be fyt for her." Throckmorton, who had a sight of the letter, wrote to Cecil that he "could wyshe that the Quenes Majestie, you and my Lord of Leycestre had seen the pennynge of the matter" . . . "you would have said that ther had nyther wanted eloquence, dispyte, anger, love nor passyon."[1] She further instructed Maitland that after giving this message to Elizabeth, he was to repair to France in order to obtain the support of that country for the marriage. The messenger met Maitland between Newark and Grantham ; but Maitland, instead of obeying the Queen's instructions, made what haste he could in his journey north, and overtook Throckmorton at Alnwick.

On learning that, in his absence, Mary had been proceeding so impetuously in Scotland, Maitland was quite driven out of his accustomed self-command. Throckmorton had never before seen the cool and ready diplomatist "in so great perplexity nor passion," and could have little believed "that for anye matter he could have so been moved." On account of his deep agitation, Throckmorton inferred that he was "as lytle affected to this marryage as any other" ; but this inference hardly hit the mark. Maitland seemed to see his whole diplomatic castle almost already in ruins, and the "wonderful tragedies" to be close at hand. Knowing his sovereign as he did—her total disregard of consequences when

[1] *Scottish Papers*, ii. 159.

the fit was on her—he probably expected that Scotland, in a day or two, would be in the throes of revolution.

Not that Maitland was necessarily devoid of courage, when mere courage alone was imperative. Indeed his return to Scotland, in the face of Mary's commands to the contrary, was an act of high moral courage : it might mean not only the permanent loss of her favour, but the loss also of his own affianced bride, Mary Fleming. He saw, however, that no good was to be gained by mere angry words to Elizabeth ; and that the more quietly Mary could accomplish her purpose, the better it would be both for her and Scotland.

The objections of the English Council were, Maitland well knew, largely founded on suspicion as to Mary's ultimate intentions ; that suspicion had been increased by the report that she was already affianced to Darnley ; and Mary's best policy was to seek to disarm that suspicion as much as she could. Up till now, Elizabeth had been entirely in the wrong ; and never more in the wrong than in permitting Darnley to go to Scotland, and then objecting to Mary's proposal to marry him. Maitland wished, if she were now determined at all hazards to oppose the marriage, to keep her in the wrong ; and he therefore deemed it incumbent to be meanwhile as conciliatory towards her as possible.

If Knox had all along been striving for Mary's overthrow, and if Moray was now gradually coming into line with Knox, the aim of Maitland, on the contrary, was to preserve Mary in power. That could best be done by preventing an open quarrel between the two queens ; and by means of a cautious and conciliatory policy there might still be the possibility of inducing Elizabeth to accept with a good grace what it was really beyond her power to prevent.

To transmit to Elizabeth Mary's fiery message, would, Maitland saw, be simply to play into Elizabeth's hands. The fact was, that acute and artful though in some ways Mary might be, she was a mere child compared with Elizabeth, as a political schemer. She was at once too ardent a friend and too bitter a foe, to act on her own initiative with the prudence required in her difficult dilemma.

The situation might have been saved had Mary been less impetuous ; but it was already half lost. By refusing to transmit her message to Elizabeth, Maitland did the best that could now be done. Necessarily Maitland's return must have given Mary deep offence ; but it is difficult to say how far this was permanent, though he was now partly superseded in his duties by the Italian Riccio, who had been acting as Mary's French secretary since the dismission of Raulet in December. When Maitland reached Edinburgh on the 13th, he received an order to stay Throckmorton from proceeding to Stirling for two or three days, on the ground that no lodging was yet prepared for him. This message he gave Throckmorton, and, leaving him to act according to his " own liking," hurried on to Stirling. Apparently he reached it on the evening of May 14th ; and on the morning of the 15th Throckmorton, who had staid the night at Linlithgow, descended from his horse at the castle gates. Middlemore, his servant, had been sent in advance to ask an audience for him ; but such precipitancy was by no means relished by Mary. Throckmorton therefore found the gates of the castle shut against him, and in a few minutes two members of the Council appeared who, in reply to his absurdly presumptuous demand for an immediate audience, desired him, in the Queen's name, to retire to his lodgings, but stated that the Queen would receive him after he had rested himself.

On being brought to the castle in the afternoon by Lords Erskine and Ruthven, Throckmorton found Mary surrounded by others of her Council—Châtelherault, Argyll, Moray, Morton, and Glencairn—to whom and to her he set forth at length Elizabeth's " mislyking and disallowance " of her hasty proceeding with Lord Darnley, " as well for the matter as for the maner, wherein she erred by unadvysedness and rashness." [1] To his tirade Mary now replied with remarkable restraint and prudence, to the effect that she had acted with " less preciseness " than she would otherwise have done, because she thought that no marriage could be more agreeable to all parties—Elizabeth and England, as well as her subjects and realm of Scotland—than the marriage to Darnley.

Finally, Throckmorton learned that though the marriage was practically determined on, it would not take place for three months, during which everything would be done to arrive at an amicable understanding with Elizabeth. For Elizabeth, Throckmorton thought that one of two courses was open : either to make use of her power to dissolve the arrangement, which Throckmorton was sanguine enough to suppose still possible, or to agree to it with such conditions as would be to Elizabeth's " honour, safety and felicity." Throckmorton seems to have favoured the latter course ; and, had Elizabeth been persuadable, an arrangement might have been arrived at that would have endangered neither Elizabeth nor Protestantism.

There was thus no break in the chain of causes that, almost from the first moment of her existence, was linking

[1] *Scottish Papers*, ii. 162.

Mary to disaster. Knox, Moray, and Elizabeth were now ready to do their part. Hitherto their hostility had by a variety of causes been held in suspense : the Darnley marriage was the solvent that brought it into action. Unlucky as Mary was in being faced by this strong combination of hostilities—hostilities emphasised, it may be, by certain imprudences on her part, but almost inevitable in the nature of the case—she was still further unlucky in the disposition and character of the husband whom, also, an almost unavoidable fate had assigned her. Another equally fateful element in the case was the prominent Catholicism of Darnley's mother. True, Lennox himself was nominally a Protestant, and Darnley could possibly have been made nominally anything ; but, on the other hand, had the family been Protestant, Mary might have found it not less advisable—her difficulties being such as they were—to marry him, and in such a case she might have been saved from the worst of her woes. But as it was, the Catholicism of the family and the folly of the son fitted in exactly with the hostile elements that were working together for Mary's ruin.

But meantime the main hostile elements at work against Mary were represented, on the one hand, by Moray and Knox, and on the other by Elizabeth, and those two elements were fused into a seeming unity by means of Elizabeth's deceptiveness. Elizabeth had really no zeal, as Moray seems to have thought she had, for Protestantism : and she had no real intention—for various reasons, but especially because she dreaded lest Spain might pounce upon her—of aiding Moray against his sister by force. Her seeming incitements to Protestant revolt were, like most of the diplomatic contrivances of her wonderful brain, deceptive : they were to prove too much for the secret and reserved Moray, who, for once in his life, was to succeed in making an entire fool of himself. His religious zeal and his personal ambition were merely utilised by Elizabeth for her own personal ends ; and it thus came about that instead of Elizabeth and the Scottish Protestants uniting their efforts to render the inevitable marriage as innocuous as possible to Protestantism, they devoted their whole attention first to the vain task of preventing it, and then to that of punishing it.

Meantime Mary, mainly, we must suppose, on Maitland's advice, was doing her best, at the eleventh hour, to adopt a prudent policy towards Elizabeth. Darnley, immediately after Throckmorton's first interview on the 15th, was created, as had been arranged, Lord Ardmarnock and Earl of Ross ; but his elevation to the Dukedom of Albany was postponed until Mary heard how Elizabeth allowed her proceedings. Though also she had taken care to secure privately the assent of many of the principal nobles to the marriage, no formal vote on the subject was taken. Her aim now was, if possible, to disarm Elizabeth's opposition, by seeking to persuade her that her intentions were in no way hostile to Elizabeth's sovereignty. All now, therefore, depended on the manner in which Elizabeth received her friendly advances; but had there been any chance of winning Elizabeth's assent, it would have been lost by the extraordinary letters now being penned by Randolph.

Randolph had been a double dupe—the dupe of Elizabeth as well as of Mary ; but knowing now how the wind was blowing in both regions, he was doing his best to shift his sails so as to prevent the wreck of his own

craft. Yet he could not conceal his secret conviction that
neither Scotland nor Mary had been dealt with quite fairly
by Elizabeth. To Leicester he did not scruple to write
that the Scots had good cause to suspect the dealings of
Elizabeth "for sendinge of hym home, whome nowe ye
wolde seeme so myche to mislyke " ; [1] but he also affirmed
that Darnley was "quite unwordye to be matched with
such one," as he had known and seen Mary to be. This
was, doubtless, true enough ; but, had the Darnley match
been agreeable to Elizabeth, Randolph would not so have
changed his tune ; and therefore due allowance needs to
be made for his changed point of view, when he now wrote
to Leicester of Darnley's display of furious passion on
learning that his creation of dukedom was deferred, or
when he asserted to Cecil that Mary's conduct was gaining
for her "the utter contempt of her best subjects " ; while
such statements as that " her majesty is laid aside—her
wits not what they were, her beauty not what it was, her
cheer and countenance changed into I wot not what,"
are clearly as arrant nonsense as the reports that she was
bewitched, the parties who had wrought the enchantment
known, and the " bracillettes " daily worn that contain
the "sacred mysteries." [2]

Yet all this showed that there was a full English gale
now blowing against the marriage ; and when at last the
Protestant John Hay, specially chosen, doubtless, on account
of his irreproachable Protestantism, set out, on June 14th,
to cast oil on the troubled waters, his errand was merely
hopeless. While expressing astonishment at Elizabeth's
opposition to a match which she had done so much to
bring about, and while intimating that she could not now

[1] *Scottish Papers*, ii. 167.   [2] *Ibid.*, 172.

resile from her engagement to marry Darnley, Mary proposed, in the interests of friendship between the two kingdoms, to refer the points of difference between her and Elizabeth to a commission. The Scottish commissioners, named for Elizabeth's approval, were Moray, Morton, Glencairn, Ruthven, Maitland, Bellenden, and Carnegie of Kinnaird—a sufficient guarantee that everything would be done that was possible, to guard the interests both of Protestantism and Elizabeth. But Elizabeth had made up her mind finally and absolutely. Though she knew that Hay was on his way with proposals, she, without awaiting his arrival, sent letters to Lennox and Darnley recalling them to England ; [1] and on the 24th, the very day that Hay arrived, Lady Lennox was sent to the Tower. The reply sent by Elizabeth to Mary with Hay was also as curt and decisive as it well could be : she was sorry to find so small satisfaction, after such cause offered of " offence and mislike," as she had " plainly and friendly given him to understand." [2] If however we are to believe Hay, Elizabeth, though sufficiently plain with him, was by no means friendly. His story to de Silva was that she flew into a rage, directly the subject was introduced, and treated all his efforts to induce her to consider his statement, in such a fashion that he could do nothing but take his leave.[3]

And since Elizabeth was so arrogantly and implacably hostile, it is small wonder that Hay, stern and decided Protestant though he was, was " highly delighted " on learning that Philip's reply to the query of Maitland

[1] Randolph to Cecil, July 3rd, in Keith, ii. 297.
[2] *Scottish Papers*, ii. 178.
[3] *Spanish State Papers*, 1558-67, pp. 441-2.

After a picture formerly in the possession of Lord Carteret.

LADY MARGARET DOUGLAS, COUNTESS OF LENNOX,
Mother of Lord Darnley.

transmitted by de Silva, was of an entirely favourable kind. But of course neither Maitland nor Hay intended, as some seem to suppose, to betray their country to Philip ; what they needed was merely a guarantee that Philip would not permit Elizabeth to interfere against the match by force of arms—and this was all that Philip promised, if he even promised so much.[1] De Silva, in fact, advised that Mary should act as prudently as possible, and that " the declaration respecting the succession should not be pressed."

What chiefly commended the marriage to Philip was that it put an end to the possibility of a French marriage ; but his cordial attitude was as balm to the wounded heart of the Scottish commissioner ; for Elizabeth, by her angry rejection of all compromise, after luring Mary into the match, was treating the Scots with the same arrogant bad faith as that displayed by Henry VIII. ; and she thus awoke old slumbering animosities which were stronger than the newly created influence of Protestantism.

Meantime Mary had also, in May, sent Castelnau to win the support of Charles IX., who on June 30th wrote to Elizabeth that he approved of the marriage of the Queen of Scots and hoped she also did so.[2] The truth was that Catherine de Medici was glad enough that Mary should be maritally fixed in such a manner as would not interfere with her interests ; and, besides, for France to show a lack of friendliness to the match would be merely to play into the hands of Spain. Naturally, how-

[1] We do not possess the terms of Philip's reply handed by de Silva to Hay, but his message to Beaton, through the Duke of Alba, was in substance that, so far as Spanish interests were concerned, nothing could be more satisfactory (Granville, *Papiers d'État*, iv. 323).

[2] *For. Ser.*, vii. No, 1276,

ever, the Cardinal of Lorraine was sore at the discomfiture of his own plans ; and although, in the case of suitors of supreme royal rank, he regarded the personal qualities as of secondary importance, he evidently thought that his beautiful and brilliant niece was, in marrying Darnley, throwing herself away. Like most persons, he had discerned that Darnley, whom he termed "ung gentil hutaudeau "[1]—apparently a slang term of the time, and probably implying intellectual and moral softness—was by no means fitted for the difficult and responsible position, which would be his as the husband of the Queen of Scots. Towards the end of May he sent to Mary a letter with a view to persuade her against the marriage ; but finding her firmly bent on it, at all hazards, he undertook to write to the Pope for a dispensation.[2]

So much for France and the Catholics. In Scotland matters were proceeding as favourably as could be expected. If the hatred towards Darnley, even amongst the Protestants, was not so " mervilous greate " as Randolph represented, there was already evidence that the more precise nobles, led by Moray, intended to proceed to such extremities as they could against him ; while even amongst those devoted to him by " bond of blood," the enthusiasm for him was in nowise excessive. But Elizabeth's ridiculous procedure had more than reconciled many to the marriage who had no great liking for it ; and the bulk of the nation seemed to be with the Queen.

To commissioners from the Kirk sent to her, on June 26th, with certain articles,[3] the first of which proposed

---

[1] Teulet, ii. 199.
[2] See especially *Papal Negotiations*, pp. 200-1.
[3] Knox, ii. 484-5.

that the Mass should be abolished throughout the realm,
" not only in the subjects' but also in the Queen's own
person," no definite answer was meanwhile given ; but the
Council, on July 12th, issued a proclamation in which she
disavowed all intentions of molesting any of her subjects in
" the quiet using of their religion." [1]   The final answer to
the articles, dated July 29th, if not issued until a later date,
was to the effect that she could not, in conscience, leave the
religion " wherein she had been nourished and brought up " ;
that to do so would lose her the friendship of France and
" other great Princes her friends and confederates " ; that as
she had not pressed, nor intended to press, the consciences
of any, so she hoped that none would seek to press her
conscience ; and that the formal establishment of religion
would be deferred until the three estates of Parliament were
agreed. [2]

A good deal of discussion has been devoted to the
question as to whether Moray contemplated a plot to kidnap
Darnley as the Queen and he were passing through Fife on
their way south from Perth ; but there can be no doubt
(1) that Mary received news to this effect, (2) that Randolph
had been sounded about a project to capture Lennox and
Darnley and send them to Berwick, and (3) that both
Argyll and Moray were within striking distance. [3]   Further,
a rumour was spread by them that Lennox and Darnley had
conspired to slay them in a back-gallery of Mary's lodgings
at Perth.   Darnley may have been guilty of some wild boasts
of the kind ; but they were evidently utilising the rumour for
ends of their own, and probably would have made it their
excuse for the kidnapping adventure.   In any case, Mary,

---

[1] *Reg. P. C.*, i. 338.   [2] Knox, ii. 488-9.
[3] See Randolph's letters in Keith, ii. 339. sq.

desirous to put an end to the injurious back-gallery story, did her utmost to get at its source ; and Lennox and Darnley not only denied its truth, but sent their goodwill to Moray. Yet all attempts to obtain any light on the subject from Moray proved fruitless : he would neither explain nor retract,[1] the fact being that he did not desire a reconciliation with the Queen, and was now bent on doing his utmost against her.

By whatever noble or conscientious motives Moray was actuated in the step he was now taking, his resolution was a false move. If a regard to his own safety left him no other choice, that safety had been endangered by his opposition to the marriage ; whereas, had he resolved to make the best he could of the inevitable, he would have been in a strong position for guarding the interests of Protestantism. But Knox was at his one elbow and Elizabeth at the other, and the two together were, combined with his own particular ambitions, too much for his characteristic caution. His chief blunder of course was in expecting help from Elizabeth. Apparently he did not realise how completely Elizabeth had been checkmated by the understanding between Mary and Spain ; but his long uneasiness under his sister's rule has also to be considered.

On July 18th, therefore, Moray and other recalcitrant lords had a private meeting at Stirling, and in their name the drivelling Châtelherault (again trotted out by Moray for his own purposes), Argyll (also, like Châtelherault, a hereditary enemy of Lennox), and Moray himself (the now strenuous, if tardy, champion of Protestantism) sent a joint request to Elizabeth virtually to aid them against their

[1] *Reg. P. C.*, i. 340-7.

SETON HOUSE.

From a print in the British Museum.

sovereign, in the same manner as, in a like extremity, she had aided them against Mary of Guise. They did so, they said, because they understood from Throckmorton and Randolph " the guid and gratius mynd your Majestie with continuance beareth to the meyntenance of the gospell " ; [1] and it is probable that before they sent the letter, they had Elizabeth's assurance of the 10th that, if by doing their duty they were forced to inconvenience, they should " not find lack" in her " to regard them in their trouble." [2]

It is further evident that, had they been able, they would have sought to hinder the marriage by force of arms ; and their menacing attitude caused it to be celebrated sooner than was orignally contemplated. Randolph even reported on the 16th that on the 9th Mary had been secretly married in her own palace, and had gone that same night to bed at Seton. On the same day he communicated a budget of news and gossip to Cecil, including the in nowise remarkable story, that two days afterwards Mary and Darnley had come to Edinburgh Castle to dine, and " had walked up and down the towne dysguysed [whatever that may mean] untyl supper tyme "— all this on a fine summer afternoon and evening. According to the same Randolph, " thys manner of passage to and fro gave agayne occasion to maynie men to muse what might be her meaninge." [3] But they were not kept long in suspense. Mary had not the least thought of making a clandestine marriage. She held the wrath both of her brother and Elizabeth in utter despite ; and she was neither ashamed, nor in dread, of what she was about to do.

---

[1] Keith, ii. 329.

[2] *Scottish Papers*, ii. 181 ; Randolph's letters in Keith, ii. 329-35.

[3] Stevenson's *Selections*, p 119.

On learning what Moray had been about at Stirling, Mary, on July 22nd, issued a proclamation in which, while denying the false report that she intended to " stay or molest any of them in the using of their religion," she summoned all the lieges to appear at Edinburgh in all haste " boden in fear of war," and with fifteen days' provisions ;[1] and that some day Darnley was created Duke of Albany, and the banns of marriage proclaimed in St. Giles and the Chapel-Royal. The marriage took place in the Chapel-Royal of Holyrood Palace on July 29th,[2] the officiating clergyman being John Sinclair, Dean of Restalrig.

It has been usually supposed that Chisholm, who arrived from Rome on July 22nd, brought with him the dispensation needed in the case of the marriage of cousins ; but Father Pollen, who has given great attention to the subject, has apparently proved that the dispensation could not have arrived until some months after the marriage.[3] If so, the fact is but additional evidence of Mary's disregard of Catholic authority, when it interfered with her own interests. In this particular case she had clearly made up her mind to defy the Pope, should it be necessary to do so.

Mary was probably a little doubtful of the *bona fides* of her uncle in the matter of the dispensation ; and she knew that he and the Pope between them had deprived her of Don Carlos. Ample time had been given for the dispensation to arrive ; and since it was needful that the marriage should take place before effective means could be taken against Moray and his confederates, she boldly—and it

---

[1] Keith, ii. 339-41.

[2] Randolph says the 29th, and various considerations seem to show that he was correct, though the *Diurnal of Occurrents* (p. 80) and the *Liber Responsium* (*Exchequer Rolls*, xv. 475) give the 28th.

[3] *Papal Negotiations*, pp. 190-231.

may be disdainfully—resolved to dispense with the customary formality, and took Darnley for better or worse without the leave of Rome. It was really as regardless a step as that of Henry VIII. ; but on this occasion it was condoned ; and it was reserved for Father Pollen, some three centuries and a half after the event, to reveal to the world this striking act of royal irregularity in the case of a sacrament of the Holy Catholic Church.

Though the author of the *Diurnal* affirms that Mary was married with " great magnificence," the magnificence was but paltry compared with the gorgeous splendour and glittering pomp of the ceremony in Notre Dame. The only detailed account of the marriage is from the pen of Randolph, who of course could not be present.

" The manner of the marriage," says Randolph, " was in thys sorte. Upon Sondaye in the morninge, betwene five and six, she was conveide by divers of her nobles to the chappell. She had upon her backe the greate mourninge gowne of blacke, with the great wyde mourninge hoode, not unlyke unto that which she wore the dolefull day of the buriall of her husbande. She was ledde unto the chappell by the Earles Lenox and Athol, and there she was lefte untyll her housband came, who also was conveide by the same Lords. The ministers, two priests, did there receive them. The bans are asked the thyrde tyme, and an instru-mente taken by a notarie that no man sayde agaynst them, or alledged anye cause why the marriage might not procede.

" The words were spoken, the rings, which were three, the middle a riche diamonde, were put upon her fingers, theie kneel together, and manie prayers saide over them. She carrieth owte the * * * and he taketh a kysse and leaveth her there, and wente to her chamber, whither in a space she followeth, and there being required, accordinge to the solemnitie to cast off her care, and lay asyde those sorrowfull garments, and give herself to a pleasant lyfe. After some prettie refusall, more I believe for manner sake than grief of harte, she suffereth them that stoode by, everie man that coulde approche, to take owte a pyn, and so being commytted into her ladies, changed her garments, but wente not to bedde, to signifie unto the worlde, that it was no luste moved them to marrie, but onlye the necessitie of her countrie, not, if she wyll, to leave it destitute of an heire. Suspicious men, or such as are given of all thyngs to make the worste, wolde that it sholde be believed that theie knewe eache other before that theie came there. I wolde not your Lordship shold so believe ; the lykelyhoods are so greatly to the contraire, that if it were possible to se such an act done, I wolde not beleve it.

" After the marriage, followethe cheere and dancinge. To their dynner theie were conveide by the whole nobles. The trumpets sounde, a larges cried, and monie thrown abowte the house in great abundance to suche as were happie to gete anye parte. Theie dyne bothe at one table upon the upper hande. There serve her these Earles— Atholl, shower, Morton, carver, Crauford, cupbearer. These serve him in lyke offices—Earls Eglinton, Cassels and Glencarne. After dyner theie dance awhyle, and retire themselves tyll the hower of supper, and as theie dyne so do theie suppe. Some dancing ther was and so theie go to bedd." [1]

On the night before the marriage, " very near nine

[1] Wright's *Elizabeth*, i. 202-3.

After a print by R. Elstrake.

MARY QUEEN OF SCOTS AND LORD DARNLEY.

o'clock," proclamation was made in Mary's name that her will was that Darnley should "be namit and stylit King of this our Kingdom and that all our letteris to be direct eftir our said marriage sua to be compleitit, be in the names of the said illuster Prince, our future husband and us, as King and Quene of Scotland conjunctlie."

The honeymoon of the couple so hastily united was passed amidst the stir, excitement, and bustle created by the possibility of having to face a formidable revolt. The musters had begun to arrive in Edinburgh some time before the marriage ; and it was now resolved to warn Moray to appear before the Council within six days, "or be pronounced rebel and pursued under the law." Letters were also directed to Châtelherault and Argyll, ordering them, on their allegiance, not to assist him or his party ; and various persons suspected to favour him were ordered into ward in the north of Scotland. Moray meanwhile retired to Argyll to watch events ; and, as Thomworth and Randolph wrote to Leicester he and his sup-porters were taking courage, "in hope that her Majesty" [Elizabeth], "having so many just occasions of offence, will so proceed that she" [Mary] "may taste what it is to have provoked her displeasure." [1]

Moray's main supporters—besides the Duke and Argyll—were the Earls of Glencairn and Rothes, Lords Boyd and Ochiltree, and Kirkcaldy of Grange. They formed the nucleus of a powerful opposition, had the burghs and the "rascal multitude" been in the same mood as during the campaigns against the "monuments of idolatry" ; but so little general sympathy was there with the up-rising, that Elizabeth's agents were convinced that unless

[1] *Scottish Papers*, ii. 190.

"these noble men have some support of her Majesty they in end will be overthrown."

The kindling influence of the Knoxian enthusiasm had not affected the great bulk of the nobility ; now nominally Protestants, they were so chiefly from considerations of self-interest ; and while Darnley could count on the support of those related to him by " bond of blood," others, who were no friends of Lennox and had little respect or love for Darnley, were not disposed to see the Queen, who was generally popular, worsted by the jealousy of the Duke and Argyll, the offended pride or Protestant zeal of Moray, and the arrogance of Elizabeth.

Those whom Randolph, as early as June 3rd, recognised as of the Marian party, were Atholl, Caithness, Erroll, Montrose, Fleming, Cassilis, Home, Lindsay, Ruthven, and Lord Robert. Being a Stewart by his father's side, and a Douglas by his mother's, Darnley could claim the " bond of blood " devotion of two of the most powerful families in Scotland. The bulk of the Stewarts, including Atholl, were with him, and not with the " bastard." He also claimed kin with Lindsay and Ruthven ; and Morton —son of the notable Sir George Douglas of the time of Henry VIII.—who, during the minority of Angus, was nominal head of the Douglases, also cast in his lot with his kinsman, so soon as Lady Lennox sent him an instrument resigning her claims to the earldom of Angus.[1]

It was also immediately determined that Lord Gordon, who had been in prison since Corrichie, should be set free, and that Bothwell should be recalled from France. If Lord Gordon—to be better known as Huntly—never forgave Mary for her stern measures against his house,

[1] Hist. MSS. 3rd. Report, p. 394.

his grudge against her was as nothing to his implacable hate of Moray, whom the Clan Gordon, had he fallen
into their hands, would have torn in pieces with unspeakable joy.

Bothwell was also in like case with Lord Gordon.
As Moray himself said, Scotland could not hold both
Moray and Bothwell. Moray, cautious and calculating
though he was, lacked nothing in bodily courage; but he
felt uneasy in near proximity to this "rash and glorious
young man," who combined in himself the daring law-
lessness of the Border chief with the gay recklessness-
of the French bravado. Moray had done his utmost, in
Randolph's phrase, to "keep him short." It was also to
him that Bothwell—involved or not in the insane Arran
project—owed his imprisonment. Like Arran, he had been
imprisoned solely in Moray's interests. Doubtless it was
because he had learned that Moray was losing favour
with the Queen, that he had ventured in the spring to
return to Scotland; but as yet Moray's power was un-
broken, and Bothwell had to go again into exile. He could
hardly have liked the Darnley marriage; but Mary and
Darnley were now man and wife, and they were happily
at feud with the chief author of his misfortunes. True,
the fact that Mary had permitted her brother to treat him,
the old champion of her mother, as he did, had clearly
deeply wounded him. While in France, he had reviled
her in his own choice vocabulary, asserting that she and
Elizabeth between them would not make one honest
woman, and gloating with ribald spite over certain absurd
surmises as to Mary's relations with her uncle of
Lorraine. But if hitherto he had no good reason to be
well affected towards the Queen, he well enough knew

that she was in no way ill-disposed to him ; and what reasons of complaint he had against her were forgotten in his ardour to have a share in effecting his great enemy's downfall.

Morton, Lindsay, Ruthven, Huntly, Bothwell—what omened names of evil to Mary's future, had she been able to read its riddle ! Morton was to be, next to Moray—and was to be after Moray was dead and gone—her " greatest enemy." The stern and pale face of Ruthven was, in after years, to rise vividly to her memory whenever that memory in any way dallied with the painful reminiscences of dismal Holyrood. With scenes of what impotent misery was she to associate the name of the rude and implacable Lindsay ! And what tragic memories were to gather round those of Huntly and of Bothwell ! But of such dread possibilities she did not then dream ; and those five notable nobles, with others of less prominent and sinister importance, were now banded together in unity to champion the cause of the lady-faced lad, whose pride and inane folly were to be a curse to her and to them. Each of those five nobles was to contribute his own special quota to the sum of Mary's woes ; but their relations to her destiny might have been innocuous, but for the peculiar qualities of the contemptible youth, whose fortunes certain, apparently unlawful, ceremonies of the Church had now bound up with hers.

The irony of the situation was that the fates, bent—even as Maitland was bent—on the union of the Kingdoms, had to choose for their instrument such a consort as was Darnley for the Scottish Queen ; but in politics the mean and noble things of this world have ever been strangely and intimately combined ; and thus the muster of the Scottish lords in defence of a marriage, in its essence as a

personal bond, so foolish and untoward, was destined to
rank as an epoch-making event in Scottish and British
history.

On July 30th Elizabeth thought good to send
Thomworth as a special ambassador to explain to Mary
how in her former proposals—respecting Leicester, for-
sooth !—she had had Mary's best interests at heart, to
express unfeigned astonishment that Mary was now treating
her so strangely, and to warn her against any attempt " to
suppress and extirpate out of her realme the manner of the
religion already received by her subjectes." After hearing
what Mary had to say in answer to this tissue of diplomatic
nonsense, he was to seek to induce her to receive Moray
and his party into her favour, and procure "continuance of
peace and amity, that she [Mary] be not provoked to renew
the old league with France." Yet with characteristic in-
consistency the ambassador was instructed officially to ignore
the marriage, and if required by Mary to speak to Darnley
" as to her husband," to refuse to do so. [1]

What had moved Elizabeth to adopt this attitude of
mingled menace and cajolery and mingled friendliness and
insult was a significant reference in a letter of Mary to " the
princes who were her allies." Elizabeth apparently dreaded
the renewal of the old league with France, and she had also
uneasy presentiments as regards Spain. She was also
beginning to discover that the Protestant opposition to the
marriage was in nowise so strong as she had hoped ; and
we must suppose that what she mainly desired—though the
circuitous fashion of her diplomacy was all against success—
was to patch up a reconciliation between Mary and her rebels,
so that there might again be in Scotland a strong and united

[1] *Scottish Papers*, ii. 187.

Protestant party to hold Mary's foreign practices in check. But she had discovered, too late, her blunder in not consenting to negotiations. Thomworth found that there was now no hope of such a reconciliation as she appeared to desire —that is, unless Elizabeth entirely changed her tune both to the rebels and to Mary, and ceased either to seek to encourage them or to bully her. Mary remained "in mind to persue them to the uttermost," while they, quite without any suspicion of Elizabeth's total lack of good faith, were so pressing Randolph "upon her Majestie's [Elizabeth's] promes for their relief," that he could do no less than forward them the money left for this purpose at Berwick.[1]

To Thomworth, Mary answered (1) that she had offered to delay the marriage until the conditions had been considered by commissioners, but after Elizabeth declined to agree to a commission she had no further reason for delay, since the marriage had the allowance of "the principal and greatest princes of Christendom," (2) that she could not but marvel at Elizabeth's objection to the marriage, since both Darnley and his father had been specially recommended to her goodwill, (3) that by the marriage she meant nothing but amity, and to be dealt with as her good sister's "next cousin," (4) that as she had no desire, unless compelled, to "enter in practices" against Elizabeth, she expected that Elizabeth would in "no wise meddle with any matters within the realm of Scotland," (5) that she intended to make no innovation of religion, "but that most convenient for the state of herself and realm, by the advice of her good subjects," and (6) that as regards Moray, she desired Elizabeth to meddle no further in these private matters concerning him

[1] *Scottish Papers*, ii. 190.

or any other Scottish subject than she was disposed to meddle with any "caises concerning the subjects of England."

Further, in order to show the sincerity of their good-will to Elizabeth, Mary and Darnley offered (1) that during Elizabeth's life and of that of the lawful issue of her body, they would do nothing to the prejudice of the title of either, directly or indirectly, (2) that they would not meddle with her subjects nor reset offenders, (3) that they would not enter into any league with a foreign prince against her, (4) that Mary would enter into one with England, and (5) that if called to the succession, she would make no innovation of the religion, laws, or liberties of England.

These offers were made on condition (1) that Elizabeth by Act of Parliament should establish the succession of the crown, failing herself and the lawful issue of her body, (a) in Mary and the lawful issue of her body, and (b) failing this in Lady Margaret and her lawful issue "as the persons by the lawe of God and nateur nexte in heritable to the crowne of England and appurtenances thereof," (2) that she would not meddle with any practice in Scotland, or reset offenders against Mary and Darnley, and (3) that she would not league with any foreign prince against them.[1]

Unless we admit that no understanding between Mary and Elizabeth was possible, we must recognise the reason-ableness of these proposals ; but what Elizabeth desired was to deprive Mary of everything and grant her nothing. As to the plea of danger to Elizabeth in establishing the succession, it may be answered (1) that her own Council over and over again urged that she should establish it,

[1] *Scottish Papers*, ii. 192-3.

(2) that Mary was illegally debarred from it, and (3) that what Mary dreaded was that some other successor than she should be nominated before Elizabeth's death.

The analogous case of Queen Anne has been referred to, who objected to her successor coming to England in her lifetime, but (1) Queen Anne's case was a peculiar one, (2) Mary had no desire to go to England in Elizabeth's lifetime, and (3) Parliament settled the succession in Queen Anne's lifetime. But of course the time for a really amicable understanding with Elizabeth was now past, and it may be that Mary's proposals were made more in bravado than in earnest. Whether, from a strict regard to her own interests, Elizabeth was so far justified in treating Mary as she was now doing, may be a moot point; but since Elizabeth treated her as she did, Mary, as ever, appears in the part of the adversary who received the provocation.[1]

Meantime, matters between Mary and the lords were rapidly nearing a crisis. Apparently to remove the anxieties of the Protestants, Darnley, who since his arrival had posed as a Protestant, went, on August 19th, to " the sermonde " as usual. The discourse of Knox, on this critical occasion, was afterwards written out by him from memory, and it is the only one of his sermons that has been preserved. It is of inordinate length, and, according to Knox, or his continuator, " because he had tarried an hour and more longer than the time appointed, the King (sitting on a throne made for that purpose), was so moved

---

[1] What chances of final reconciliation between the queens there might have been, were lost by the refusal of Thomworth to accept a passport signed by Darnley as King. This both involved his detention for some time in Scotland, and introduced a new subject of quarrel.

at this sermon that he would not dine; and being troubled
with great fury, he past in the afternoon to the hawking." [1]
The King's dinner may well have got out of season by
his long detention; but the veiled insolence to him throughout the tirade must have galled him so much, that probably,
but for the fact that he was there for a political purpose,
he would have bounced out of the church.

Notwithstanding the deep emotional piety pervading
the sermon, it was plainly not one of Knox's most un-
restrained performances. It lacks something of the Knoxian
vehemence and fire. Though it abounds in malevolent
insinuations, more is implied than is directly expressed,
and it is pervaded by a tone of almost hopeless melancholy,
produced by the defection of so many Protestants and
the conviction that Moray and his confederates had no
chance against the Queen.

"Let the faithfull," he says, "not be discouraged, although
they be appointed as shepe to the slaughter-house; for
he for whose sake they suffer, shall not forget to revenge
their cause." "Give us," thus he addressed the Most High
in his peroration, "O Lorde! hartes to visite thee in time
of our affliction; and that, albeit we see none ende of
our dolors, that yet our faith and hope maye conduct
us to the assured hope of that joyfull resurrection, in the
which we shal possess the fruite of that for the which
nowe we travaile. And in the meane season graunt unto
us, O Lorde! to repose ourselves in the sanctuary of thy
promise, that in thee we may find comforte, till that this
thy great indignation, begunne amongst us, may passe over,
and thou thyselfe appeare to the comforte of thy afflicted,
and to the terrour of thine enemies." The main interest

[1] *Works*, ii. 497; for the Sermon, see *Ibid.*, vi. 230-73.

of the sermon is that while it shows the relentless antipathy of the extreme Protestants to Mary, it also mirrors the state of utter dejection into which they had fallen on account of the rigorous methods adopted by Mary against the rebels ; but it is more than a pity that, as he says in his preface, Knox of purpose " omitted persuasions and exhortations which then were made for alluring suche unto the feare of God, whom gladly I would have pleased, if so I could have done, and not have betrayed the manifest truth of my God."

Knox had never a doubt as to what was " the manifest truth " of his " God " ; but if we are to judge of the character of his " allurements " by the specimen of them preserved by his continuator, they were a little eccentric : amongst other things he said was " that God sets in that room (for the offences and ingratitude of the people) boys and women." And amongst some other words which appeared " bitter in the King's ear," were that " God justly punished Ahab and his posterity, because he would not take order with that harlot Jezabel." Small wonder that after listening to such " allurements," the King " appeared bitter," and felt the need of an afternoon of hawking to restore his spirits ! It was but a light punishment, for this outrageous political offence, to prohibit Knox, as the Council did, from preaching for fifteen or twenty days ; but the aim of the Queen was meanwhile to avoid hurting the susceptibilities of the Protestants. The prohibition for this short period was also useful, as it prevented Knox from inflaming further the minds of the people. His leisure was spent by him in preparing his sermon for publication, but the spell of his spoken eloquence could not be transferred to paper.

Meantime the rebel lords had on the 15th begun to muster their forces near Ayr, so as to be ready to take the field on the 24th, and thus attack the Queen before her preparations for resistance were complete. But as soon as Mary learned their intentions, she, on the 22nd, issued an urgent summons to the men of the middle shires to meet the " King and Queen's Majesties " within certain dates at Edinburgh or other convenient towns on the way westwards to Glasgow, her purpose being to go as rapidly as she could in pursuit of the rebels, collecting her forces at different stages of her journey.

Mary's words against Moray were, according to Randolph, " outrageous," and she affirmed that she would rather "loose her crown than not be revenged on him " ; but she was really fighting against her brother for her crown. On the afternoon of Sunday, 26th, she left Edinburgh to pass the night at Linlithgow, 600 "harqubussiers " and 200 spearmen following her on the morrow. By the time she reached Glasgow her followers had increased to over 5,000 ; but Moray and the Duke adopted the bold and clever ruse of marching on Edinburgh, which they entered on the last day of August with 1,200 horse, Argyll being expected to join them on the following Monday with as many more.

The aim of Moray and the Duke was to gain recruits from Edinburgh and other towns, and, if possible, to hold the city until a force of 400 harqubussiers—a vain dream !—could be landed from England at Leith. Moray's hope of adding to his followers proved delusive ; however we may account for it, Edinburgh, blessed though it was by the ministrations of one whose tongue God had made " a trumpet to forewarne realmes and nations," now proved quite lukewarm in the support of the rebels. Moreover, Mar, who held the castle in the Queen's behalf, threatened that if Moray remained longer in the city, he would turn his cannon against it ; and he actually began firing, to the utter consternation of the prophetic Knox, who was just then penning the concluding portions of his sermon, and, in his utter dismay, perorated thus :—

"Lorde ! in thy hands I commend my spirit ; for the terrible roring of gunnes and the noyce of armour, doe so pierce my heart, that my soule thirstith to depart " * * * "Be mercifull to thy flocke, O Lorde ! and at thy good pleasure, put an end to my miserie."

Never perhaps, in his whole life, had Knox been so overwhelmed with despair. At last, at his urgent entreaty, Moray was seeking the Queen's overthrow ; and if Moray were taken—as seemed now most likely—Knox and Protestantism seemed doomed to perish with him. So hopeless was now Moray's plight, that he and the lords who had set at defiance the summons to appear before the Council, sent Mary a meek letter, begging her to leave off pursuit and permit the Council to try their case.[1] But now that she had laid her hand to the plough, she was not so weak as to think of turning back. Her strength lay in the fact that she, alone of the main persons concerned, was quite regardless of consequences. Her brother Moray was brave enough, and he was now at bay ; but he had quite failed to kindle general Protestant enthusiasm ; and cost what it might, Mary would never again be at his beck. Nor was Elizabeth's policy of hide-and-seek of any use in such a crisis. The French ambassador, in dread lest Mary should throw herself

[1] *Scottish Papers*, ii. 200.

into the arms of Spain—as indeed she proposed to do
—seconded the hypocritical pretensions of Elizabeth in
her new rôle of mediator; but Mary treated such
attempted interference in her affairs with mere scorn.
Some of her own followers were no doubt lukewarm;
though they thought Moray was acting foolishly, they
were averse to extremities against him; but in the
mood with which Mary was now possessed, they had
no choice but to obey her. Amazed, and secretly dis-
gusted, at Elizabeth's hesitation, Randolph assured Cecil
that by a bribe of £8,000 or £10,000, it might easily
" be brought to passe that one countrye maye receave bothe
the Quenes before yt be longe." [1] He may have had
good reason for what he said; but the money was not
forthcoming, and the desired consummation was longer
deferred than Randolph hoped.

Moray, almost caught in the neighbourhood of Edinburgh by Mary's rapid march eastward in the face of
very tempestuous weather, left the city on the afternoon
of Sunday, September 2nd; and, to avoid capture, had
nothing for it but to hurry southwards towards Dumfries—
there to await in vain the expected help from England.
Mary went back by Stirling to Glasgow, to keep
watch on the movements of Argyll; but afterwards
returned to Edinburgh to organise a more powerful force
against the rebels in view of their possible reinforcement
from England. Meanwhile, the rebels sent Robert
Melville, on September 10th, to England to ask from
Elizabeth definite external support, including a fully
appointed force of 3,000 men, with field-pieces and a siege
battery; [2] but though Randolph was backed up by the

[1] *Scottish Papers*, ii. 202.   [2] *Ibid.*, 207

urgent representations of the rebel lords, and though he
abounded in exaggeration of Mary's difficulties and the luke-
warmness of her followers, his enthusiastic attempts to
spur Elizabeth towards active measures for the ruin of
her rival were all in vain. Elizabeth hinted, encouraged,
promised ; but, in view of possible foreign complications,
she dared not permit an English soldier to set his foot
on Scottish soil. The Moray fiasco need not, therefore,
detain us long. Mary, quite in the dark as to what
Elizabeth might be intending or doing, resolved to prepare
as best she could for the worst ; and while sending
messages both to the Pope and the King of Spain for
support, she gathered together a powerful force to attack
her brother before any large reinforcement could reach
him. Amongst her new recruits was Lord Gordon (who
on October 6th was restored to his earldom, and who
brought with him a large force from the north) and
Bothwell, who, according to the envious and anxious
Randolph, was taking great things on him and promising
much : " a feete capitayne," adds the sneering ambassador,
" for so loose a compagnie " [wild Border rievers] " as nowe
hange upon hym." [1]

But Mary was now setting out against a merely
imaginary foe. Before she left Edinburgh, the insurgent
army had dissolved, like a fairy vision, and its leaders had
vanished into England. Moray himself, who had gone to
Carlisle, in order apparently to meet reinforcements which,
through Leicester, he had been urging Elizabeth to hasten,
so as to put an end " to their troubles," received there,
instead of the hoped-for armed help, a letter from Elizabeth
to the Lords, informing them that she could not grant

[1] *Scottish Papers*, ii. 219.

them the aid they required without " open war " ; but that if they could get no terms from the Queen, she [Elizabeth], out of her private love and clemency, " will not omytt to receave them into hir protection, and save ther persons and lyves from ruyne." [1]

To complete the comedy, the crestfallen Moray had, practically on condition of his obtaining refuge in England, to undergo the famous scolding ordeal in the presence of the two French ambassadors. His hopes when he took up arms must have been high, and Elizabeth must have guessed only too well what they were. Could he, with Elizabeth's help, have captured his sister and her husband and handed them over to Elizabeth's keeping, his elevation either to the regency or the crown would have been the reward of his great achievement. Now, baffled and disgraced, he had to choose to which of the two queens he would entrust his fortunes ; and Elizabeth's insults were not so terrible as his sister's wrath. Writing to Leicester on October 19th, Randolph reported that the " Queen is nowe retorned from her paynefull and greate yornaye. She roode farre with great expedition, myche troble of the whole countrie, and found not them whome she soughte, when she cam to her yornies ende." [2]

[1] *Scottish Papers*, ii. 216.
[2] Add. MSS. (B. M.), 35,125 f. 14.

END OF VOL. I

From the picture at the Hermitage, St. Petersburg.

MARY QUEEN OF SCOTS.